Reviews of *Divine Betrayal*

"Fusing nature's breathtaking beauty with life's agonizing cruelty, this astounding true life story is a triumph in every sense of the word. Little Grace Kolenda and her missionary parents depart terra firma in Michigan over treacherous seas to an unknown life in Brazil. With the strength of someone far beyond her years, Grace cries out against the heartbreaking world around her, yet to the dishonor of her parents, devours the wonders of Florianopolis with all the zeal of a child who simply can't get enough of all that is life and living."

—Julie Peterson Freeman, Ph.D.

"Graceann's life story is a marvel that transported me to places I never knew existed."

—Moira Lieberman

"*Divine Betrayal* is about the long journey of a young missionary daughter to deliverance and self-discovery. It is the story of a young girl who had to resolve, on her own, the titanic struggle within her, between the power of indoctrination and the power of reason. As this narrative flows through the lives of many people, it evokes feelings of disenchantment with an honorable man who set aside all worlds except the world of him with his God. This is a compelling story that will be engaging and thought provoking for both secular and sectarian readers, the story of a young heroine who, fully aware of the consequences, stood alone in the face of a daunting force. The author, Graceann K. Deters deserves our empathy and admiration.

—Sid Bekowich, Fulbright Scholar

"Chilling yet uplifting tale of a child's 'coming of age' in a strict missionary family in Brazil. So compelling, I can hardly wait to read it again."

—Nancy McLachlan

"*Divine Betrayal* is the hopeful memoir of Graceann Kolenda Deters, who came of age in Brazil during the 1940's, a time of war and worldwide political upheaval. Personal upheaval comes early for Grace who was 5 years old when her father felt the religious call to uproot his family from their home in Michigan and bring them to Brazil, a place of breathtaking beauty and shocking poverty. Grace mourned the loss of her life in the United States and soon learned to mourn for much, much more. The story is beautifully and sensitively written. It is not a bitter diatribe against her parents or a church, but a true story of a girl who 'died' in Brazil and was, in her own words, 'reshaped from the dirt and the water of a place that seeped into me in the night.'"

—Eileen Peterson, Essayist and Reviewer

"A story, rich in detail . . . downright adventurous . . . her depiction of her family members rings true because it draws them as real people, complete with both altruism and pettiness."

—The Rev. Dr. James R. Beebe

"Graceann's entire family made a serious, sustained and uncompromising effort to live their ideas of what Christianity is (i.e. classical fundamentalism). It is one of the best such stories because of the many insights Graceann has about it. She reflected on her intelligence to analyze her experiences and express her insights in non-dogmatic language that helps readers to learn."

—Woodard A. Ching, Ph.D.

DIVINE BETRAYAL

An Inspirational Story of Love, Rebellion and Redemption

GRACEANN K. DETERS

with Jeannine Ouellette

GRAND
SIERRA
PUBLISHING

Incline Village, NV

For information about this title or to order other books and/or electronic media, contact the publisher:

Grand Sierra Publishing Company
774 Mays Blvd #10, Suite 452
Incline Village, NV 89451
www.divinebetrayal.com
775-832-9516

Library of Congress Control Number: 2008909957

ISBN: 978-0-9821869-5-4

Printed in the United States of America

Book and Cover design by: 1106 Design

Publisher's Cataloging-in-Publication
(Provided by Quality Books, Inc.)
Deters, Graceann K.
    Divine betrayal : "an inspirational story of love, rebellion, and redemption" / Graceann K. Deters ; with Jeannine Ouellette.
    p. cm.
    LCCN 2008909957
    ISBN-13: 978-0-9821869-5-4
    ISBN-10: 0-9821869-5-9

1. Children of missionaries--Brazil--Biography.
2. Children of missionaries--United States--Biography.
3. Missions--Brazil--Biography. 4. Assemblies of God--
Missions--Brazil--Biography.   I. Ouellette, Jeannine.
II. Title. III. Title: An inspirational story of love, rebellion, and redemption.
BV2094.5.D48 2009   266'.0092
                    QBI08-600344

DEDICATION

To Bill: my husband, best friend, lover,
and life's partner for over 50 years.

Table of Contents

PART II – 1945 to 1949 – And Back Again: America

PART III – 1949 to 1952 – With Fresh Eyes: Brazil

ACKNOWLEDGEMENTS

THIS BOOK WAS inspired by my three wonderful daughters, Angela, Elizabeth, and Martha. They listened to my many stories throughout their childhood years and encouraged me to put them into writing. When they grew up, they wanted me to record as much as possible so they could pass the stories on to their children.

I wish to thank my many relatives from both the Kolenda and Westmark families for saving the stacks of letters my mother and father sent from Brazil. These letters helped rekindle my memory, and many of my stories would not have surfaced otherwise.

I also want to thank my friends for putting up with my idiosyncrasies and for pointing them out to me, gently and lovingly, especially Molly Poole, who said to me: "Grace, you are different, not in a bad way, but different from anyone I know." Molly's observation sparked in me a need to know why I was "different" and led me on a journey into my past to find out.

And many thanks to several special friends who kept believing in and asking about my book, and who encouraged me to continue writing: John Appert, Dianne Kendall, Eileen Peterson, Carole Frommelt, Sunny Pouliot, Jan Lee, Nancy McLachlan, Mary Ann Linderman, and many others.

Other special friends who gave me encouragement and help during this process were: Sue Rock, Sara LaFrance and Jan Saunders, who referred editors and possible agents to me; Lawrie and Moira Lieberman, Mike and Shannon Hess, Cate Pons and Dan Lee, my neighbors and friends who helped in so many ways from printing numerous copies of my manuscripts to offering opinions and suggestions when asked; Kim Wyatt, who painstakingly edited the manuscript and also volunteered many helpful suggestions; Julie Freeman, Ph.D. who is always enthusiastic for my work; Laurry Harmon, also a writer, who shared some of his work with me and was a big fan of my story.

A special thanks to Dr. Woodard A. Ching, Ph.D. who, as my therapist for many years, helped me work through enough of my own conflicts to seize the courage to write this book.

Special mention to my son-in-law, Matt Rohde, who took the manuscript with him on a week-long trip to Italy, where he edited and creatively critiqued everything I wrote.

I must also give a special mention and thanks to Rollin and Henrietta Severance. As my parents' best friends and co-missionaries, Uncle Rollin and Aunt Henrietta provided both financial and moral support to my parents throughout their lives, and their decades' worth of saved letters from Mom and Dad provided a treasure trove for this manuscript.

My sister Dorothy Sakazaki deserves special mention and loads of gratitude, as many of the stories in this book were enhanced by her vivid memories. She was never impatient with my many telephone calls, as I tried to pick her brain and reclaim memories of long ago.

Words cannot say what a pleasure it was to work with Jeannine Ouellette as a collaborating writer. I compare our relationship to a painting. I provided the sketches and Jeannine brought them to life by adding the color, background, and composition. Thank you, Jeannine.

And, last but not least, none of this could have come to pass without my husband Bill. He gave me constant encouragement with every page I wrote. He read and re-read every word. Sometimes he laughed, and a few times he cried. But he was always positive and full of excitement and encouragement.

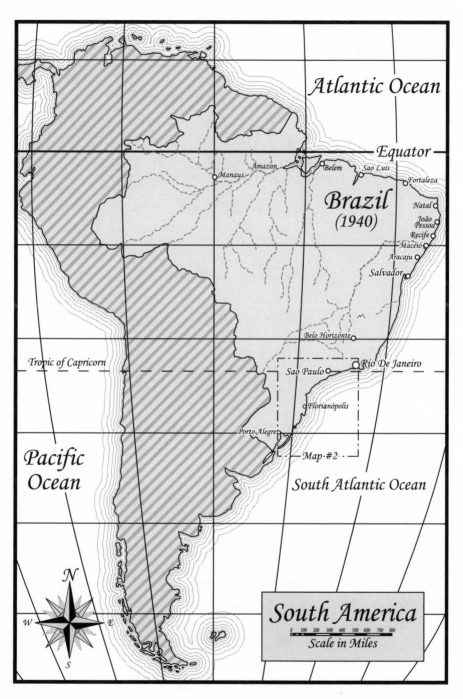

Atlantic Ocean

Equator

Manaus
Amazon
Belem
Sao Luis
Fortaleza

Brazil
(1940)

Natal
João
Pessoa
Recife
Maceió
Aracaju
Salvador

Belo Horizonte

Tropic of Capricorn

Sao Paulo
Rio De Janeiro

Florianópolis

Porto Alegre

Map #2

Pacific
Ocean

South Atlantic Ocean

N

W   E

S

South America

0 100 200 300 400 500 600 700 800
Scale in Miles

Map 1

Map 2

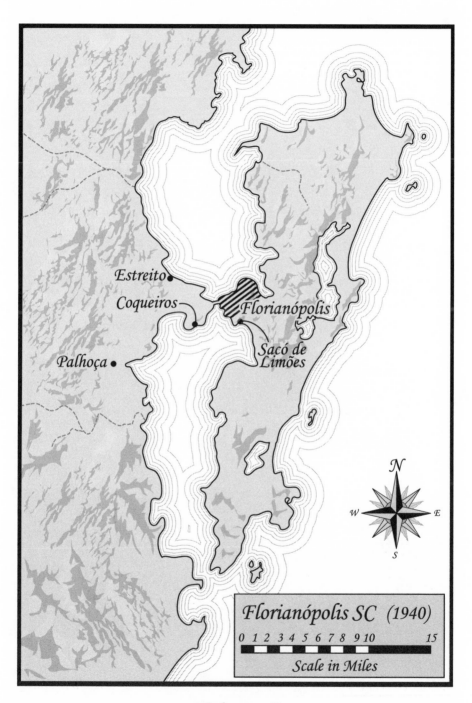

Estreito

Coqueiros

Palhoça

Florianópolis

Sacó de
Limões

N
W   E
S

Florianópolis SC (1940)

0 1 2 3 4 5 6 7 8 9 10   15

Scale in Miles

Map 3

PROLOGUE

FOR THE PAST fourteen years I have relived the phone ringing in my kitchen in Minneapolis, and hearing the voice of my grown daughter, Beth, coming ever so softly over the line from Brazil: "Mommy, I've been shot." My daughter's trauma, as it unfolded, became an uncanny metaphor for my own past. Beth's blood and pain, and the prevailing grace that marked the months of her healing, became the first seeds for writing this memoir of faith's recovery.

Beth was shot on March 30, 1995. Five decades had come and gone since my own childhood in Brazil. Beth was a twenty-eight-year-old aspiring singer with hopes of performing Brazilian concerts and improving her Portuguese, and she had sojourned alone to Copacabana, a district of Rio de Janeiro, to stay with my lifelong friend, Carmem Pacheco. Carmem's upscale condominium was just two blocks from the famous Copacabana Palace Hotel. Carmem had lived in this beautiful area for more than fifty years.

On the evening of Beth's shooting, the air outside was clear and oppressively hot. From a nearby construction site arose a steady cacophony of clanging hammers, along with a succession of fireworks, irregular and arrhythmic, like the first kernels of popping corn. Beth and Carmem sat in a corner, practicing Portuguese. Carmem said the words slowly and deliberately, and Beth reformed them carefully in her own mouth as little sculptures of sound.

A sharper, louder bang exploded outside—gunfire? More fireworks? Beth and Carmem went on with their language lesson. In the corner, the television droned to no one.

A second shot was fired just after the first. As the noise broke, Beth cupped her hand to her mouth to capture eruptions of warm blood and sand. But the blood splattered through her fingers to stain the walls, the furniture, and the beautiful Persian rug. The "sand" in Beth's mouth was shattered tooth and bone from her jaw, and also from her ring finger, which had rested upon her smooth cheek, directly in the bullet's path.

It was a little after six in the evening in Minneapolis when my daughter called me. Five thousand miles away, all I could do was pray—both in desperation for my daughter's well-being and in utter gratitude for her life. The margin was inches. If Beth had been leaning forward a bit more—perhaps setting her cup upon the table, or distracted by something surprising on the television—she would have been gone.

Four hours later, Carmem called me with an update. Beth's first operation (she would have dozens more over the next ten years) was over; the plastic surgeons had skillfully closed the wounds. Beth had lost six teeth and part of the bone under her nose. Her ring finger was also badly injured. With serious risk of infection looming, she was forbidden to travel for four days in order for the doctors to monitor her progress and ensure the effectiveness of the antibiotics. Meanwhile, Carmem's son Ricardo, who was manager of the Rio airport, arranged for Beth's first-class flight back to Minneapolis on the fourth day of April.

At the time of the shooting, Beth shared an apartment with her boyfriend, Matt, in Atlanta, so Ricardo arranged a three-hour layover there. In those pre-9/11 days, airport reunions still happened right at the gate, with the raw tension and immediacy only possible in the very first moments off the plane. Matt's wait for Beth was electric. He paced edgily until the jet taxied up to the gate. Beth was the first passenger to emerge. Her face was darkly bruised and swollen to a tight shine. She smiled hesitantly—and toothlessly—at Matt. He laughed. Then he cried.

Matt took Beth's hand and her luggage, and drove her to their apartment. He looked into her eyes and told her she was beautiful. Very gingerly, they made love, with their eyes open. Matt kissed Beth's forehead, her hair, and the bandages around her finger. She felt so wholly loved. My husband saw this as an example of the deep sincerity and love in the man who later became Beth's husband. I recognized this as a radiant example of God's grace in our lives. That belief—that a tender hour of lovemaking in the midst of grief could actually embody divinity—illustrates the vast distance between the rigid beliefs of my childhood in the Assemblies of God Church and the gift of my faith today.

In the months and years after Beth's shooting, as she slowly recovered and steadfastly clung to her joy of living and her thankfulness to God, I began to record my memories of Brazil: the intensity, the fear, the love, the longing, and the transcendence. Through writing, I rediscovered the trajectory of my life, from its early days under the harsh watch of my father's God, through my emancipation from my parents, and the enduring yet vastly different faith I uncovered inside myself in the years that followed.

End of the Sermon

SATURDAY, JUNE 23, 1984. I opened my eyes to watch the blue and red lines drift in from the Bay Area and over Livermore on the Channel 5 *Accuweather* map. Cold and warm fronts crossed, spreading a trail of tearful, eulogizing showers throughout the valley.

It was a perfect day for a funeral: clouds, fog, damp chill, and even the odd, temperamental shower. Modesto was almost never like this in the middle of June. Typically, the valley would be baking by this time of year under a relentless sun and clouds as evasive as an unfaithful lover. But these mournful skies were none but a sign; a sign that John Peter Kolenda was deeply loved by his maker. Surely, such dismal weather had to be for my father. Why else would God ruin what had been predicted to be a typical sunny Saturday with highs in the mid-eighties? It must have taken God some time to arrange weather so unseasonable.

I was still contemplating the mystery of fog when the car pulled up to the front entry of Calvary Temple Assemblies of God Church. It was ten thirty in the morning; the service was due to begin at eleven. I squared my shoulders and walked into the sanctuary. There were about two hundred guests milling about. I greeted several of my relatives and only knew

I was doing my best to think about anything but the open casket at the front of the room.

"Aren't you coming up?" It was Dorothy, tugging the sleeve of my gray sweater. "Grace, we're supposed to go up to the casket. You can't sit down yet."

But I pulled away and dropped my shoulder, shaking my sister's words to the floor between the pews as I lowered myself to a seat, third from the aisle, next to my husband and three daughters. Dorothy paused just long enough to make sure I at least caught a glimpse of her troubled, questioning gaze—it was time to get in line, though, and she had to turn around and continue down the aisle, leading our mother toward the body of the man who, only days before, had slept beside her as husband.

I sat for a long time in my pew, looking down at my firmly clasped hands. I didn't want to view the casket because I did not want to super-impose that last memory over the one I now held of my dear father. Only four days before I had conversed with my father, celebrated with him, sung with him, and prayed with him. That's when we said goodbye, when he was full of life. I didn't need anything more. I sat now, silent, just as I did as a child when my father's voice had filled the room with inspired zeal.

Mother and Dorothy returned to our front pew. Mother sat next to me, and Dorothy on her other side. I held Mother's hand and none of us said a word. Suddenly, a gasp rose from the congregation, and we looked forward in shock and disbelief.

There at the front of the hall, before Father's casket, stood Uncle Ernie, the youngest of my father's brothers. He was clasping his brother's lifeless body by the shoulders and hugging him passionately. He appeared to be yanking Father completely out of his casket. Even in death, my father seemed to wear an expression of vague surprise at this unexpected turn of events. The brothers rocked together; one shaking, crying, and wailing in heavy sobs, the other placid and lifeless.

If the guests tried, out of decorum, to look away, they apparently could not. It was such an un-Protestant mingling of the quick and the dead. All eyes were fixed on Ernie in his display of abject heartbreak. Aunt Goldie,

Uncle Ernie's wife, pleaded with him to let go, and several cousins went forward and were finally able to pull Uncle Ernie away from his brother and lead him to his pew. He and Aunt Goldie sat directly behind us. I looked at Mother. She was shaking her head, her lips firmly clenched together. She whispered, "Even in death Ernie can't be dignified, he is such a shame to his family!" I was shocked and asked, "What do you mean?" She whispered, "There's a lot you don't know!" And she turned her head, looked straight ahead with her lips tightly clenched and head erect.

Pastor Blakeley clutched his Bible but was clearly dumbfounded. I was in shock. I'd had no idea that Uncle Ernie loved his brother so much. My memories of Uncle Ernie and Dad were dominated by the men's loud, arguing voices, as they passionately debated this or that tangent of biblical theory. Most recently, Uncle Ernie had taken up a belief in the "Jesus Only" biblical theory—whatever that meant, and Mother would whisper to me, with obvious disapproval, that it was hard for Dad to accept these ideas of his brother Ernie. And now, here he was, Uncle Ernie, carrying on this way, moaning and screaming and clutching this man who in life—and even in death—held such sway over us all.

Uncle Ernie quieted down and sobbed softly as he sat behind us. Dorothy, also in shock, instinctively reached back, patted Uncle Ernie on his knee and said, "Don't cry, Uncle Ernie, everything will be fine." Instead of quieting him, this only resulted in yet a louder wail from Uncle Ernie, as if Dorothy had triggered another memory of his departed brother. Dorothy looked at me with surprise, Mother looked straight ahead, and I lowered my head and prayed.

Please Lord Jesus, help Uncle Ernie get control of himself, so we can continue with the funeral.

The hour-long funeral went by too fast. I felt like I was in a dream. Speakers from South America, North America, Germany and other parts of the world gave lovely eulogies of what Dad meant to them; "our cherished spiritual father," "a prince and a great man fallen," "a valuable servant of God," "a man of peace," and so on.

This was my father. As an adult woman, I loved him deeply, but as a little girl he meant everything to me. He was my idol! He was perfect!

He knew everything! He was the rock of my life! Dad was the ideal man and without fault!

As for Uncle Ernie's unexpected brotherly passion, it would be many years before I understood the source.

I was five years old when Father, Mother, and my sister Dorothy disembarked with me in Rio de Janeiro. My father, John Peter Kolenda, was a missionary in the Assemblies of God Church, an evangelical denomination based on a literal belief in the Bible and an acceptance of the Holy Ghost manifesting itself through converts speaking "in tongues."

Dad was a preacher of extreme passion. He passionately loved my mother. He passionately loved my sister Dorothy. And he passionately loved me. Most of all, he passionately loved Jesus, and winning souls for his church. He believed without question in the extremity of his religion, including its prohibitions against virtually everything.

Fast chutes to hell lurked everywhere from the wrong music to a short haircut to befriending unbelievers (which included everyone outside of Assemblies of God). As a small girl, I basked in the total security of my father's fundamental zeal. As long as I kept my hand tightly in his, I would never lurch down a trapdoor to damnation. My father's convictions afforded me utter safety. All I had to do was serve God as Dad saw fit—and help him convert others along the way. It was simple enough, but impossible.

Divine Betrayal tells the story of my life as my father's daughter, and paints a microcosmic portrait of the power of the Pentecostal missionary movement in South America, a major event in twentieth century religious history. Beginning in 1910, under the leadership of two Swedish missionaries, the Pentecostal movement in Brazil soon catapulted Pentecostalism into its current position as the major Protestant force in Brazil.

Unwinding against the exciting and dangerous mid-century Brazilian coast in the context of my German-American family at a time when speaking German was against Brazilian law—and having a shortwave radio could get you arrested for being a spy—mine is one of the oldest stories in the world. It is a story of believing, losing your belief, and finding it anew—but changed.

This story is not about John Peter Kolenda, but about his daughter Graceann.

J.P. Kolenda had a profound effect on everyone he came in contact with, and most of all his immediate family. I could not tell my story without including my father's story, and my recollection of what it was like to be his daughter.

My earliest recollections were as a three-year-old girl in Lansing, Michigan, where Dad had accepted a pastoral assignment after serving several years as the pastor of Riverside Tabernacle in Flint, Michigan during my birth and infancy.

Part I

1937 to 1945
From Here to There: Brazil

My father's frequent quotation in reference to his
calling to be a missionary in Brazil:

Isaiah 52:7

How beautiful on the mountains are the feet of those who bring
good news, who proclaim peace, who bring good tidings, who
proclaim salvation; who say to Zion, "Your God reigns!"

Chapter One

Watching for Christ

FROM THE KITCHEN window of our parsonage house in Lansing, Michigan, I watched for Jesus. He was due to arrive at any moment. I knew this, because my father said so all the time in church.

Our house had three small bedrooms and a small living room. Every wall was painted white. In the kitchen sat a dining table, and from above the kitchen sink, a small window let in the sun. That window also let in a little of the promise of God's presence. Part of me was sure that when Jesus did finally come, he'd peek in that window first to make sure we were home. Our house had one exterior side door, and another interior door that led to the front of the church, right onto the platform from which my father preached about the end of the world and how we should all be preparing for it every day of our lives.

My father was an important man. He was extremely busy with his Assemblies of God ministerial duties. And Mother had an important job too, which was to help Dad. She was busy as church pianist, choir director, and Sunday school director. We had church every Wednesday night, and evening choir practices throughout the week. Sunday mornings were for Sunday school and church services. And on Sunday evenings the main church services were held, usually beginning at seven o'clock and lasting until at least nine. When a visiting evangelist came to town, we had church every night of the week. My parents made home visits to the ill and needy, and in addition, held funerals, weddings, board meetings, and the like.

My sister Dorothy, nine by then, had light brown hair that she wore short with bangs. Her sparkling blue eyes always lit up when she smiled. She had a lively sense of humor and ended most comments with a laugh. Dorothy was old enough to go with Mother and Dad on church activities. I was not quite three, and too much of a nuisance to take along.

"Grace cannot be counted on to keep quiet or sit still," Mother said. "And Dorothy is too young to be responsible for her."

Consequently, Mother left me in the parsonage when she went to church in the evenings, figuring she'd be only a few steps away in an emergency. I found it hard to resist the urge to follow Mother. As soon as she left my room, I would find a way to climb out of my crib and watch as my family filed from our foyer into the church. Once they were gone, I'd follow at a safe distance behind them.

Mother soon devised a clever system to keep me contained in my room. She pounded a large nail into the wall outside my door, about eight inches from the doorframe, careful to first knock her fist against plaster to find a solid spot. That way she was sure to drive the nail into a wooden stud rather than the flimsy plaster and lathe.

When evening came, she put me in my room and tucked me into bed as usual, with a pat to my forehead. As she walked away, she was just a large shape, dark and indistinct: brown dress, or navy or black, dark stockings, sturdy black shoes. Her brown hair was tied tightly at the base of her neck. *Don't go,* I prayed silently in the direction of my Mother's round back. Sometimes she turned and told me once more to count my blessings and sleep tight. Usually, though, she kept walking through the doorway, and shut it behind her with a click. After my Mother left, I gnawed at bits of my fingernails, searching for the sharp edges against my tongue.

Through the wooden door, I could hear her in the hallway, the thin rustle of fabric and the creaking of the glass knob as she tied an old silk stocking from the doorknob to the large nail. She pulled the knots securely to make certain I couldn't open the door from inside.

The paint in my bedroom was not bright, but old and mellow, the color of the sky on winter mornings. Worn, but clean. I liked the room in the daytime, but hated it at night after my mother left. It closed in around me. When my mother's footfalls faded away, I'd start to scream. I screamed until my throat burned, until it hurt. I screamed until I fell asleep, sweaty and exhausted.

Sometimes, I tired of screaming. On those nights, I climbed out of bed. The wooden floorboards were cool under my feet, the glass knob smooth in my hand. I'd twist the knob and pull on it as hard as I could until my arms ached too much to continue. I'd climb back into my bed and scream a little more before going to sleep.

One night, however, something wonderful happened. I was yanking on the doorknob with my feet braced against the floor. But my feet were covered up inside my one-piece flannel pajama, and I slipped and fell backward onto my bottom in utter surprise. When I stood up, I saw that the door was ajar. The silk knot had given way.

I stepped cautiously into the hallway and followed the sounds of rhythmic chanting and a strange male voice. The parsonage connected directly to the stage and pulpit of the church by way of a heavily polished oak door in our foyer. I opened that door soundlessly and looked out into the church's sanctuary. I saw a man who was not my father—but a guest minister—in the middle of an animated sermon. I walked onto the stage in my footed flannels and stood behind the young preacher. The congregation erupted in laughter as I hiccoughed loudly from the effort of crying. Mother leapt from her seat at the piano to grab me. From then on, Mother brought me along to church services.

I suppose I always understood that Brazil was part of my life, even before there was any direct talk of going on a mission there. I knew my father had spent his early years in Brazil after my Grandpa Kolenda had emigrated from Germany in 1902. But Grandpa Kolenda had found it difficult to support his family in Brazil as a modest preacher, and had moved them all to the United States in 1909. All but my Aunt Martha, that is. Martha had been left behind because she was pregnant and had to get married.

So when Martha came to visit us in Lansing in 1937, no one in the Kolenda family had seen her since 1909, when they'd all left Brazil without her for America. Over the years, Martha and her husband Rodrigo had eight more children. The youngest, my almost five-year-old cousin, Edison, came with his mother. The entire Kolenda family erupted into an absolute flurry at this thirty-year reunion with their long-lost sister.

Aunt Martha was forty-seven, but to me she looked about a hundred. Heavy streaks of gray divided her brown hair in the front, and she wore her braids fastened tightly behind her head. Her face was cross-hatched with lines of hardship from so many years in Brazil raising nine children on a pittance. Still, she smiled nonstop and her arrival prompted a string of family reunions, with constant company through our daily lives. Good-hearted Aunt Elizabeth bought Martha some nicer dresses and a pair of new black leather shoes—modest, of course—and a fancy black felt hat, the kind most women wore in those days.

Dad was the only one of us who spoke Portuguese. He acted as the interpreter for Martha when German didn't suffice. Poor Edison didn't speak a single word of German or English. He was almost my age, just ten months older. He was shockingly thin for a boy his age, just a tangle of wiry arms and legs, but he was comical and spirited. Dorothy had no use for playing with me; I was a bother.

"Get away from me and do something useful with yourself," she said whenever I asked her to play.

Edison, on the other hand, seemed to like me, even though we couldn't say much to each other. We quickly became friends, and developed a crude sign language.

What Edison liked most was to play with the coal-fired furnace in the church basement. His hand sign for this game involved a pat, pat, pat with one hand over the other to signify the basement stairs, and the waving of ten fingers to suggest fire. Edison couldn't get enough of the furnace. Since there was no need for central heating in Brazil, our massive coal burner held his fascination. It must have seemed like something from another world to him, perhaps a hungry, hot-mouthed monster or a portal to the fires of hell.

My cousin and I fed the furnace with old magazines and newspapers we gathered from the stacks against the church basement walls. The fire crackled as we stuffed in the paper and radiated such intense heat that I had to take off my cotton sweater. Edison unbuttoned the collar of his shirt, stained with perspiration. We smiled at each other, both our faces streaked with soot and grime, hairlines dripping.

Upstairs, adults in the living room took off sweaters and suit coats as the temperature rose. Sweat broke out on their foreheads. Grandma Kolenda started fanning herself despite the crispness of the fall day. That's when my father took the basement stairs two at a time and found us cheerfully stuffing armloads of paper into the furnace.

Horror spread across his face. "Drop those newspapers!" he demanded, as Edison was about to throw in another armload.

Dad slammed and fastened the furnace door shut then stamped on the smoldering papers. When he'd extinguished every spark, he marched us up the stairs by our elbows. Stern old Grandma Kolenda sent me to sit in the corner.

"Ha, ha," Dorothy mocked, "you get what you deserve."

But not Edison—he didn't get in any trouble at all.

Grandma drew nearer to him. "Come stay by me, my sweet boy. You should not do anything that bad girl tells you to do."

Dorothy laughed with delight at my shame.

I never liked my Grandma Kolenda after that day. I went out of my way to avoid her. And I was especially glad I didn't have her big ugly nose.

Grandma Kolenda thought I was a bad girl, and certainly Dorothy agreed, but Jesus knew better. I felt like the luckiest girl in the world. Just as I was watching for Jesus and his second coming, Jesus was also watching over me. For the most part, I could expect what I deserved, and I deserved mostly good things because I tried hard to please God and my parents.

I found life in Lansing comfortingly predictable, punctuated alternately by small deprivations and pleasant indulgences. Dad was home most of the time during those years, and our family seemed close and safe. There were definitely good things to be had from life; it was simply a matter of learning where and when to find them.

Chapter Two

Giant at the Pulpit

SUNDAY MORNINGS were my favorite time. At Sunday school I got to see my friends, and we sang fun songs and listened to fascinating Bible stories. After the morning service, Dorothy and I were expected to greet members of the congregation. This task was also enjoyable, and both of us looked forward to doing it, especially since some members would bring us small treats—butterscotches, pillow mints, strings of red licorice, or even chewing gum. We quickly caught on that the same people tended to bring treats again and again. Soon we knew whom to look for as we said our hellos.

"Come on, slowpoke," Dorothy would say, grabbing me by the sleeve. "Mrs. Johnson is over there! If you want a licorice you better hurry."

I learned that the church's chairs had hinged seats that could be raised as needed. The underside of these seats was a goldmine of discarded gum. I scampered hurriedly off to our kitchen for a knife and a paper sack. Then I set about the harvest.

The first few wads I stuffed into my mouth were a bit hard, but after some vigorous chewing, an amazing mixture of flavors emerged.

Just as I was popping another piece into my mouth, Dorothy's shout rang through the nave. "Are you crazy, Graceann? What in tarnation are you doing?" She ran at me and yanked the knife out of my hand. "Open your mouth!" she demanded.

"Leave me alone! You're mean, mean, mean!" I mumbled through my gum. I pursed my lips shut.

"Open!" Dorothy shouted again.

I shook my head.

"Open that mouth or I'm telling."

I opened my mouth, just a little. But a little was enough. Dorothy saw my huge glob of gum.

"Spit it out, Graceann," she ordered, grabbing my paper sack and holding it open under my chin.

I shook my head.

"NOW!"

Reluctantly, I parted my lips, and let my treasure fall. I began to cry. Dorothy ignored my tears and dragged me to the parsonage to deliver me to our father. She was telling on me anyway, even though I'd spit out the gum.

Dad gave me a memorable lecture on germs, and I didn't collect the chewed gum anymore. But still, I felt its sticky sweetness beckoning from under my seat during every church service. I longed to answer that call. Sometimes, my mouth would water with the thought of it. But my father's voice was more compelling.

How could it not be? I believed every word he said. Day after day and night after night, I watched him preach with a passion that inspired, soothed, and converted souls for God. Dad's influence on his congregation is impossible to separate from any other impression of my childhood. One memorable service took place on October 30, 1938. I was four-and-a-half years old and was sitting obediently in the church waiting for the beginning of the service, when the front doors shot open and a crowd of people— members and non-members—rushed frantically into the pews. They listened raptly to every word my father said, their faces filled with fright and desperation. He went on preaching, with more conviction than ever.

As soon he finished the sermon, he gave the "altar call," his direct invitation to those in the congregation ready to be saved. Dad asked them to come forward and give themselves to Jesus. "Don't wait another minute," he said. "The moment is now, Jesus is here for you now!"

I stole a furtive glance over my shoulder, but I didn't see Jesus yet.

A large group of the congregation hurried forward, most of them crying. These people were really anxious to repent of their sins.

Dad couldn't figure out what was happening, but kept on calling. When finally the altar call wound down, Dad asked one of the nonmembers to explain what was happening. "Why are you all here now, on this night, when Jesus calls every night?" he asked the gentleman.

"There's no time," the man answered. "The world is ending!"

"What are you talking about?" my father asked.

"It's on the radio!" he said, sobbing through his words. "It's happening right now; it's an alien invasion!"

Again, I craned my neck to see if Jesus was possibly making his entrance at this very moment.

"Pull yourself together, my friend," my father said, placing his palms on the gentleman's shoulders. "Be specific. Who said the world was ending?"

"It's the *War of the Worlds!*" the man said. "The Martians are invading! I heard it on the *Mercury Theater.* Everyone did!"

My father returned to his pulpit and demanded the attention of the entire congregation. He promised salvation to any who would accept it, and he converted one sinner after another that night. All of these terrified people rushed forward, crying as they knelt before the altar. Dad commanded they repent of their sins, ask for Jesus's forgiveness, and promise to be a Christian and serve Jesus for the rest of their lives.

My father raised both arms, with tears in his eyes, and prayed out loud: "Dear Jesus, hear the prayers of these sinners, forgive them, and accept them as your children, and help them to follow your ways. We thank You for salvation. In Jesus's name, Amen."

Then everyone rose, and went on their way.

Orson Welles's 1938 CBS radio drama convinced more than my father's congregation that the world was ending, but the congregants, at least, knew where to go to be saved.

Surely in the following days and weeks these people realized, along with the rest of America, that the Orson Welles broadcast they'd heard was fictitious. As a young child on that frightful night, I saw only my father's power to quell the hysteria of the terror-stricken and bring to them the solace of the Lord.

THE CHRISTMAS SEASON that year was agonizing. I was burning with desire for a very special rubber doll. I'd seen her in a store window and fallen madly in love. This baby wet her diapers. She drank from a bottle. She had hair of flaxen gold. I talked of her nonstop. I dreamed of her at night, and I prayed to God for her, loudly, to make sure Mom and Dad would hear me.

Dear Jesus, I'd yell from my bed. *Please, please, please let me have the baby doll.* I would pause to consider what I might offer in exchange. *Please, Jesus, I have been so good,* I'd continue, yelling even louder. *I will take care of her, and I will not quarrel with Dorothy.* Did it count if Dorothy quarreled with me but I didn't quarrel back? I decided it was good enough, and went on. *I will not quarrel with Mother. I will not covet anything else, not one other single thing, if I have this doll.*

I had to have her. I asked Mom and Dad, and reminded them how good I'd been.

"Don't get your hopes up," warned Dorothy. "They haven't got any money, what with Aunt Martha's visit."

She laughed a little, and for a moment, I hated her. Then I remembered my promise to Jesus. I couldn't quarrel with Dorothy now. And it was true that Aunt Martha's visit had involved a lot of extra expenses, and there was no money for Christmas gifts. I had heard Mother and Dad say it themselves. Still, Dorothy was mean to rub it in like that.

But she didn't know that I had covered all my bases—I'd asked Santa Claus, too. "And Santa Claus doesn't need money," I told Dorothy smugly.

"You mean he wouldn't need money," Dorothy said, "if he existed. Which he doesn't."

Dear Jesus, I hollered at the top of my lungs that night. *Please help Dorothy believe in Santa Claus as I do! Please make her be nicer to me! Please let me have the baby doll for Christmas. I promise to be even better, to obey and to follow in your footsteps. Amen.* With my throat sore from shouting, I felt satisfied and confident. I knew Jesus was on my side.

"Graceann," Mother said the next morning as she set my plate of eggs in front of me on the kitchen table, "you needn't shout your prayers at night. It's simply not pious. The Lord can hear you plenty fine without such a racket."

Finally, Christmas Eve arrived. Our family celebrated in the church sanctuary on the platform where my father preached. There, we'd decorated a tree together with the congregation. My gift was under the tree, but it was not in the right-sized box. I scrunched my eyes and hoped anyway as I carefully peeled back the paper. Inside was a raincoat, bright yellow rubber, with a wide hood. My heart sank.

It was practical. And it was pretty. It was actually the most beautiful raincoat I had ever seen. But it was not my doll. Dorothy's gifts were practical items as well, mostly clothing. When the gift opening was over, we sang "Silent Night" and "Angels We Have Heard on High." We prayed thanks to God for His gift of love and His goodness to us. I tried hard to be sincere. I tried to be grateful. I failed on both counts.

Back at the parsonage, I felt ashamed of myself. What a selfish, sinful girl I was. Father would be disappointed in me if he knew how ungrateful I really was. I was horrified at the darkness inside my heart.

Then Dorothy said casually, "Grace, you should look behind the couch."

My heart caught in my chest. I walked slowly to the couch and stood there in front of it. I held my breath. Then I crawled onto the blue floral seat cushions and looked over the back. I screamed. There she was! My baby! She was in a box, not wrapped in Christmas paper, just a box with a cellophane top, through which I could see her. She looked up at me, her glassy blue eyes wide open beneath thick, black lashes. My doll! I thought I would die of happiness. I hugged and kissed Mother and Dad and then I ran to hug and kiss Dorothy, too.

"That's enough," my sister said, wiping my kiss off her cheek.

I named my doll Ruthie, after one of my favorite Old Testament stories. She wore a fancy pink dress and came with her own bottle and extra diapers. I barely let Ruthie out of my arms, let alone out of my sight. And when my father began to speak of a journey we would make to Brazil, that faraway place of Edison and Aunt Martha's home, I held Ruthie tighter and whispered to her of the adventures we would have together when my wonderful father took us traveling.

WE LEFT the parsonage in the summer of 1939 and set up housekeeping in a small rental cottage while we prepared for our move to Brazil. That fall, Mother enrolled me in a kindergarten about one hundred yards from our cottage. Dorothy was in middle school by then.

"See to it that you are a good girl and a good example for Jesus," Mother warned her.

Dorothy rolled her eyes behind Mother's back.

"You shouldn't disobey Mother," I whispered fiercely.

"Just you keep quiet," Dorothy warned me. "You don't know anything, little Miss Goody-Two-Shoes. Your day will come, just you wait and see. Mother will be watching you soon enough."

As it turned out, she already was. My kindergarten had a morning music class, and that's where I learned that I was not like everybody else. It started when the pretty young teacher took out the Victrola. She and the other children and I happily danced along to "Charley My Boy," by Gus Kahn and Ted Fiorito. On the other side of the same record was a song called "Little Old Clock on the Mantel," and a cheerful foxtrot. It was great fun for everyone.

But when I told Mother about it, her face turned red and the vein near her left eye bulged. "So this is what music class involves!" she snapped. She scrawled a note to my beloved teacher, saying that under no circumstances should I "be allowed to dance with the other children during what you are calling music class."

My teacher, unsure what to do with me during the dancing, announced the conundrum to the class. "Does anyone have an idea for what Graceann might do during dancing?" she asked. "Please raise your hand in the air if you do."

Blood rose hot to my cheeks, as the other children looked around silent and confused. A plump little girl in blond ringlets raised her hand. "She could turn the handle on the record player," she said sweetly.

My teacher found this idea grand. Starting that morning, I cranked the handle of the old Victrola while the other kindergarten girls and boys stamped and twirled across the wood floor. Outside, cold rain streaked down the windows in time to the beat. I wished I could have joined them and was confused and embarrassed to be singled out in this way. I could feel a tightness in the pit of my stomach, and I forced myself to hold back the tears.

As I walked home that afternoon, the small neighborhood beagle hound, a scraggly light brown beast, started trotting after me. This dog often chased me to and from school, running along behind me, nipping. On this day, he ran faster than usual, and his long, floppy ears flew behind him as he chased me. His barking grew nearer, and I began to run, too, crying through the falling rain, my yellow raincoat slapping my bare legs as I went. But I wasn't fast enough. The dog reached me, and bit into my coat, tearing a large chunk off the back hem. My beautiful raincoat was wrecked, just like that.

Chapter Three

The Send-Off

"**B**UGS IN BRAZIL aren't like here," said my cousin Albert. A slender Box Elder bug scurried through the dust near the toe of Albert's brown leather shoe. He leaned over in a flash and held the bug between two fingers. "See this fella?" he said. "He'd die if you swallowed him. But his cousins in Brazil are tougher and meaner. If they get in your mouth, they'll shoot down your throat and live inside your stomach for years."

Albert dangled the Box Elder bug six inches from my nose. Its legs wheeled frantically against the air, thin as eyelashes.

"Don't!" I hollered. It was the summer of 1939. I was five years old, and this was our farewell family reunion in honor of our impending departure to Brazil.

Albert dropped the bug loose and it skittered away into the grass. Then he reached into his pocket and pulled out a pack of Wrigley's spearmint chewing gum. "Here," he said, "have a stick."

With wariness, I eyed his outstretched hand, the half moons of his short fingernails edged with dirt, and the foil treasure he offered.

"Come on," he coaxed. "Have a piece while you can. They don't have chewing gum in Brazil."

Albert was the son of my beloved Aunt Elizabeth and Uncle Fred Brenda. At eleven, even though he teased a lot, I adored him, and I loved the attention from my older cousin.

"The people there don't wear clothes," said Fred, Albert's older brother. At the advanced age of twenty-one, Fred knew just about everything. "They go stark naked in Brazil. Even to church. You and Dorothy will have to go naked, too."

"No, we won't!" I yelled, stamping my foot. "I don't believe you!"

A hot wind whipped my short brown hair into my face, sending billows of dust upward. My eyes watered and stung. I gripped Ruthie tighter to my chest, and jammed her plastic bottle into her pink mouth. Naked people in church! No way would my father let anyone come into his church without clothes. I wasn't even allowed to dance to the music on the Victrola in my own kindergarten!

"Believe it or not," said Albert. "Suit yourself. But you'll see when you get there."

The following morning, we loaded the Chevy for our southward trek to Louisiana. From there, we would board a ship bound for South America. Would all these people really help us go through with this? All told, counting Dorothy and me, there were forty cousins on Dad's side of the family, so, if you subtracted the nine Brazilian cousins, there were thirty-one of us at any typical reunion. On this day, there were at least that many milling about the yard. The Kolendas were a close-knit and family-oriented bunch. During the summer, reunions sprouted up fast as dandelions, over the least excuse. Always festive and prayerful, these gatherings were lively celebrations of family and faith. The many cousins played games, such as cricket, hide and seek, and kick the can, and the adults shared the latest family news and current events. But this particular day, on the brink of our departure, was more emotional and intense than usual. Ham sandwiches, mounds of thick yellow potato salad, and pitchers of ice-cold lemonade set the oddly cheerful backdrop for my mother's sobbing. Even Dad wept, while his brothers and sisters gathered on the porch and prayed for our safekeeping in Brazil.

"They had better pray harder," Albert said, casting a glance in the direction of the porch. A long blade of grass dangled from the side of his mouth. "Yep," he nodded. "I reckon they'd better pray to the Lord a whole lot harder, 'cause you sure are going to need it."

Across the lawn, my mother slumped against the porch rail, her shoulders heaving up and down, up and down. A lump pressed up my own throat. I wasn't sure how long I could hold it back.

"Don't cry," said Fred. "It's not allowed in Brazil. If you cry there, they'll throw you in jail. And they aren't even real jails. Just cages in the jungle. Full of people crying. You don't want to end up in something like that."

All of my cousins liked to tease, but Albert and Fred had a genuine passion for it. I looked up to these older boys. I admired them, simply because they were older and, I was sure, much wiser. I took their every word as gospel, no matter how I protested outwardly. I ignored him this time, and looked down at Ruthie, who lay in my arms with her head askew and her eyes closed. I tucked her bottle into the pocket of my pinafore.

"You'll want to be careful with that one there," Albert said, gesturing to my doll. I clutched her tighter and shifted several inches down the bench. "Brazil is wild country," he said. "A backward sort of place. No lights, no running water, no cars. No dolls. Just think what will happen when you pull up in your dad's '39 Chevy with that soft rubber dolly of yours. Oh, what I wouldn't give to be there for that! All the naked people who've never seen a car will swarm around you, and then they'll see that baby there. Their eyes will be popping out of their heads." He demonstrated by holding his breath and opening his eyes as wide as he could. All the veins along his temples snaked blue and ugly. "You better remember to bring your bananas," he said, his head lolling back and forth on his neck.

"Why?" I asked, sensing a trap.

"Man-eating monkeys," Fred said.

"Brazil is crawling with them," said Albert. "Those killers love bananas, so you have to remember to bring plenty every time you go in the car. If you toss bananas out the windows, the monkeys will catch them and run away. But if you don't have bananas, the little devils will crawl right over your car and smash the windows open. They'll grab you however they can, and they'll eat you up. They can eat a whole person, bones and all, in minutes flat."

"Dear Lord," I could hear Uncle August praying loudly from the porch. He swayed back and forth slightly as he spoke, and he raised his face and his arms toward the sky. "Please, Lord, look down upon these servants of yours, and their helpless children, and bless them with your mercy and compassion as they begin this difficult voyage. Please keep them safe from the dangers that will plague them on the way, please hold them . . ."

Please, Jesus, I prayed silently, frantically. *Please don't make us go. I'll be good, I promise.* I stroked Ruthie's rubber head as I implored the Lord. *Please don't make us go to Brazil, please not now!* I considered a possible future date I could offer to God as an acceptable alternative. After a brief moment of consideration, I added simply, *Please don't make us ever go, God! Please, not ever!*

OUR SHIP, the *Del Valle,* sailed from New Orleans on Halloween. Aunt Elizabeth and Uncle Fred came along from Michigan to Louisiana to see us on our way, and so did Uncle Ernie and Grandma Kolenda, cranky as ever. Other Kolenda relatives came too, packing themselves into a caravan of cars. Oddly, my parents were still seen as "the young missionary couple," despite being forty-three and forty-one years old. Still, their departure into the great unknown to do the work of the Lord was somehow glamorous, and the Kolendas wanted to be there when John Peter and Marguerite boarded the big ship with their small daughters.

In 1939, a forty-nine day luxury Atlantic cruise on the Delta Line's *Delmundo* was about five hundred dollars. But for two hundred dollars you could get to Brazil on a fine boat like the *Del Valle.* It was a medium-sized cargo freighter that delivered goods to ports in South America—Rio de Janeiro, Santos, Montevideo, Buenos Aires, and Victoria—and it could accommodate twenty-five passengers. Our voyage was fully booked.

Mother wore black on the morning of our departure, but her dress was neither sleek nor stylish. Her eyes, ringed with red, watered steadily, and she kept a handkerchief tucked into the sleeve of her dress to dab them as needed. Our possessions lay stacked beside us on the dock, ready to be loaded. Mother had packed up all of our earthly belonging into boxes and crates. She had even packed her Havilland china. The Havilland, with its delicate blue print, was a wedding gift from her parents, and each fragile piece was painstakingly wrapped in newspaper and wedged tightly into heavy boxes sealed with packing tape and twine.

I had treasures of my own from my grandma on Mom's side, Grandma Westmark, who, unlike Grandma Kolenda, doted on me. To prepare for our trip, Grandma Westmark had taken Dorothy and me shopping at Dayton's in downtown Minneapolis. Dayton's was a stylish and expensive department store. There, in those heavily perfumed aisles adorned with tall, beautiful mannequins gazing down from brightly lit pedestals, Grandma Westmark spoiled us rotten. For me, she bought a brand new navy-blue coat, with smart brass buttons down the front and on the sleeves. It came with a matching pillbox hat. And she bought me a new dress, too, a calico print with a wide belt and ruffled hem. I wore the dress and the coat for our departure.

"You look ridiculous," Dorothy sneered at me.

But I knew she was just jealous. Her own dress, a brown calico, was much plainer. I felt like a princess! I had no idea that this would be my last new outfit until our return from Brazil six years later.

When the *Del Valle's* horn sounded the boarding call, all twenty-five passengers filed excitedly, and in some cases, tearfully, onto the ship. Dorothy and I were the only children on board. As we pulled away from the port, everyone gathered on the narrow promenade deck. Mother and Father waved goodbye to those who waved from shore, so I waved, too. Grandma Kolenda scowled up at us, and Aunt Elizabeth's mouth was moving, but I couldn't hear the words. She was too far away, and the ship's roaring engine and blaring horn drowned out everything else except my father, singing "God Bless America" with Dorothy smiling at his side. She looked so happy next to Dad. Her short curly brown hair was ruffled by the wind, and her eyes were filled with tears. He had that effect on everyone. Other passengers joined in with the song, loudly and through their tears. It was a wailing rendition of the song, tinged with the hysteria of the unknown.

As I watched the expanse of deep gray water widening between us and the port, and as I listened to Dad booming out those patriotic verses, horror and fear filled me. My father seemed so unfamiliar, his voice unlike the one I knew from the pulpit. I wanted him to stop singing. I wanted the ship to turn around. I wanted to be back in Lansing. But the shore only grew more difficult to make out, just a papery gray strip of horizon. I couldn't believe my parents were going through with this terrible mistake.

Chapter Four

Over the Equator

EVENTUALLY, I HAD NO CHOICE but to explore the novelties of our temporary, floating home with Dorothy.

"Come on," Dorothy said. "Stop blubbering. There's lots more to do here than at home."

I tucked Ruthie under my arm and followed her.

We began with our tiny stateroom, unpacking our clothing and placing it neatly into the drawers of our small, shared dresser. Then we climbed onto the bunk beds—Dorothy on the upper and me on the lower. The bedspreads were chenille, criss-crossed with navy diamonds. We poked in and out of the ship's public spaces. The lounge was carpeted in dark blue wool and outfitted with velveteen chairs and couches and mahogany tables. Exposed oak beams, stained dark brown, lined the ceiling. An enormous, dark oil painting hung on the main interior wall. It was a painting of a large schooner sailing on a stormy ocean with mountains in the distance.

The painting lured me, with its rich colors and shiny surface that looked like it was still wet. I reached up to touch the painting, but couldn't quite get there. The paint was so textural, so luminous, my mouth practically watered with curiosity. I climbed onto the velveteen chair and balanced myself on my knees to reach up again. This time, I made it. But the paint felt disappointingly dry to the touch.

"Gracie!" scolded Dorothy. "Get down from there!"

Bells started to ring, and a loud whistle blew. What had I done? I scooted back off the chair so fast that I toppled off onto my bottom and Ruthie rolled out of my arms and across the carpet.

"Come on!" shouted Dorothy. "Back to our room!"

I grabbed my doll and we ran through the ship back to our stateroom door, and there in the hall, we bumped into Dad. His arms were full of orange lifejackets that he'd pulled out from under our beds. Mother stood inside our stateroom and was fastening her lifejacket; Dad helped us fasten ours. Then we all ran back to the deck. By now, I was crying.

"Stop crying," said Dorothy. She turned to Mother. "Make her stop crying."

Mother glared at Dorothy and pulled me closer to her. "It's just a fire drill, Gracie. Don't worry."

I cried anyway, and clung to Ruthie, as Dorothy scowled in my direction. But even she became distracted as crewmembers lowered a lifeboat over the ship's side to the water below. I would not be getting into that little boat, no way. I cried harder. Then a loud, sharp noise, like a firecracker, exploded from behind us. Mother jumped. An iron-weighted rope flew past us, over the deck rail, into the ocean. Then the crew drew the rope back in. That really got me to sobbing, until the captain finally gave the signal that the fire drill was over, and I was allowed to take off my lifejacket.

During the aftermath of the fire drill, Mother connected with Mr. and Mrs. Emrich, a couple from Minneapolis who were pleasure-tripping to Bolivia.

"No doubt they are wealthy people," Mother wrote in a letter to her youngest sister Edna, who lived in Minneapolis. "They have a bakery on the corner of Bloomington Avenue and Lake Street, I think."

Mother also wrote about eight Mormon boys aboard the *Del Valle*, heading to Brazil as missionaries. She was especially proud of Dad's enthusiastic efforts to convert them. Mother said Dad talked to them about the Bible every chance he had. "We are so glad the Lord has made us a blessing to them," she wrote to Brother and Sister Severance, who were the main financial supporters for our mission in Brazil. They were also Mom and Dad's best friends. Dorothy and I called them Uncle Rollin and Aunt Henrietta, although they were not related to us.

That first night at sea, I lay stiff and awake on my lower bunk until the sun rose. Ruthie lay stiff and awake beside me. Her diaper was wet, but I was too afraid to get up and change it. The ship's engine roared on through the dark hours, making time through the night. I didn't like the sound of it. Nor did I trust the roll and sway of the ship against the water. When morning sunlight finally brightened enough to penetrate the floral drapes over the small, round windows of our room, relief washed over me.

During the night, the air in our stateroom was close and stale, even a little musty. Worst of all, it was strange. I couldn't wait to get back out on deck where the air was fresh and somehow more familiar, despite its saltiness. Plus, the deck was full of distractions and surprises. Like the small saltwater swimming pool that I nearly stumbled into one afternoon early in our voyage. The pool was literally a water hole, about ten feet by ten feet, with mesh around all four sides. A short ladder hung on one end. There was no way for me to know how deep the hole was, because none of us could touch bottom.

Once I made my discovery, Dorothy and I began to spend every spare moment playing in the make-shift pool. Dorothy enjoyed the pool as much as I did, and it was easy to talk her into joining me there even though she preferred to explore the ship without me now that we both knew our way around. Often Ruthie swam with us in the pool, too, bobbing up and down in the saltwater waves.

Dorothy was busy helping Mother with something in our cabin one day so I went alone to the pool. Halfway there, I realized I had forgotten Ruthie. I would have turned back, but I was in too much of a hurry to swim, especially since it looked like rain was on the way. The sky above was gloomy, and the ocean waves were rolling high, so the ship tossed about vengefully. So did the water in the swimming pool. It rocked and threw me back and forth and up and down, which was fun until I lost my hold of the pool's mesh sides. Now I was being tossed back and forth under the water, and I panicked. Although I loved the pool, I could barely swim. I went down, down, down beneath the surface, dark saltwater pressing down from overhead. I thrashed and spun, and in my panic, I tried to scream. Saltwater filled my open mouth and burned my throat and nose. I swallowed and gagged. I felt fear like I had never known. I kicked and flailed until something scratchy brushed the fingers of my left hand. I grabbed and held. It was the mesh wall of the pool. I clung to it and pulled myself up until my head was above water. Then I breathed and breathed and breathed.

That night when Dorothy and I were in bed I told her what happened.

I was surprised by Dorothy's response. "Gracie, don't you ever go swimming alone," she said. "Even if I don't want to swim, I'll sit by the pool and watch you."

Although Dorothy was my constant tormentor, at times like this I knew she really loved me.

By FIVE O'CLOCK each afternoon, dusk settled over the ocean and the *Del Valle*. And dusk meant danger. All passengers were required to pull the shades and drapes tightly against the night. Lights were for emergency use only, because the *Del Valle*'s captains were worried about being spotted by a German submarine. The war was simply too close for comfort. Even though the United States was not officially engaged in battle, we could be mistaken for a British ship in the dark. Here on the ocean, life was one big scary surprise after the next. I was getting used to being scared.

I was on the promenade deck with Mother and Dorothy, watching the waves roll by, when Dad emerged from the ship's interior covered head to toe in blood. I screamed at the top of my lungs.

"Right this way," Dad said, "right this way!" He snapped a long leather whip in the air and laughed. He was dressed in shorts, and the streaks of red ran down his arms and legs.

All around him, passengers gathered to whoop and yell. I screamed again, and started to cry. I buried my head—and Ruthie's—in Mother's skirt.

"Shush, now," Mother said. "Your father's not hurt. He's celebrating. It's fun." She didn't sound convinced. "Dorothy, get your sister a drink of cool water. Quickly."

"Oh, for heaven's sake," Dorothy snapped. "Does she need to cry at every little thing?"

"Stop your insolence this instant," said Mother.

Dorothy gave her a dark look and went to find a drink of water for me.

Father had volunteered to be a "Trusty Shellback," someone who has already crossed the equator, in the spirited ritual of initiation for the "Pollywogs," those passengers who were passing over the equator for the first time. I didn't understand that the "blood" all over my father was ketchup, and I couldn't accept that such screeching and shouting was not a deadly fight. It looked and sounded at least as dangerous as the invisible German submarines lurking beneath the ocean's dark surface. What was wrong with my parents, once so safe and predictable? Nose to nose with Ruthie in the folds of my mother's wool skirt, I began to sob in earnest.

NOT LONG after we crossed the equator, the *Del Valle* sailed into a violent storm. We had to veer off course for several days in order to avoid a full-blown hurricane at sea. Our ship reeled in the huge waves, and seawater deluged the *Del Valle's* bow and flooded the ship's decks. No one could venture up from the bowels of the ship without risking being swept overboard. As I huddled with Dorothy in our bottom bunk, clutching Ruthie to my chest, I cried and prayed.

When I wouldn't stop crying, Dorothy finally said in exasperation, "I'm going to kill you if you don't shut up."

But I couldn't help myself. The oily, metallic scent of the *Del Valle* mixed inextricably with the smell of my own fear. For three days and nights we hid below, waiting out the storm. I watched for Jesus the whole time. I was sure the end was coming. I wondered if Jesus would take me up. I was pretty sure he would. But I wasn't sure about Dorothy. I cast a glance at her through my tears. Maybe Jesus knew why she was so mean and would take her up anyway. But I had my doubts, and that made me cry even harder. I loved my sister! Jesus had to take her up with us!

Mother, though, remained incredibly stoic as the ship pitched in the deep sea. And just as she had insisted it would, the storm eventually passed and the *Del Valle* sailed back toward Brazil. If Mother had any misgivings during our ocean journey, she never showed them. As each day passed, the United States receded further and further into the distance, literally and figuratively, and by the time the storm died down and we were back on course, it seemed that my father's destiny was immutable and that even nature could not outwit my father and God.

Finally, on Sunday morning, the eighteenth day of November, after nineteen long days at sea, Mother woke Dorothy and me so that we could look at what she saw through the porthole window: the distant sparkle of Rio de Janeiro.

"No," I mumbled, and pulled the sheet back over my head. I clutched Ruthie tighter and tried to force myself back to sleep.

Above me, I heard Dorothy stir and climb out of bed. "Go ahead," she whispered as she passed my pillow, "sleep through the landing. See if anyone cares."

"Oh, go back to bed," Mother said curtly. "You've had your look, there's nothing more to see."

I felt the sting of Mother's words to Dorothy. Why, I wondered, was she always so sharp to my sister?

Mother was right, of course. It was Rio that she'd seen across the water. We docked later that morning. Alongside us was a huge British aircraft carrier. The *Ark Royal* had been combing the South Atlantic for a German warship said to be somewhere near Argentina. Sailors in white uniforms stood at attention along the carrier's upper deck. I wore my beautiful dress, and Dorothy wore her brown one, and we waved at the sailors from the *Del Valle*'s deck. Many of them waved back.

"Marguerite," Dad said, "get my camera!" Mother quickly ran for the camera, and Dad started photographing the first of what would eventually become thousands of scenes depicting our Brazilian experience.

At the bottom of the gangplank, we stepped onto solid but utterly unfamiliar ground. Late November is high summer in Brazil, and the air was wet with humidity. Sweat ran down my forehead and into the corners of my mouth, salty and tart. Ruthie's rubber skin was slippery against my palms. The smell of Brazil was overpowering. The air was thick, humid, and musty, with a hint of rotten fish, and other strange smells I could not identify. I breathed it in as deeply as I could, and at the same time, I wanted to cover my nose.

"Stop it, Grace," said Dorothy, as I sucked in a nose full of air.

"Do not start that quarreling," Mother scolded Dorothy. "Leave your sister alone for once." Mother took my hand in hers and walked faster, leaving Dorothy to trail behind.

High on the side of Corcovado Mountain, looming over the Rio port, stood Cristo Redentor (Christ the Redeemer)—the colossal statue of Jesus that had been erected a few years earlier. His outstretched arms reached toward us, and my father pointed out the statue in admiration. He aimed his camera again, jostled by waves of passengers and other passersby. All around us, the musical sounds of Portuguese rang out. I strained to understand, and at the same time, I was desperate to cover my ears. Then I remembered.

"Dorothy," I said, turning around and letting go of Mother's hand. I ran back to where my sister lagged behind and started tugging on her sleeve.

"Stop it, Grace," Dorothy answered.

"But Dorothy, we need the bananas."

"What in tarnation are you talking about?"

Something in her tone stopped me. I looked around and didn't spot a single monkey. Every person wore clothes. Along the portside roadways, cars hummed steadily along, just as they had in Lansing. Albert and Fred had been lying about the naked people and the cars and the monkeys. They had probably been fooling about the law against crying, the cage jails in the jungle, and the bugs that could slip down your throat and live in your stomach, too. Probably, they'd lied about all of it. So I should have felt relieved.

But I didn't. I was still afraid, and so was Ruthie.

Chapter Five

Roots of Divinity

MY FATHER TOOK LOADS OF PHOTOGRAPHS during our voyage to Brazil. Indeed, he kept meticulous records throughout my childhood. He filled many reels with movie footage, including scenes from our trip on the *Del Valle*. This was novel and exciting, because home movies were so rare in the 1930s. No one else's father was taking moving pictures on board the ship! No one else's father was as amazing as mine. His whole life, every detail, held my interest and fascination. What he didn't tell me in his stories, he preserved for my discovery later in his hundreds of pages of notes and letters. Nothing was more exciting to me than my father's stories.

"My fourth birthday was the most memorable of my life," he told me one night on the *Del Valle* as the ship sliced through the dark waters. "I celebrated the occasion in the middle of the Atlantic Ocean."

"Where on the ocean, Daddy?" I asked.

"Oh, I can't be exactly sure," he laughed. "But I can tell you that the view was majestic, and the purpose of the journey was a noble one."

That trip, when my father turned four, was his first trip to Brazil, when his parents, Emilia and Ludwig, emigrated from Germany. Ludwig had originally worked as a coal miner in the Ruhr Valley, but he abandoned mining after a back injury, and took up a milk dealership in Gelsenkirchen instead. My father's mother, Emilia, was a smart woman and well educated. She was talented with languages—with a fluency in five tongues. She ran a successful seamstress operation for extra money.

After years of saving, the couple purchased a six-unit brick dwelling on two acres of fertile land. There they built several stables, a barn, a chicken coop, and a blacksmith shop. Ludwig and Emilia lived in one unit and rented the others to relatives and friends.

But changes were on the horizon. It was the end of the 1800s, and the Brazilian government was offering free transportation to Brazil and endowments of land—from forty to sixty acres—for German citizens willing to settle in Brazil for two years or more. Many of Ludwig's friends and family members had accepted this enticing offer and were already living abroad in Brazil's untamed countryside.

Ludwig and Emilia's pine-plank dining table was stacked with desperate letters, pleas from the expatriate relatives. "Dear Ludwig," the letters began, in the ornate script of the era, "our children are illiterate and quickly becoming uncivilized. They have no knowledge of God or church, they have only what we can teach them. But we are so busy trying to make a living, we have no time. Please, won't you lend your help to your loving family?"

Ludwig, a devout Christian and part-time lay minister, couldn't just turn his back on the plight of his countrymen. With little fanfare and even less discussion with Emilia, he sold the brick apartment house, packed what he could, and moved with his wife and children to Brazil. The year was 1902.

There were five children by then, three daughters and two sons: Mamie and Martha were fifteen and thirteen years old, perfectly capable of teaching the children in Brazil arithmetic and writing. Elizabeth, who was eight, could help Emilia with keeping the house, and Ludwig Jr. (Louis), already ten years old, would help his father with the ministry. So, too, would my father, John.

Ludwig could never have known then just how seriously his youngest son would take up the charge.

ATLANTIC CROSSINGS WERE LONG and arduous at the turn of the century, taking a good month at least. November had arrived by the time Ludwig's ship landed in Porto Alegre, Brazil. From there, Ludwig and Emilia and the five children pressed on for another twenty miles. They rode by horse-drawn wagon for two long days before reaching their destination. At night, they spread blankets and pillows rummaged from their belongings over a ground covered with unfamiliar flora, and went to sleep under a sky full of strange new stars. Finally, they arrived in the town of Triunfo, in the interior of the state of Rio Grande do Sul. In Triunfo, they settled in a makeshift dwelling, a small hut cobbled together quickly and poorly by the local relatives. Between its unpainted wooden wall planks were open gaps several inches wide in spots, and the floor was plain dirt.

More than forty people gathered in Ludwig's temporary house for his first sermon. Everyone was eager to hear what the new Lutheran minister had to say. Finally, the expatriates had an official to lead a proper church service. They leaned against the edges of the plain, quilted beds, they perched on logs, they even squatted on the floor. Having gone so long without the word of God, they practically held their breath in anticipation. So when the horsewhip cracked against the dirt floor, it shocked them all. Young Johnnie shot three feet into the air in a cloud of dust. He landed unbitten by the whip but stunned, and that's when he saw it: a huge snake curling through the outstretched legs of the worshippers. The man with the fast whip struck again and killed the snake before it could attack anyone. And thus began my father's first worship service in Brazil.

LATER, THE KOLENDAS MOVED into a bigger, better house, one Ludwig built by hand. He kept his family there for two years, deep in the Brazilian interior, serving the German colonists. Emilia gave birth to a sixth Kolenda child, Ernest. Times were tight, though, and soon after Ernest's birth, Ludwig took action. His family needed better schools and better job prospects than could be found in the under-populated interior. He moved his wife and children back to the capital city of Porto Alegre, where they'd first landed in 1902. There, he continued to work with and minister to the German population.

The German residents of Porto Alegre were quick to take advantage of the religious and educational services of Ludwig and his family. But they had little to offer in return, and Ludwig couldn't feed his family on the meager donations and small sums he earned from odd jobs.

There had to be an easier way. If he were to believe the glowing reports from Germans who'd settled in the United States, maybe there was. Could it be that the land to the north was "the right America," the America where he could fully realize the potential of the New World? By the light of the fire at the end of each long day, Ludwig read and re-read the letters he received from the U.S. Germans. Their promises tantalized him.

Meanwhile, he worried about his daughter. Martha was now a young adult, dating a Brazilian man, Rodrigo Lemos. Time was running out on Ludwig. If he was going to pull up stakes and head for new ground, it had to be soon, before his children started marrying and settling permanently in Brazil. In 1908, six years after landing in Porto Alegre, Ludwig took off to America to scout for jobs.

He landed work almost immediately, work that took him back to his roots as a young miner in Germany. Soon he was crawling down the dusty coal mines of Pennsylvania. Every cent he earned, he saved, until he could afford to send for his family in Brazil. My father, John Peter, was almost eleven when Emilia and the five children left for America in early 1909. Martha was pregnant by then and decided to marry Rodrigo Lemos. She stayed behind.

Ludwig couldn't meet his family's ship in the port of New York, so he made arrangements with his ticketing agent, who promised Ludwig he'd be on hand for Emilia's arrival. Unfortunately, the agent forgot his promise, and when the ship pulled in to dock, no one was waiting. A clerk from the shipping company asked Emilia about her husband's whereabouts.

"Pennsylvania?" she ventured. "Or Michigan? Or maybe . . . Colorado." The confused Emilia envisioned these places nestled as tightly as the neighboring countries of Scandinavia.

The frustrated clerk, after several long hours, shuttled the Kolendas to Ellis Island, where they were held, examined, and processed before entering the United States.

Immigrants stayed on Ellis Island in segregated dormitories where two to three hundred people sprawled on canvas cots. My young father watched as immigration officials herded his mother and sisters away to the women's quarters. While they waited, the Department of Immigration posted the names of the Kolenda family members and a call for help in the newspaper. The announcement included a matter-of-fact deadline for a deportation date. When Ludwig's ticketing agent caught sight of that small ad, he remembered his forgotten vow. But when he contacted the authorities at Ellis Island, they told him that only a relative and responsible party could "receive" Emilia and the children. He dispatched a telegram to Ludwig, who rushed to New York in two days. By then, the Kolenda family had been on Ellis Island for almost two weeks. They were on the brink of deportation when Ludwig arrived to take them home.

LUDWIG SQUIRRELED AWAY HIS EARNINGS diligently until he had enough to buy a patch of land in Caseville, Michigan. There, my father got himself a grade-school education and an impressive set of sinewy muscles. He built up his shirt-sleeve knowledge through seven years of backbreaking physical labor on the farm. At eighteen years of age, he set out for Detroit to look for work.

What he found instead was Aimee Semple McPherson. The legendary McPherson was the most visible Pentecostal of the 1920s and possibly the most famous female evangelist in the world. Irrepressible and complex, she satisfied the public's need for spirituality, sensationalism, and sex appeal. McPherson was a stylish woman whose passionate sermonizing could mesmerize huge throngs of believers at her tent revivals. Her multi-day crusades were extravaganzas of praising the Lord, speaking in tongues, and faith healing for anyone who needed it. Her 1912 jet black Packard—a personal "Gospel Car"—had the words "Jesus is Coming Soon—Get Ready" painted on one side, and "Where Will You Spend Eternity?" painted on the other. Wherever McPherson went, she attracted good press and plenty of it. After years of working her way up and down the Atlantic coast, pitching her tent, playing piano, and perfecting her fiery preaching style, she decided to go West. She set off in 1918, and by some accounts,

Aimee and her mother were the first women to travel across the country by car unaccompanied.

People everywhere flocked to see her. My father flocked, too, and the impression she made on him altered the course of his life. He was one of thousands who took to Aimee Semple McPherson without reservation. He became, as he later put it, "one of her boys." It took a lot of man-power to run her revivals. The tents had to be moved from town to town, and the crowds that came to hear her had to be controlled, directed, and managed.

Dad traveled with McPherson throughout that first summer after leaving the farm in Caseville. He converted from Lutheranism to Pentecostalism. And he decided to become a minister, which meant making a move to Pasadena to enroll in what was then the only Pentecostal Bible School in the country, now known as Vanguard University of Southern California.

In the ocean air of the west coast, my father's plans crystallized like salt. He wanted to return to Brazil, where his sister Martha was still living and raising her family, too busy and tied down to travel. He wanted to pursue ministry with fervor and complete conviction. And to put his plans into action, he would need a "helpmate." There could be no better place to find a wife, in my father's opinion, than Bible school. He took up the mission with the same matter-of-fact approach that another man might use to research an important career decision or to purchase a new appliance. Somehow, he gained access to the school's student files, and in those private manila folders filled with manually typewritten application forms and academic records, my father discovered a co-ed named Edith Marguerite Westmark. Miss Westmark's goals were strikingly similar to my father's, so he vowed to contrive a meeting with her.

He soon learned from the other students that Edith Marguerite did not use her first name, but preferred to be called Marguerite.

Since Marguerite played organ for a street meeting crew, it wasn't difficult for my father to find her. She was pleasing enough to look at and from her file, my father knew that Marguerite had a teaching certificate from the Pasadena University, today called Point Loma Nazarene University, where she graduated in 1921. This impressed him enormously, since he deeply regretted his own lack of schooling. He undertook his courtship immediately and stubbornly, despite the disappointing truth. The cultured Marguerite, who also played piano and sang like an angel, wanted nothing whatsoever to do with him. To her, my father was a strange German with a heavy accent and a collection of garish second-hand suits in bright red and green stripes. Dating him was completely out of the question.

But John was not to be discouraged. He launched his wooing at a crowded street meeting one Saturday night, by offering to escort Marguerite home to the Pasadena house where she stayed as a nanny. By the time they reached the door, darkness had fallen. Children's voices filtered through the open windows and out onto the porch.

"Marguerite," my father said, "I'm interested in you."

Marguerite laughed and closed the door in his face. The next day, she wrote him a note of explanation, a note I still have, its faded ink disappearing in the creased folds:

APRIL 13, 1922

Dear Mr. Kolenda,

I feel led to write you so that nothing more will have to be said about what you spoke to me Saturday night.

I wish to say that I can only consider you as a friend and brother in Christ.

I don't think it is necessary to go into detail telling you why I have to make this definite answer, but I believe I am led of the Lord, too, and that He would have me give you this answer.

Your friend, Marguerite Westmark

MY FATHER WAS UNDETERRED. Indeed, Marguerite's rebuff only "fueled his fires of love." Everywhere she went, my father followed. He found every possible excuse to shadow her—to classes, to church, to meetings, to special outings, to cafés, to simply walk down the street. In the beginning, she resolutely ignored him. But he persisted, and after months of this uninterrupted attention, her resolve weakened, little by little. When one day my father painted for her, with words, an impassioned picture of his plans for missionary work in Brazil, she listened, intrigued. Gradually she came to look past this unusual suitor's eccentricities and recognize him as a man. But she still could not bring herself to accept his requests to date.

My father graduated from the Southern California Bible College in 1922. Father stayed in California, determined to be near Marguerite and win her acceptance. He worked as a car salesman for a Chevy dealer that summer, and when he'd made his eighth sale, he bought himself a used car—and a new suit. He was ready to plead his case again with Marguerite. A package had been mistakenly left for Marguerite at my father's dormitory, and he took this as his excuse to make a visit. When he pulled up to the Pasadena house in his car—and stepped out of it in his new suit—he was met by a surprisingly friendly Marguerite. When he asked her to dinner, she accepted. It was their first date.

A few days later, my father planned a trip for the two of them to Catalina Island, off the California coast. They toured the shallows around the island's shores in a glass-bottomed boat. My father purchased an abalone shell scavenged from the ocean floor by a diver right before the young couple's eyes. And on the way back to the mainland, as their tour boat cut through the Pacific waves, my father asked Marguerite to marry him. It was just a few days after their very first date. To his great surprise, she said yes. I'm quite sure she was surprised, too.

Her acceptance of Dad's proposal was a foregone conclusion: She owed it to God. Wasn't Dad an aspiring missionary? To marry him was to accept another opportunity to serve the Lord—the very thing she had promised to do, on her own deathbed, just a few years earlier. Dad's proposal was a divine call; there was only one right answer.

WHEN MY MOTHER was sixteen years old, she stopped breathing. She had been suffering a terrible bout of pneumonia, and as the fluid filled her lungs, she started suffocating from the inside out. She was slowly slipping away. She saw before her a tunnel, radiating with white light and disappearing into a distant darkness. Terror-stricken, my mother offered God a fast bargain. If He would let her live, she would serve Him for the rest of her life.

At the same moment, Grandma Westmark set to work. There in the comfortable bedroom of their stately Minnetonka home, Grandma placed a hand on my mother's damp forehead to steady herself, then pressed her full lips over her daughter's papery ones. She breathed into Marguerite's stilled mouth. Almost immediately, Marguerite began to gulp and choke. She was breathing again. From that day forward, my mother recounted this story to anyone who'd listen: the doctor, the grocer, the drugstore clerk. She told every person she met, within the first five minutes, about her near death experience and the divine promise that saved her life. This drive to divulge her moment of faith's discovery persisted throughout my mother's life, much to my embarrassment as a teenager.

In order to keep her promises to God, my mother left the Minnetonka Community Church and joined the intensely fundamentalist Nazarene Church. For Marguerite, religion was not taken for granted, or considered simply a pastime. She had an obsessive need to be active in a church twenty-four hours a day. It was all-consuming and she had a strong desire to serve Jesus one hundred percent of her time in whatever capacity God so desired. She enrolled in a two-year course to earn her teaching certificate from the University of Minnesota, but then taught only briefly before catching wind of a new Bible school underway in Pasadena, California. She felt she had to go. Grandpa Westmark pitched in for the tuition, but Marguerite was on her own for room and board. She signed on to be a nanny in a home near the Bible school's campus. It was there that my father later pulled up in his "new-used" Chevy and convinced her to accompany him on that first date.

In becoming Mrs. J.P. Kolenda, my mother severed herself from her previous identity. As my father's wife, she adopted a strictly defined role: To please God through being the perfect helpmate for John.

They held the wedding in Marguerite's home city, at Minnetonka Mills, on December 9, 1922. My father won over the Westmarks easily with his charismatic personality and energetic sincerity.

After the wedding, my parents settled down in Pigeon, Michigan, where my father started a tire shop with his brother-in-law, Fred Brenda. The duplex where they lived and hosted Assemblies of God meetings was "simple," so simple that when Marguerite's parents visited from Minnetonka, they were shocked. And when Dad's car broke down on his way back from a meeting, Grandpa Westmark could stand it no longer. He bought the newlywed couple their first brand-new Chevrolet.

For the next twenty years, my parents lived in Michigan and worked as ministers for the Assemblies of God. They started new churches all over the state, especially in upper Michigan, and in their own eyes, at least, they prospered—right up until God called Dad back to Brazil.

Chapter Six

Dodging Waves

WE WERE BACK IN BRAZIL, my father's childhood home. The missionary community in Rio de Janeiro put us up in a one-bedroom furnished apartment one block off the water. As soon as we arrived and I saw the shore I forgot my fears, at least temporarily. Dorothy and I scrambled into our bathing suits and started jumping over the waves of the beautiful Copacabana beach.

Just before leaving America, Dorothy and I had our hair cut short and curled. It was perfect for after salt water swimming and travel. We were shocked to learn that the Assemblies of God in Brazil did not allow short hair, much less artificial curls on women. Soon we learned there were endless restrictions imposed by the Swedish missionaries who were the first to establish the Assemblies of God missions in Brazil, such as:

- Females must wear long dresses with long sleeves and collars up to the neck.
- Females must wear hair long and in braids.
- Females are not permitted to wear make-up or fingernail polish.

- The only jewelry allowed is a modest wedding band to be worn on the right hand when engaged, then moved to the left hand when married.
- Males and females must be segregated in church.
- Members must not associate with non-believers.
- No movies.
- No card games.
- No dancing.
- No secular music.
- No secular books.
- No radio except news programs.

Although my dad disagreed with many of these policies, he was careful not to upset the establishment. His priority was saving souls; he was not concerned with changing these insignificant rules.

My parents' plan had always been to continue on to Aunt Martha's house in Porto Alegre, in the state of Rio Grande do Sul, eight hundred miles to the south. But first, Dad had to get our car and other belongings out of customs. It was a grueling and cumbersome process that took at least a month. It really put Dad to the test. The first phrase he learned was *da um geitinho,* meaning more or less, "find a little way." Put bluntly, if you are making a request of any kind, you need a bit of cash in your hand. You extend the bills casually, bow slightly, and smile. Then you say to the person in charge, *"Da um geitinho."*

In North America, this is considered bribery. In Brazil, this is a necessary, expected, and even respected way to get things done. You're sending a clear message—in this case to the customs agent—that he is important, that you respect him, and that he has the power to accomplish the task at hand. A little gesture goes a long way with uniformed individuals, including police officers, who are woefully underpaid. Still, this practice was tough for Dad at first. He had to reconcile his resistance to the underlying principle of *da um geitinho.* But once he did, Dad became an expert at getting things done. He got our car, refrigerator, washing machine, and the rest of our trunks out of customs in record time. We were finally on our way to Aunt Martha's by mid-December.

MARTHA'S SON ALBERT came to meet us in Rio de Janeiro and guide us back home with him to Porto Alegre. This wasn't easy. The only "highways" were dusty dirt roads with hairpin turns over jutting mountain peaks. And the old-fashioned tube tires on the Chevy went flat three or four times every day. After the car clunk-clunk-clunked to a stop on the rim, Dad and Albert patched the tubes, refilled the tires with a hand pump, and set us back on our way—until the next flat tire, or until a herd of cattle decided it was time to meander across the road, or until ocean waves along the beach routes swelled to mountainous proportions and threatened to swallow up our car and everything in it, including us.

The Chevy was tightly loaded with Dad, Albert, and Mother squished into the front. They'd yanked out the back seat back in Rio de Janeiro, and strapped it to the roof alongside a steamer trunk. In the space where the back seat had been, they had jammed in one more steamer trunk, and Dorothy and I perched on that for the entire eight hundred miles.

"Move over," Dorothy yelled at me. "Your leg is touching mine." She drew a line with her finger down the middle of the trunk. "This is the middle. Keep to your side, or else."

Our bottoms slapped up and down on its hardwood surface as the Chevy bounced over rocks and rough terrain. Not one of us had room to move. "Are you okay, Ruthie?" I whispered to my doll. She looked up at me with her clear blue eyes and I wished with all my heart that she could talk.

Dad tried his best to entertain Dorothy and me. First he taught us to sing in Portuguese. It was Christmastime, even if it didn't feel like it in this strange country. Soon, we'd be singing hymns and carols in a new church, with more new members from this bizarre new world. Dad also taught Dorothy and me to say, *Eu não comprendo Portoguez,* or, "I don't understand Portuguese." Dorothy caught on with aplomb, but I was clumsy with the accent. When I said the phrase, it came out sounding like, *Eu não comprendo porco diz.* "I don't understand what the pig says," which everyone found overly funny, especially Dorothy.

"I don't know what the pig says," she sneered at me, over and over.

Of course, I found this infuriating. But Dad's diversions did keep the time clicking as we bounced along on the steamer trunk.

Sometimes, though, the way was so harrowing that there could be no diversions. Like when the road dwindled off and disappeared altogether. For a hundred miles along the Atlantic, where there was not so much as a trail, let alone a road, we were forced to drive along sandy beaches close to the waterline, where the sand was wet and dense enough to support the car's weight. At the top of the beach, farther from the shore, where the sand was too soft and loose, the Chevy's wheels would just sink and spin. This meant Dad had to quickly maneuver around fast-crashing waves with enough height to swell over and engulf our car.

Even more dangerous were the shallow rivers that flowed down the beach into the sea. If we were caught in one of these rivers just as a big wave hit, we could be easily dragged out to sea. We'd roll to a stop whenever we came to one. Greedy seagulls squawked around our car begging for crumbs as Albert waded the river to get a feel for it and to figure out how long it would take to get across. We had to guess the intervals between waves rushing in and out from the ocean.

Mother always prayed before these crossings, which were frequent. She would close her eyes, lower her head and say: "Dear Jesus, please help us to get to the other side of this river, and protect your servants from all harm. We ask you in Jesus's name, Amen." By the end of her prayer she would usually have tears in her eyes, and she'd thank God copiously when we made it to the other side.

After five long days, dozens of flat tires, countless close calls with an angry sea, and a string of endless prayers, we finally reached Aunt Martha and Uncle Rodrigo's house in Porto Alegre.

A FRAGRANT POT of *feijoada* bubbled on Aunt Martha's stove when we arrived, bedraggled and happy, on Christmas Day. Everyone—children, friends, neighbors, and strangers—had assembled for our arrival. Dorothy and I dutifully hugged each person and kissed every cheek, even the cheeks of those we were meeting for the first time. The more my stomach rumbled, the faster I hugged. Such delicious smells wafted from the kitchen I could barely contain myself.

By the time Aunt Martha scooped ladlefuls of thick, steaming black beans over the rice into dark crockery serving bowls, the saliva was pooling under my tongue. Traditional preparation called for cooking *feijoada,* the staple dish of Brazil, for three or four hours, along with onions, plenty of garlic, various types of meats and vegetables and whatever else was on hand, even bananas. *Feijoada* had been my father's favorite meal during his childhood in Brazil. Our family ate it three-hundred-and-sixty-five days a year throughout our time in Brazil. And I took to it like a local.

FOR THE FIRST two months at Aunt Martha's, local schoolchildren were on vacation from school. But by March, classes resumed, and continued for the next four months. Dorothy and I attended the nearby public school with our cousins Edison, Rudolfo, and Albertina. We were thrown headfirst into Brazilian culture. Not one word of English was spoken in our daily lives, except by our parents. And even then, Dad was practically never home. He was busy helping Missionary Nordlund, the Swedish missionary in charge of the entire state of Rio Grande do Sul. The main church in Porto Alegre had many outstations. These were smaller congregations, from twenty-five to over two hundred people, in the nearby suburbs and villages. Most of these congregations did not have a full-time pastor, but were ministered to by preachers who traveled from village to village. There was never enough help, so Dad kept busy the whole time he was there, going from place to place. He seemed to enjoy helping Brother Nordlund, and it also gave him an opportunity to preach in Portuguese and get a feeling for what his future work would entail. At the same time, he was scouting for a permanent place for his own mission. Mother was around, of course, but she was busy with her adult responsibilities and we really didn't cross paths except at dinner and bedtime.

The upside of all this was that Dorothy and I mastered Portuguese quickly. Though we quarreled as much as ever, Dorothy and I spent more time together during these months at Martha's than ever before. We had to, since often we were each other's only source of easy communication.

"But don't get any ideas," Dorothy teased me. "You're still just as much of a nuisance as always. And your doll is filthy. If you were more grateful, you would take better care of her."

I held Ruthie tighter and stalked out of the room. Ruthie was a bit worse for the wear. Circles of grime shone on both her cheeks, and her blond hair was matted into an unseemly square on the back of her head. I vowed that later, when I was certain Dorothy wasn't watching, I would tidy Ruthie up. *Dear Jesus,* I prayed. *Please forgive me for being ungrateful and for not taking better care of Ruthie. I do love her. Please make Dorothy be nicer to me. Amen.*

In April of that year, Dad received a letter from the neighboring state of Santa Catarina. A Swiss missionary, Albert Widmer, invited Dad to visit him in Florianópolis, the capital city of Santa Catarina. Dad was intrigued. By then, we'd been living with Aunt Martha and Uncle Rodrigo in Rio Grande Do Sul for four months, and Dad was becoming impatient about securing a permanent mission. He arranged to meet Widmer in Santa Catarina.

It must have been a heady month for Dad, cruising the mountainous region with Widmer. Their route was mostly rugged dirt roads. Santa Catarina is roughly the size of Michigan, and populated only along the Atlantic coast except for scattered ranches, squatters, and a handful of settlements in the interior. The sharp curves and deep ruts of the mountain passes would have raised the hair on anyone's neck, especially when experienced through the billowing dust on a motorcycle. Rain, when it came, turned the roads into rivers of red, sticky clay.

Widmer was in his mid-thirties and wore his sandy hair cropped short and neat. His large blue eyes were wide-set and kindly, with rows of crinkles at their corners, made more noticeable by his usual expression, a wide grin. He was gregarious, charming, and exuded a certain magnetic restlessness. On the road, he opened his bike up all the way to take it as fast as it would go.

Another minister, a native preacher, had confided in Dad prior to departure that he, too, had once gone riding with Widmer, and had bounced off the back of the bike when it hit a bump. For thirty minutes he'd sat, bruised and indignant, in the weeds on the side of the road, because it had taken that long for Widmer to notice that his passenger had been tossed.

Dad implored Widmer to slow down on the sharp turns, out of genuine fear, but more potent than the fear was the thrill: My father was only in his early forties himself, and he was as handsome and charismatic as Widmer. Dad's dark brown hair, now bleached from the sun, was lighter than it had ever been. He kept his stocky farm-boy build, walked erect, and exhorted enthusiasm.

Everyone loved my father, and everyone was drawn to him. Adults respected him and deferred to him, and children adored him and flocked after him. He loved children, and made a point of taking candy or a small gift for the children in the homes he visited. He also enjoyed telling stories and making funny faces, which the children loved. My father was a powerful man, and he had his own deep craving for adventure and risk. Why else would he have dragged his entire family to the wilds of Brazil?

Dad loved what he saw. Santa Catarina is the coldest state of Brazil, and the only one cold enough for winter snow to fall in the highlands. Thick groves of Brazilian pine covered Santa Catarina's central areas, and the southwest prairie lands yawned open as far as the eye could see, while the east and west wore strips of forests. He thought it was a perfect place for a permanent settlement, and Widmer was thrilled.

"If you take over for me here," he told Dad, "I'll move on to Argentina." Apparently, Widmer had his sights set on forging southward with his missionary work. It seemed as if God had stepped in to arrange this turn of events, just for my father. Dad was certain he'd found a place for his mission.

In the early part of June 1940, Albert Widmer came to Aunt Martha's house in Porto Alegre to visit Mother and Dad for a week, mostly to talk with Dad about taking over his mission territory of Santa Catarina. Winter was coming and the evening air was already cool. I had just turned six years old. We had been in Brazil for over six months, and by this time my hair had grown enough for short braids, which also helped hide the permanent wave. I was very proud of my braids.

It was just past dusk when Brother Widmer came to me on the first night of his visit. "Gracie," he said, "if you come to my room in the morning, I'll tell you a story."

Even at barely six years old, I knew Brother Widmer was a handsome man. And he was so much younger-seeming than my parents. With his motorcycle and his dashing moustache, Brother Widmer was my prince from the moment I saw him. He paid me a lot of attention, too. He lavished me with it in a way that my parents never could.

"Well, dearie," he said, tugging my braid. "Will you come keep me company in the morning?"

"Yes!" I said.

"Delightful. I shall expect you then." He pressed his face toward mine. I could see the individual hairs of his moustache, gold, brown, and a little bit red. He winked, then giggled like a little boy. His eyes crinkled up in the kindest way. I would have died for Brother Widmer.

Soon after the weak light of earliest morning washed through my window, I stepped out of bed and crept through the house; Ruthie was tucked safely under my arm. Brother Widmer's room was across a short, wide hall from mine. I paused briefly at the end of the hall to examine Aunt Martha's foot-pedal sewing machine, a black Singer. I pumped the treadle first slowly, then faster and faster. The bandwheel made a pleasing whir as it spun crazily. But I thought it best not to risk waking Aunt Martha or my parents. Reluctantly, I turned back toward Brother Widmer's room and knocked softly on the closed door. I held Ruthie up to the door to listen. I pressed her ear against the thick paint, the color of heavy cream, with large chips and scratches around the tarnished brass doorknob plate. Many layers beneath the cream, the paint was blue, like the sky. This color streaked through where the door was most scarred. My doll stared back at me blankly. I knocked again, louder. I heard a stirring behind the door, then Brother Widmer's voice. "Come in, I am waiting," he said.

I opened the door and stepped across Aunt Martha's rag rug to Brother Widmer's bed. He smelled odd, but good, like something growing in the shade of the woods. He lifted the faded quilt, with its cut-square pattern of yellows and browns, and beckoned me under it. The bed was musty and warm with the heat of his body. Ruthie fell to the floor beside the bed.

"Do you know about the Indians, Gracie?" he asked, patting my head. "There are savages in the interior, and in the south. Let me tell you a story." His soft voice was so unlike my father's clipped, staccato speech. Brother Widmer's words were liquid glass, utterly smooth.

I repeated these visits two or three times during Brother Widmer's visit to Aunt Martha's house. All he requested of me was to massage his big toe, which had been severely injured, and was always hurting.

In July, my father brought my mother on the fourteen-hour, three hundred and seventy-five mile car trip to Florianópolis. Mother's reaction to her first glimpse of Widmer's property and cottage was pure joy.

"It is so beautiful," she wrote. "I can't think of a lovelier spot in the United States. It just seems too good to be true."

Chapter Seven

Florianópolis and Coqueiros

MY PARENTS RETURNED from their trip to Florianópolis full of enthusiasm. They could talk of nothing else. On August 3, 1940, we began the trek toward our reason for being in Brazil in the first place. As we loaded our belongings into a borrowed Chevy truck, a feeling of weight settled over me, solemnity tinged with excitement. Our life here, I realized, was real, and it was about to begin in earnest.

"Ruthie," I whispered to my beloved doll, "it's time to go. But don't worry, I'll take good care of you."

Martha's two oldest sons and a friend of theirs insisted on accompanying us on the journey. This made it possible to take both the truck and our own '39 Chevy. We set out at five in the morning, and for the first hundred miles along dirt roads, we did fine. Dorothy sat beside me and talked to me for the first hour, until I got on her nerves and she forbade me from speaking. "I mean it, not one word," she threatened.

"Dorothy, that's enough out of you," Mother interrupted. "Gracie can speak if I say so. She's done nothing wrong. Stop being such a hateful sister."

"Girls," Dad interrupted. "Stop bickering and pray. We're heading into some dangerous driving."

Dorothy and I looked out our windows. We'd entered a part of the journey where there were no passable roads, and the only possible driving route was along the beach. For the next hundred miles we'd be doing ocean driving, just like the journey from Rio to Porto Alegre. Except this time there were even more rivers and creeks flowing down the beach into the ocean, and the ocean was rough, crashing wave after wave onto the shore. All the while, a hard rain came from the South, pelting almost sideways in the driving wind. The waves were nearly impossible to dodge, and inevitably one finally crashed over the truck, killing the engine.

"Get out!" Dad yelled. "We've got to unload the truck!"

Unlike many other trucks, buses, and cars in those days, we were not dragged into the sea. But the terror made me cry. I hugged Ruthie tightly to my chest and sobbed quietly.

"Oh no," Dorothy moaned, burying her head in her hands. "Please stop, Gracie. Your crying is going to be the death of us all."

Much later, my father sent a letter to his brother, describing the scene: "You should have seen it," he wrote. "Marguerite, Dorothy, and Gracie, barefooted, carrying suitcases up on higher ground. The trunks, the refrigerator, everything had to be carried and rolled away in what seemed to be no time. With the waves dashing against us, we were able to jack up the truck, place boards under the wheels and, with my Chevy car, pull the empty truck to higher ground."

To add to the mayhem, the truck wouldn't start. We didn't have a starter for it, only a crank. There was so much violent wind, and such a roar from the waves, that my cousin Isaac didn't notice his brother Albert turning the crank. Isaac had his hand near the fan belt, and in an instant, as the engine caught, the fan belt sliced the tip of Isaac's finger clean off, including the nail. I could see a sliver of white bone through the blood, and I nearly threw up.

The nearest town was forty miles away. When we finally arrived there, one contingent headed out to find the town doctor, and the rest of us tracked down the local mechanic to work on starting the truck. It was ten o'clock that night before the engine turned reliably, too late to cover the final fifty miles of beach driving.

I don't think I've ever prayed so desperately, so earnestly, and so continuously as I did the next morning, as we chugged along the treacherous shore. I never once let Ruthie out of my arms. When the dirt roads finally appeared—rutted and full of deep potholes and sticky dust—it was like heaven, because at least we were safe. At nine that night, after two full days of travel, we arrived in a darkened, sleeping Florianópolis.

MORNING BROKE beautifully that first day in our new home, Albert Widmer's cottage. I rose early to see it. I couldn't believe my eyes. Straight ahead, an expanse of pasture sloped down toward the sea. The water was smooth and calm, and sunlight shimmered in an unbroken sheet of light. Jagged rocks towered as high as fifteen feet above the water's surface on the shoreline. To my left, there were lush mountains, and to my right, hills in the foreground and more water in the distance. Ahead of me, I saw sailboats gliding past, and even a small steamer slicing the still water.

Albert Widmer's cottage was on the side of a hill, overlooking the ocean and the whole island of Santa Catarina. The cottage itself was in Coqueiros. This village lay snugly in the outskirts of Florianópolis, the largest city on the island. Florianópolis was the capital city of the state of Santa Catarina.

South of the Tropic of Capricorn, winter happens June through August just when summer is at its peak in the northern hemisphere. Everything has a way of turning upside down. Soon I learned that even the name of Florianópolis had gone topsy-turvy. It was meant to be a tribute to Marshal Floriano Peixoto, second President of the Republic of Brazil from 1891 to 1894. Up until the end of Floriano Peixoto's rule, the city had been called *Nossa Senhora do Desterro,* or Our Lady of Banishment. Now, groups of citizens were clamoring to change the name of the fair city back, alleging that Floriano was a dictator who ordered the death of hundreds of people from Santa Catarina.

Brazil's southern Atlantic coast is rich with beaches, islands, bays, and inlets, and the island of Santa Catarina itself is pristinely wrapped by forty-two paradisiacal beaches. A series of fortresses built to withstand invasions by the Spanish and Dutch during the sixteenth centuries still stand along the Santa Catarina shoreline. Now saved for history and tourism, these forlorn fortresses rise in sharp contrast to the busy fishing villages that thrive alongside Santa Catarina's waters. Villages such as Coqueiros still operate today much the same as they have for hundreds of years.

Florianópolis was connected to the continent by a cable bridge, about a kilometer long. We had to cross this bridge in order to reach Florianópolis from Coqueiros. During this time Florianópolis had a population of about 30,000 people. Widmer's cottage was about five miles from the city, and from where I stood I felt like I could see the whole world.

The cottage was small, with a closed-in front porch decorated with flower boxes planted with red geraniums. Brother Widmer had painted the cottage entirely white except for the light brown wooden planks of the floor. The windows had bright blue shutters and no curtains. Outside the front door, I met Nero, Albert Widmer's dog. Nero was a big German Shepherd.

"See the doggie, Ruthie?" I crooned, holding my doll up to the dog for him to sniff her. Nero licked her dirty rubber face, and tried a tiny bite of her hair. "Nice doggie, nice doggie!" Albert was Nero's number one master, of course, but I would soon become his master number two.

The front yard had a flower garden, with many rose bushes, daisies, and small palm trees. Next to the cottage there was a beautiful red poinsettia tree, which had flowers year-round. On the hill was a large and productive vegetable garden with potatoes, pumpkins, onions, peas, and carrots. Widmer kept a few chickens and rabbits in a fenced back yard. Behind the house was a large banana grove—which caused a horrible problem for Mother's allergies—and in the grove were several papaya and guava trees, one avocado and one cashew tree.

Inside the cottage were two small bedrooms, a living room, and a kitchen. The kitchen had a wood stove and a small oven in which my mother miraculously produced extraordinary, complicated daily feasts. But in the end she had no choice. Dinner had to be made, whether it was easy or difficult. Life in Coqueiros was about getting the work done, just like always.

The dapper Widmer, a lifelong bachelor, enjoyed our presence from the first day. "Amazing, Marguerite," he crooned when dinner was served. "I can't imagine how you do it. You are amazing. I've never eaten such wonderful cooking!"

Mother beamed. She couldn't help but be thrilled at the young Widmer's constant barrage of compliments.

WHEN NIGHTTIME FELL in Coqueiros it fell hard, and for this I was unprepared. Electricity in our cottage was spotty, at best. When it worked, which wasn't often, it came on between the hours of seven and eleven in the morning, and then again between seven and eleven at night. At night, when most people were using electricity for lighting, our light bulbs would barely glow. On our first night in Coqueiros, I lit a candle and held it beside a bulb; the candle was by far the brighter of the two. We relied primarily on kerosene lamps to light the house against the pitch blackness.

For water, we had a well nearby that we pumped by hand for drinking and bathing. We had an outhouse in the wilds behind the house, surrounded by banana trees. Oftentimes, I opened the outhouse door to greet a poisonous snake coiled lazily upon the dirt floor, or even on the outhouse seat. As a result, I seldom visited the outhouse. Instead I poked around out back for a clear patch where I could discretely relieve myself.

Before long, I developed a fear of snakes. Where we lived, there were two types of poisonous snakes. Coral snakes were very common, with their black, red, and yellow bands. My head swam with the tales of children, fooled by the bright colors, mistaking coral snakes for shiny beaded necklaces, reaching down to grab them, and learning of their mistake too late as they stiffened and choked to their deaths. Coral snakes cause their victims to convulse into a state of ruthless paralysis and respiratory failure. Along with the coral snakes, there were also jararacas, some as long as three feet, with ominous rattles at the tips of their tails, and bites that send shards of pain straight to their victims' hearts.

COQUEIROS was full of children my age. Across the street lived the Dutras, with eight children, including two girls my age, Ina and Iolanda. Down the street from the Dutras was one large family after the next. I was free to play nearly all day when we first arrived in Coqueiros, because the Brazilian school year was nearly finished. I wouldn't begin my own studies until March 1941. Soon, my circle of friends widened even more to include Lourdes, Neuza, Lahir, Dida, Vavau, Edesia . . . Everywhere I went, I was surrounded by five or ten other children, and most of them were usually willing to follow my commands. I taught them my favorite songs and children's verses about good and evil. My friends would follow behind me, chanting loosely translated songs from English to Portuguese:

> *Um, dois, tres, o diabo quer me pegar.*
> One, two, three, the devil's after me.
> *Quatro, cinco, seis tijolos vae jogar.*
> Four, five, six, now he's throwing bricks.
> *Sete, oito, nove, não consegue acerta.*
> Seven, eight, nine, he missed me every time
> *Hallelujah, Jesus meu Salvador!*
> Hallelujah, hallelujah, I'm saved!

On Saturdays, I made beautiful things. I melted down cast-off bits of old wax and precious ends of colored crayons, and poured the steaming mixture—so pungent my eyes watered—carefully into the dark hollow stems of papaya leaves.

"You may never use my pans for your candles!" Mother warned me. As a serious cook, Mother was certainly not interested in having my smelly wax mucking up her cast iron cookware.

As a result of Mother's stern rule, I was always scouting for the best wax-melting container to use for my candle-making, which I took just as seriously as Mother took her cooking. One day in the middle of my inspiration, I found the perfect container, sitting on a high shelf in the garage. It was a large Calumet Baking Powder can, and when I pulled it down, I was delighted to find it so light that it had to be empty. I set it on the counter and took off the lid to peer inside. It was empty except for a small black thing on the bottom of the can. I reached in and was about to grab whatever it was, when suddenly I noticed that it was moving. I threw the can to the floor and out crawled, or maybe tumbled, a huge black tarantula. Its long, bendy legs were furry and thick, and it took an impressive jump away from me.

"Help!" I screamed.

My cousin John dashed to my rescue, brandishing a long stick. He edged the stick in toward the spider from as far away as he could while still being able to reach, and coaxed it gently back into the can. Then he snapped the lid back into place. I noticed then, for the first time, that the lid had little holes poked into it, so that the spider could breathe. John said that the boy who was helping him with the garden had caught the spider several days ago, and was holding on to it until he could get into town and sell it for a good price to a laboratory that purchased spiders and snakes for research. How close I had come to getting bitten!

Eventually, I'd find something or other in which to melt my wax, though, and while it hardened inside the papaya stems to form long, smooth candles, I would go about my chores. When my father was gone it was my job to slaughter the chicken for Sunday dinner. Although I dreaded this job, I became very skilled at it. My father had taught me to swiftly chop off the chicken's head with a hatchet. I was always amazed at the way its headless body would jump about for several seconds before falling to the ground. Then I would return to check my candles and resume playing with my friends.

Dad found my magnetic power over the neighborhood kids amusing, and soon he took to calling me "the General." Dorothy, in retaliation, called me a lazy Goody-Two-Shoes.

DAD AND ALBERT WIDMER searched for a church hall in Florianópolis, and they quickly located a place that could seat about two hundred. It was a long, narrow hall with chairs on either side of a center walkway. The sidewalls, whitewashed and plain, pressed in on the seating space. This hall became the beginning of our church in Florianópolis.

As the preacher's daughter, I had a front-row seat, all the better to hear my father's sermons—those long, long sermons. The chair was hard against my legs, the back stiff and straight. In contrast, my father's voice was smooth and deep, rising and falling over the peaks and valleys of his beliefs, undulating with his passion for the Lord and his predictions of the end of the world.

Somewhere along the route from Michigan to Brazil, I'd stopped watching so hard for Jesus. I wasn't sure exactly when it happened, and I still believed he was on his way eventually, but his arrival no longer felt quite so imminent or urgent. I was most alert for a sighting of him when I was terrified for some reason. On a normal day in church, my father's sermon was often enough to put me straight to sleep. My mouth would fall agape to make way for a trickle of damning drool to creep down my chin and onto the front of my dress.

This infuriated Brother Widmer, who watched me relentlessly. "I will teach you," he warned me one day, "to stay awake." The coarse hairs of his moustache were moist with humidity. "Next time you fall asleep during the sermon, I will put a *barata* in your mouth!"

Brazilian cockroaches are big ugly creatures, brown and slick, their bent-up legs and wicked antennae squirming with menace. I would do anything to keep one out of my mouth. Anything. Except the impossible, which turned out to be staying awake during Dad's sermons.

I tried so hard to keep my eyes open. The weight of them pulled like anchors through the waters of my exhaustion. I tried to find distractions, but it was difficult since I was not allowed to bring Ruthie or any other toy into the church. Nor was I allowed to crane my neck around during services to watch the people behind me. So unless I paid attention to my father's sermons, there was little to occupy my attention. Sometimes I would recite the words to my favorite songs, or pinch my legs in desperation as sleep swept me into its relentless current. But finally, eventually, like a swimmer in the undertow, I would give myself over to the force of nature, and my eyes would close.

Rattle, rattle. My eyes popped open in fear. My father's voice was rising and falling, beckoning and threatening. And there was Widmer, standing beside me, leaning in, with a red and yellow matchbox in his hand. He was shaking the box, and something inside was making the noise. Widmer smiled at me, and I could see the grooves in his teeth glistening behind his lips. His eyes flashed with pleasure as my eyes came into focus, taking it all in. I knew that the box held a barata. I wished it would jump out of the box into Widmer's open mouth, crawl past his grooved teeth and tonsils and down his throat. But of course, it didn't.

I would have to be more careful when Widmer was in town. Luckily for me, he traveled a great deal. When Widmer was away, his dog Nero became my closest friend. I fed him, made sure he always had water to drink, and spent a lot of time playing with him. Nero stayed outside tied to a wooden post with a chain that reached the front door and the kitchen door. He was an amazing watchdog. No one came near Nero—or our cottage—without our permission. And Nero warned us dutifully whenever we had passersby.

Nero loved Widmer. He really did. If it hadn't been for Nero, we'd never have known when to expect Widmer back from his travels. With unreliable electricity and no phones, communication was spotty and slow. But Nero knew when Brother Widmer was on his way home, and he let us know, too. On the evening before Widmer would appear back from a trip, Nero would howl mournfully toward the horizon for hours on end.

The first time Nero did this, I worried that he was hurt, or sick. He never made this sound at any other time, and I had never heard anything like it before. The next day, Widmer pulled up to the cottage on his motorcycle, and Nero barked ecstatically and wagged his tail with delight.

The next time Nero did his mournful howling—once again, while Widmer was traveling—Mother wiped her hands on her apron and said, "Well, I see Albert will be coming tomorrow. I suppose I had better do some baking for him."

And like clockwork, Widmer appeared the next day. During the year that Widmer stayed with us in the cottage, Nero howled on the eve of his master's return every time without fail, predicting Widmer's appearance with uncanny accuracy.

Chapter Eight

Trial of Fire

IN THE BEGINNING we shared the tiny dwelling with Brother Widmer. And until my father finally built an addition on the cottage, we were limb upon limb. My parents placed their rubber mattress in the only bedroom. They bought twin beds for Dorothy and me, and arranged them in the room that had been Brother Widmer's study. Brother Widmer slept on the couch, or sometimes on an army cot in the front entryway. The couch was grey and utilitarian. It did not open into a hide-away bed, but still, it was quite comfortable. The cot, on the other hand, was dreadful.

We had no sooner settled in Coqueiros, when Albert Widmer approached me and said: "Gracie, if you would like to hear some more stories, come and see me tomorrow morning, early." I could hardly wait, as I was so excited to hear more of his adventures.

I never lay with Brother Widmer on the gray couch—only on the cot in the front entryway. The couch was in such plain view, I'm sure Brother Widmer worried about what my parents might see. My parents had to know that on occasion I would be in Widmer's cot while he told me stories, but in their eyes, he was a "Man of God" and I'm sure it never entered their minds to be concerned. As it was, we had plenty of company from the *lagartixas,* small green lizards that climb up and down the walls, especially at night. There were dozens of *lagartixas* in every room of our house.

The front entry where Brother Widmer kept his cot was an unusual space, almost like a small room. It was long and narrow, with one window and two doors. One door opened up to the front porch and the outside, and one led into the living area. This narrow space was where my father would lock up a schizophrenic young man and attempt to exorcise the boy's demons. It was where he would one day beat me bloody with a wooden hanger. But in the beginning, it was the room where I crawled in bed with Brother Widmer.

Brother Widmer traveled constantly, and I missed him when he was away. He always had a smile and a wink for me, and he made time for me. And I loved his stories. I'd wake up at sunrise and knock on the door to his entryway. He'd let me in, and I'd crawl into his nice warm bed. We'd press our heads together under the thin gray blankets of his cot, and he'd whisper to me of his adventures in Argentina and Uruguay. I'd ride with him along the currents of his warm breath deep into the Amazon, with the crocodiles and the brown-skinned Indians with exotic shards of polished bone stretching the soft flesh of their ears and nostrils.

Brother Widmer asked very little of me when weighed against all he gave. I had only to rub his big toe, which he said always hurt from an old wound. Brother Widmer's toe was not like my father's, which was bony and calloused with a sprouting of dark hair beneath a thick nail clouded with age. The toe that Brother Widmer slipped into my palm in the darkness of his cot was completely smooth. It was always warm, and sometimes damp and slippery. I wondered why this was so, but feared that asking would be rude. Finally, as I rubbed and rubbed one morning, I could no longer resist. "Brother Widmer," I said, "why does your toe have no toenail?"

"Gracie," he moaned, pulling my hand off his toe and propping himself up on his elbows. A *lagartixa* scurried up the wall beside us and froze, its lizard legs splayed and clutching. "The day I lost my toenail was a terrible one, child. I'm lucky to be alive. I was in the wilds of Argentina, saving souls for Jesus in the backwaters of the rain forest. A thick billow of steam rose from the water, unlike anything I'd ever seen. That steam was bewitched—it nearly made me insane. Before I knew what was happening, I'd lost control of my canoe, and next thing I knew I was flailing in the river. That's when I saw the wicked beast, those sulfurous yellow eyes bulging out of the water. Have you ever seen a crocodile, child?"

"No," I said, wide-eyed.

"You should hope you never do. I wish I hadn't. But I'm strong and fast," Brother Widmer said as he twirled one of my braids with his trembling hand. "I swam hard and was nearly pulling myself ashore when the croc overtook me. He tore off the tip of my toe with his ugly teeth. Good thing I was near the site of an Indian encampment. The Indians dragged me to their village and wrapped my toe in a poultice with special herbs. Those herbs stopped the bleeding lickety-split, and the next morning, I couldn't believe my eyes. My toe was completely healed."

Brother Widmer closed his eyes and sucked in a long breath. "Except for the nail. That never grew back. And the ache. Always the ache." He pulled my hand away from its anxious twisting of my short braid, and guided it back under the blankets. His toe was hot and throbbing now. "It hurts, Gracie. You can't imagine how it hurts. Keep rubbing, child. Don't stop rubbing."

At about the same time we moved in with Brother Widmer in Coqueiros, a sixteen-year-old village girl accused him of molesting her. The girl's younger sister accused him, too.

Mother was enraged. "It is inconceivable that such a godly man could have violated those young girls," she said.

Father was apoplectic. "It's the devil's work," he shouted, his voice cracking with fury. "Satan is working through these girls to destroy this wonderful man. We must help him fight back against this atrocity."

Despite my parents' efforts, the authorities were not convinced that Widmer was innocent. He served a short stint in the county jail. I insisted on visiting him in jail as often as possible. My parents visited Widmer daily and brought him homemade cookies and pies. However, I had no idea why he was in jail, and my parents only told me, "Some people lied about him and he should never be here; it is the work of the devil."

I was convinced of his innocence for whatever he was accused of doing. I felt so very sorry for him and prayed that he would be released soon so he could tell me more stories.

My cousin Albertina, 15 years old, was living with us at that time, and she and Dorothy were always together, laughing and whispering whenever there was any mention of Albert Widmer. I could not understand why Dorothy and Albertina did not feel sorry for him. I tried to hear what they were saying and whispering, but I could not understand what was going on. All I knew was that poor Brother Widmer was in jail for "no fault of his own." Through all of this it never occurred to me that anything wrong had happened during the special story times in Brother Widmer's bed. However, I sensed that it was best not to say anything to Mother and Dad, as they might not let me bother Brother Widmer.

After thirteen days in jail he was released on probation, but still, he was able to travel freely. And Nero continued to predict his master's homecomings, to which we both looked forward with great anticipation.

THE RELIGION of my childhood was absolute. In Assemblies of God, there is right and wrong, good and evil, and very little in between. This was explained bluntly by my parents, whom I loved and revered utterly and completely. Life was as clear as the seawater that pooled in the dark rocky crevices of our bay at dawn. It was as clear as the chorus of children's voices running through the village, or the sound of Nero's bark of joy. And it was as definite as the threat of jararaca poison, or of fire, or of my own sins. Nothing was ever separate from religion. Rewards and threats were immediate, and life in Brazil only made this dichotomy more raw and more true.

According to my childhood faith, the New and Old Testaments of the Bible were divinely inspired, unquestionable truths delivered by God. My parents and their fellow worshippers considered the Bible the supreme guidepost for how to structure one's life and faith. With that clarity came comfort. It was a huge comfort knowing exactly what to expect from life, in the present and beyond.

Assemblies of God believers ascribe to the existence of the "Godhead": a unified existence of God, Jesus Christ, and the Holy Spirit as one being. God is the creator and sustainer of the universe, revealed through the writings of the Bible. He existed before creation and will continue to exist infinitely. Jesus Christ was the human manifestation of God the Father, born of the Virgin Mary. He lived a sinless life and was crucified for the sins of the world. The third day after his death, Jesus Christ was resurrected from the dead and exalted to Heaven with God. The Holy Spirit is the essence of God moving among the people, touching the lives of believers here on earth. The Holy Spirit is a very important concept in Assemblies of God.

Assemblies of God worshippers understand the church to be the body of Christ here on earth, charged with the mission to spread the word of God to all nations. The church is also a place where believers come to worship their God.

Most important of all, Assemblies of God members believe that soon there will be a "Second Coming of Jesus Christ." At the first coming, Jesus was born in human form to the Virgin Mary. But at the Second Coming, in an event called the "Rapture of the Church," current and past Christians will be taken to live with Christ forever.

My father preached passionately and often about the Second Coming. "Be ready for the Lord!" he implored. "Be ready, He is coming soon and sooner than you think!" His voice would quiver with the vibrato of unadulterated belief as he admonished his congregation for the sins of wickedness that would cost them dearly, indeed, would cost them their eternal salvation, and soon.

How soon? No one knew for sure. Church scholars were always arguing about exactly how Biblical time compared to modern time, and just how that would affect Jesus's return. But one thing was certain: The Second Coming would undoubtedly occur in the foreseeable future, in my father's lifetime, and therefore, in mine. I, for one, couldn't wait.

Although I no longer expected Jesus to appear at any second, as I had back in Lansing, waiting and watching for him to peer in through the kitchen window from our small table, I did feel a vague and persistent curiosity about just when and how the Second Coming might take place. Sometimes, I would perch on the rocks behind our cottage, overlooking the sea, and watch for Jesus. If by chance Jesus was coming, I had high hopes of being the first one to see a sign of the Rapture, a sign that we believers were about to be lifted up from the bondage of earthly life.

Sometimes I watched for hours. The tide would recede into itself, drawing back its briny fingers and discarding in its wake the debris of life and death in the sea. Often, in the early afternoons, cloudbanks rolled in from the southwest, filling the bay and obscuring my view of the horizon. Though I was unsure of its meaning, this knitting of clouds seemed like a sign of God's presence, and even better, a sign of God's awareness of my presence. Once in a rare while, I would sit all the way through the waning light of late afternoon into dusk, observing the holiness of sunset and the slow retreat of light into darkness. I liked to watch for the first star to appear overhead, puncturing the seamless sky, and this, too, was a sign. One evening in early 1942, when I was seven years old, I sat on the rocks watching the night slowly fall. Nero's joyful bark pierced the air, and I knew it could mean only one thing: Albert Widmer had returned home from another trip to Argentina. After one year, his probation was finished, and he was free to move anywhere.

UPON HIS RETURN, Widmer approached my father about the property. They sat in our enclosed porch in the starlight, sipping tea and speaking of Widmer's plans. Nero lay happily at his master's feet. "It's time you bought it from me," Widmer encouraged my father. Widmer was delighted to be finished with the probation sentence, which had only fueled his burning zeal to leave Brazil and head to Argentina for good.

My parents had no money for buying the property from Widmer, though my father very much wanted to. But it so happened that Grandma Westmark, my mother's mother, had passed away in 1940, and she had left Mother a small piece of land in Minnesota. With the help of her brother back in the States, she arranged for the sale of her inherited land, and with the money from the sale, she and Dad were able to buy the cottage from Widmer for eighteen hundred dollars. Dad named the cottage in the Brazilian native Indian language, calling it *Itaguasu,* or Big Rock.

ONE SUNDAY evening at the main church in Florianópolis there was a young man who caused a disturbance during the evening service. He fell down between the chairs, started to foam at the mouth, and yelled obscenities in a deep, guttural tone. His mother began to cry and begged Dad to help her. She said her son Roberto was getting older, stronger and she was at her wits end. Dad decided that he could help Roberto, and that same evening he brought him to our house. The rest of us were surprised at the sight of him, sinewy and hard, with wavy dark hair and eyes that darted and flashed with anger. We didn't call him schizophrenic, of course; no one really knew his diagnosis. We called him "possessed by the devil," and Dad was convinced he could save him with faith and patience. But Roberto's crazed appearance scared me. And I hated the sounds that came out of him, from somewhere in the depth of his throat, like animal noises. Surely, I thought, he was going to attack me.

He was kept in our front entryway. Mom and Dad gave Roberto the cot to sleep on, but by Monday morning, he had torn it to bits. Even the wooden legs lay in splintered pieces on the entry floor. Mom and Dad figured that it didn't make sense to give Roberto any more furniture to tear apart. He could sleep on his blankets and sheets. But through the day he thrashed and ripped at these linens until they, too, were nothing but a pile of scraps and shreds. It was becoming clear that "sleeping" was not something that Roberto had a lot of interest in doing. All through Monday night, I could hear him screaming and throwing his body against the walls and floor. There was one window in the entry, facing the front of the house. Dad boarded up this window, but he made sure there was a sliver of daylight streaming into the room between the boards.

Dear Jesus, I prayed. *Please help Roberto. Please make him better and please cast out the demons from inside of him.* What I really wanted was to pray to Jesus to make Roberto leave our house, but I was afraid that Jesus would disapprove. My father certainly would.

On Wednesday morning, as Roberto went on screaming and battling in his entryway cell, I asked Mother what would happen if he did not get better.

"He will get better, Gracie," she snapped. "Don't question, just pray. That is what the Lord requires. That is how the demons are cast out." She was kneeling near Roberto's door for feeding time.

Once a day Dad asked Brother Dutra, from across the street, to come over in case Dad needed help when he opened the door and Mother quickly placed Roberto's food and water on the floor and jumped back from the door as fast as she could. I imagined it was sort of like feeding a dangerous animal in a zoo, and Mother was doing a brave and risky thing. Usually, after she gave him his food, Roberto would throw the food and dishes at the wall, so Mother switched to tin plates and cups.

In the evenings, Mom and Dad stood outside the entryway and prayed for Roberto. Dad held the Bible and read verses in his preacher voice. Sometimes this made Roberto rage harder, but mostly he seemed oblivious. At one point he screamed Portuguese obscenities that even I understood. Blood rushed to Mother's cheeks, but Dad just preached on.

Mother started fasting on Wednesday. She spent three days not eating a thing, only drinking water. She kept to herself and spent most of the time in her room praying. She felt this was the most powerful way to reach God, and have her prayers answered. Thursday and Friday dragged along the same way, with the fighting and raging in the entryway broken up by small, pregnant pauses of threatening silence that we knew by now would only be broken by more screeching and slamming. When, during one long quiet spell, I worked up enough courage to peek through the window slits Dad had left open into the entryway, I saw that Roberto had made long, vertical scratches in the paint on the wall. Dried food and shards of smashed china littered the floor and stained the walls, along with small splotches of dried blood from the damage he'd inflicted on himself. Roberto also refused to use the chamber pot, and there was human excrement all over the floor. The terrible smell seeped through the doorway to our living room. I felt my stomach clench and swallowed down a gag. This boy looked broken and pathetic; Jesus simply had to help him. I turned away and prayed wordlessly for Jesus to please, please help us all.

After that, I didn't peek in the entryway again. Instead, I sat quietly in the living room, listening to Roberto as he fought with the devils inside of himself. I had to admit that he fought hard. The battles were loud and grueling, full of banging and thumping and screaming as Roberto slammed himself into walls and beat himself. They went on for hours before he finally collapsed in a jerky, exhausted sleep. When evening fell, Mom and Dad's praying started up again.

By Friday, though, Mom's mood took a turn. The situation with Roberto was getting worse, not better, and Mom was worried he might break out of the locked entryway and hurt one of us, or worse. I could see by the tension in her neck and mouth that she was actually scared. When Mom finally approached the subject with Dad, Roberto was in his cell, flailing himself full force against the walls. An especially vicious slam against the wall by my father's desk in the living room shook the floor so hard it sent the lamp flying off, and glass shattered across the wooden floor.

"John," my mother screeched, "the Lord has to deliver Roberto soon, as he is a danger to all of us!"

As if on cue, Roberto pounded his rageful fists on the wall behind my parents. Dad contemplated. "Marguerite," he finally said, "keep praying and I know the devil or devils will be out of him. We must have faith and keep praying."

That same evening, Dad asked Brother Dutra and one of his sons to come over. Dad felt it was time to cast out the demons, but he wanted help and would not endanger his family by trying to do this alone. Mom, Dorothy and I were also present.

Dad got the vial of oil he used for anointing the sick. He opened the door, and Roberto seemed to be surprised. He approached the sick boy, and the two Dutras followed. We women stayed back, watching. Dad rubbed oil on Roberto's forehead, then placed his hand on the young man's head and in a loud, demanding voice said: "In the name of Jesus, I rebuke the devil and I command that the demons leave this Brother, now! At this very moment!" He repeated this several times, in his loud husky voice.

Mother was praying and crying loudly, and so were Dorothy and I. Then Dad started speaking in tongues for at least a minute straight, maybe longer. At the end he said, "Thank you, Lord, for delivering this young man."

Roberto became very quiet and subdued, and after a careful few hours of waiting to see if the storm was going to kick up again, Father went into the entryway, all by himself, to pray with Roberto again. The boy responded calmly. Mother thanked Jesus for delivering Roberto and for protecting us all from harm. And on Saturday, Roberto's mother came to pick him up. He was as quiet as a mouse as he shuffled down our front road, a pace behind his mother in her worn floral housedress. I felt uneasy, but it did seem as if maybe his demons had gone away.

Several months later, Father heard again from Roberto's mother. But this time, she wasn't looking for his help with the demons. She didn't need help anymore. She had put Roberto in an asylum as soon as his fits had started back up, a few weeks after he left our home.

Mother felt very sad, and I heard her say to Dad: "I was afraid this would happen. You know Roberto's mother is not a believer; she never gave her heart to the Lord, and it was easy for the devil to take over again."

Chapter Nine

Transformation

T HE NEGOCIATED PURCHASE PRICE of Widmer's cottage left two hundred dollars for Dad to apply toward remodeling. Remodeling our
own home was my father's first building project in Brazil. He drew up the
plans himself and did most of the work, with help and advice from our
neighbor, João Dutra, who was a master carpenter. João's sons also helped
with the construction, and the work progressed quickly. My father loved
working with his hands, and he often claimed that had he not become a
minister, he'd have been a builder. He eventually constructed countless
churches throughout the state of Santa Catarina and, in his later years,
built dormitories and many more churches in Germany.

During Dad's work on the addition, I celebrated my eighth birthday.
The addition had no finished rooms at the time, only a large open area
in the back of the house, its wooden beams a skeletal promise of things
to come.

I came home from school to find Dorothy waiting in the kitchen.
"Come see the addition," she said. But I knew there was nothing finished
to see. Never sure if Dorothy was friend or foe, I was skeptical. "You'll be

sorry," said Dorothy, turning away, and this was enough to compel my curiosity.

"Okay, okay! I want to see," I begged. She led me through the open door into the addition.

Twenty children screamed, "Surprise!" They jumped up from makeshift tables and benches that Dad had built. Atop the tables were steaming cakes that Mother had spent the morning baking. I was stunned. Was this a sign from God? Or simply evidence of my parents' love for me?

"Happy birthday, my little General," Dad said.

The happy surprise of my birthday party was made even brighter by the way it popped up suddenly and early, like an impatient jack-in-the-box. Dad couldn't plan the party on my official birth date, April 21, because of *Dia de Tiradentes,* the Day of the Tooth Puller, or Martyr of Independence, one of the greatest heroes of Brazilian history. This exciting national holiday happened to share the anniversary of my arrival on earth, a coincidence I proudly enjoyed. And whenever *Dia de Tiradantes* fell on a weekday, which it did on my eighth birthday, school was closed for the occasion. So Dad let Tiradentes have his day and planned my special celebration to take place ahead of time.

Dia de Tiradentes paid homage to the orphan Joaquim Jose Da Silva Xavier. I still remember the lessons we learned of him at school, and the stories my teachers told each year about this legendary rebel. Xavier was born on Pombal farm, located between the modern-day town of Tiradentes and São João del Rey in the Brazilian state of Minas Gerais. He lost his parents at age eleven, and lived after that with the town surgeon. He didn't acquire much education but nonetheless went on to great success in the fields of business, medicine, dentistry, and politics. It was the dentistry that earned him the title Tooth Puller, but it was the politics that earned him the hearts of his countrymen.

During the late 1700s, the Enlightenment was in full swing and the world around Tiradentes was in a state of upheaval and revolution. The American colonies were busily wresting their independence from Britain while the French were rallying and building steam toward a revolution of their own. So it was only natural that Tiradentes, when he learned that Portugal, which controlled Brazil at the time, was confiscating large amounts of Brazilian gold and still demanding evermore in taxes, responded with revolutionary zeal. He organized clandestine meetings in backroom pubs with likeminded revolutionaries until finally he was ready to declare independence from the Portuguese government and establish the Republic of Brazil in 1789.

But before he could wage his battle, Tiradentes was betrayed by one of his own men.

"Imagine," our teacher would say at this point in the story, "being thrown to the wolves by a brother!"

And my classmates and I gasped out loud until our teacher shushed us and continued with the story of Tiradentes' arrest in Rio de Janeiro. The capture took place on May 10, 1789, and the ensuing investigation and trial dragged on for three long and tormented years, during which time other revolutionaries were arrested and imprisoned as well. But Tiradentes honorably testified that he was the leader of the conspiracy and was responsible for it. On April 18, 1792, the court handed down the sentences. Only one of the death sentences was carried out, that of Tiradentes. Deemed "unworthy of royal mercy," he was hanged and quartered in Rio de Janeiro on April 21, 1792.

In the wake of his brutal execution, Tiradentes became hailed as a martyr to Brazilian independence. Ultimately, this orphan and dentist from the Pombal farm took a more significant place in history than his impractical plans might have earned for him had he not been betrayed. As it is, Brazilians regard him as their national hero, and in my childhood memories, his day of honor and mine are inextricably intertwined.

VADICA CAME to work for us when she was eighteen, very old for an unmarried Brazilian girl, since most of her peers had long since married and begun having babies. She had light brown hair, brown eyes, and stood about five feet tall. Vadica was very thin but after a few months working for us she gained considerable weight, which she liked, as it also made her more attractive. She was kind and good-humored, always cheerful. The opposite of Mother, Vadica never seemed to have a bad day. She smiled practically nonstop and entertained me by telling stories. My favorite was about the local werewolf.

"He lives about one kilometer from here," she whispered. "Right down the beach, in a shack with his mother." At this point, she stared meaningfully in the direction of the werewolf's house. "During the full moon, he changes from a man to a *lobo*. First comes the hair on his arms. Then on his body. And then his teeth grow long. All of the mothers keep their children inside during the full moon. But once in a while one disappears."

By this point in the story, the hair on my own arms would be standing up. But I begged her to repeat it over and over again. Vadica made it so real, I believed every word. Mother disapproved, so Vadica and I had to talk about it when Mother was gone.

Vadica didn't live with us, but she came six days a week, and worked constantly from morning until night. The ironing often took her a whole day. She had to coal-fire the iron, and its temperature was then fickle and impossible to regulate. Often, the clothes were scorched and had to be washed again. Vadica had fun apprenticing in my mother's kitchen, where she soon learned to cook like an expert. Since I was often on hand in those days, I had many odd jobs in the kitchen as well, even though Mother mostly liked me to keep out of her way. That's why running for eggs became my specialty. It wasn't unusual for Mother to realize, in the middle of a recipe, that she needed another egg or two. I was the only one in the house who had perfected the technique of knowing just when a chicken was about to lay an egg. I'd run out to the henhouse and, one by one, insert my finger up the chickens' rear-ends. If a hen was about to lay an egg, I could feel it inside her. I could predict by the texture of the shell, whether an egg was on its way or would be laid within fifteen minutes or longer. Mother was most grateful!

Vadica even perfected the art of pie baking during her years with us, with plenty of Mother's help. As long as my father was at home, a day never passed without a warm pie, so pie baking was a high-priority in our Coquieros kitchen. Dad's favorite pie was raspberry, and once the raspberry canes that he planted in our yard matured, we had fresh raspberries almost year round.

OVER THE WEEKS and months that followed my eighth birthday, my father's vision for our enlarged home materialized. Even without the advantages of electricity or running water, my father did wonders with his renovations. Within the original cottage, he created a library, an office that doubled as a small bedroom when needed (which was often, with our constant stream of houseguests), and a living room, dining room, and kitchen. He preserved the original front entryway, a narrow space where Albert Widmer slept when he stayed with us. Our cottage's front enclosed verandah was also left alone, as a peculiar and lovely room that was accessible only via the house's interior, as it had no outlet to the front yard. Dad hung two hammocks there and they were used to relax in after a meal, and also as two extra beds when needed.

The addition Dad constructed on the back of the cottage included four bedrooms, a one-car garage, and best of all, an indoor bathroom. We had relied solely on the outhouse in the banana grove for two years, which I'd avoided as much as possible. How luxurious it was to stop searching for clear spots out of view of the house! Indoor plumbing was heaven. *Thank you, Jesus, I prayed, for giving us an indoor bathroom,* and I meant it with all my heart.

On top of the addition, with its bedrooms and its heavenly bathroom, Dad built a terrace, which housed a large water tank at the far end, covered over by a terra cotta slab. The slab doubled as a large table. There on the terrace, gathered around that terra cotta table, my family shared many wonderful meals against the postcard perfect backdrop of the sea and the island of Florianópolis.

From the water tank, Dad ran a small pipe to a nearby well. He purchased a windmill to pump water from the well into the tank. When the wind blew, we'd run to connect the windmill to the well and in this way we filled the tank almost effortlessly. My cousin John, from Porto Alegre, had just moved in with us, and one of his many responsibilities was to make sure the tank never ran dry. John was eighteen and very capable. He did his best not to forget. But, when several windless days passed in a row, the tank stood empty, and we were then forced to take turns pumping the water by hand for many hours to refill the tank.

The cook stove in our kitchen was a large, wood-fired contraption with four small, open-flame areas, and to the left of those extended an iron top beneath which was a generous oven. Dad, in his ingenuity, placed copper coils that ran inside the stove with a small water tank above. The hot water in the copper pipes would rise and go into the tank above the stove. The tank connected directly to the bathroom. If we wanted a warm shower, we'd start a fire in the stove and let it burn at least a half hour. For this reason, our showers were often planned for after meals. It worked brilliantly as long as we kept our showers brief, and as long as I managed my one clear role in the process, which was to keep the firewood bin full at all times.

Behind our house, Dad built a shed for the washer and rinse sink, neither of which was connected to the main well. The sink had to be filled using a hand pump connected to a separate well. The washer was a Maytag with a ringer and a suds saver that we'd brought with us to Brazil. Our system for laundry was precise: whites first, and save the water for the darker prints, followed at last, still in the original whites water, by the darkest, dirtiest work clothes. This water had to be heated on the stove in the house in large oil cans, then hauled by hand to fill the washer.

Everyone helped, even my cousin John. Dad helped too, when he was home. Once the clothes were washed and rinsed, we'd run them through the ringer and hang them on the long, wire clothesline. Doing the laundry, by the time the clothes were actually dried and folded, was an all day ordeal, made even longer if it rained, which it sometimes did. In that case, the clothes had to be hung in the shed, in the house, or wherever else we could make room for them. We did laundry on a strict schedule, every Monday. Dorothy and I didn't expect fresh new outfits each day. We had to be very careful with the clean clothes we did have. I never, ever threw clothes on the floor. Ruthie had begun to spend most of her time naked, a neglectful state which my Mother disapproved of and for which she scolded me often.

According to my father, my mother and Dorothy should never have to collect wood for the stove. It was my job to check the bin, which was right next to the stove, every day, and collect enough wood to keep it heaping full.

"Ha, ha," Dorothy teased. "Little Gracie actually has to do some work. I hope it doesn't kill you."

The wood supply was in the back of the house, which made my task no small feat. It took so many trips back and forth that it soon became not only arduous, but worse yet, boring. While my many neighbor friends pleaded with me to play, I lugged armloads of wood back and forth from the back of our yard to the kitchen.

"Come play! Come play!" my friends shouted from the road. The sound of them made me crazy as I trekked, back and forth, back and forth, sweat running between my shoulder blades and from my hairline into my eyes. And then I came upon an idea.

"I can play as soon as I finish," I yelled back. "As soon as the woodbin is full!" This worked more beautifully than I could have imagined. My friends swarmed in like so many worker bees to help me. Sometimes I offered a reward of Mother's fresh-baked cookies, but usually all I needed was to promise I'd play when the work was done, and my friends set to the hauling. Dorothy looked on with envy and disgust as my assembly line of friends did my work for me.

Dorothy teased me relentlessly for sloughing my chores off on the neighbors. "Figures," she said. "Lazy little Miss Goody-Two-Shoes finds a way out of her chores. Don't think you'll get away with that forever."

But I was my father's daughter. He had ingenuity, and so did I.

About nine months after Albert Widmer left, he surprised us with a visit. He brought along his Argentinian bride.

Mother was shocked at how young she looked, and remarked to Dad: "I can't believe Albert Widmer could not have found a more suitable woman to be his wife!"

Dad did not reply, but Dorothy and I could tell by his expression that he agreed with Mother. She was a pretty petite blond, with short curly hair and blue eyes. She couldn't speak Portuguese, only Spanish. She was very timid and did not attempt to communicate. They stayed at our place only two nights before they went on their way to the state of São Paulo, where they planned to settle, never to be heard from again.

YEAR ROUND, we had menaces from the outdoors buzzing and slithering into our home. Snakes, cockroaches, mosquitoes, and huge flying bugs and bats—I hated them all. Dad eventually broke with local tradition by putting screens on our windows. The locals believed that healthy air could only pass through a truly open window. But for me, no amount of screen was enough to stay safe. Before I could sleep, I always closed my windows, despite the hot, muggy motionless air I trapped inside by doing so. One morning, I awoke and opened my window to find a jararaca snake coiled on the ledge. Surely he'd fallen off the terrace and landed there. But when I saw his beaded eyes, I could only imagine he'd been slithering in the night looking specifically for me.

My terror of creepies and crawlies grew so intense I couldn't sleep at night for fear something would slither or scurry across my face in the dark. The only thing to do was to hide my head completely under the covers. I pouched the fabric up around my nose slightly to create a bubble for breathing and there, in my cocoon of white cotton, with night sounds mingling with my own breath and Ruthie tucked under my arm, I willed sleep to come.

Chapter Ten

Lonesome Beach

FROM MY EARLIEST days, I understood that my father's life work was about serving God as he saw fit—and my job was helping him. It was simple enough, and impossible. But I was determined. When my father volunteered my services as pallbearer to the locals, I willingly obliged. So it was I who carried babies to their graves.

Dorothy, almost fourteen, was far too old for this task. By fourteen and fifteen, Brazilian girls were beginning to seriously think of marriage and having babies of their own. Tradition demanded that other children carry the casket of an infant. That meant I was on one side of the wooden box for the entire three miles to the cemetery, and a rotation of village children were on the other side, trading off to rest their aching arms.

The babies lay still in their open caskets, their smooth skin oddly dry in the damp heat. White calla lilies lined the boxes of fresh-hewn pine that dug into the flesh of my fingers. Lily petals grazed the babies' cheeks, while the floral scent rose thick as bread dough. I was seven years old, bearing the weight of life and death in too-close succession. Death was dressed in clean white cotton, resting in a bed of flowers. I thought the scent of lilies would press down my throat and choke me.

The funeral processions for the babies always went past my house, with its wide veranda and lush garden, set in front of a banana grove dotted with papaya and avocado trees.

Malnourishment was rampant, and I was the tallest, strongest child in our village. It was my job to help carry the casket of every baby who succumbed to the meanness of poverty. It didn't matter if I knew the baby's name, if I had ever held her while her heart was still beating, or if I had ever even seen her alive. Mostly, I had not.

Usually, of the twenty or so children walking the casket, I would only know two or three. We all dressed for the occasion. I wore my Sunday best, white embroidered blouses and colorful cotton skirts that swished across my suntanned knees as I walked. I wore *tamancos,* thin wooden-soled shoes with a leather strap to hold them on my dusty feet.

There were so many dead babies. Sometimes it was the sugared coffee in their bottles that did it—or coffee mixed, for the lucky ones, with a touch of powdered or canned milk when the privilege of the breast was passed over to a newborn sibling. Other times, parasites chewed the babies up from inside, leaving them hollowed out by diarrhea and dehydration. With no medical care to speak of, baby funerals were as common as rain and salt.

Just beyond my house, on the first stretch of our journey, was Praia da Saudades, loosely translated from Portuguese as "Lonesome Beach." The truth is: *saudades* eludes translation. There are a few words in Spanish and English that brush up against it, that hint at the danger of its melancholy, but ultimately, translations fail to convey the gripping despair. *Saudades* means to miss something or someone, but so much more. It means to be swallowed alive by an unnamed loss, to lose your mind in the pitch black of hope's destruction, to writhe with the ripping pain of a broken heart.

You can die from *saudades.*

Praia da Saudades was the natural backdrop to the agony of the mothers, fathers, grandparents, and siblings who accompanied the tiny caskets. Brazilians do not hold back in their grief. Their cacophony of sorrow would crash with the waves against the rocks.

From Praia da Saudades the dirt road continued uphill, with the ocean on the right, and on the left, the houses of Coqueiros—Spanish adobe style, of a plastered brick, mostly, and some of wood. Their modest front doors butted up against the street. There was no sidewalk. We marched straight down the middle of the one-lane road. When a truck rumbled by, we stepped aside and waited while we disappeared in a billowing cloud of brown dust. I can still taste that dust.

About one mile from my house, the winding road passed a small Catholic church. There, we turned west, and continued another two miles or so over very hilly terrain, with only a few houses and mostly open fields. Finally, we arrived at the cemetery, where the freshly dug grave gaped beneath a cloudless sky. Each member of the funeral procession tossed a shovelful of dirt onto the baby's coffin.

No one was embalmed in our neighborhood. Bodies were buried within twenty-four hours of death. Since the cemetery itself was small—only about seventy-five feet long—and deaths were constant, graves had to be re-used every few years. Any shovelful of dirt was apt to include a bone or two from a grave's previous occupant. At one baby burial, I turned over my rusty shovel to set loose a cascade of dry earth and a full set of human teeth, clenched. At the far end of the cemetery, a squat, stucco building housed a jumble of anonymous skulls and bones of those who had rested in peace too briefly before being unearthed.

Like the babies I buried, I died in Brazil. And I was reshaped from the dirt and the water of a place that seeped into me in the night, through my eyes and nose and mouth, through my pores. Brazil, like my father's voice, gripped me and made me in its image. I nearly drowned in saudades, but I came up gasping. It eventfully released me, but not completely.

THIS ALL REMINDED ME a little of Ruthie, and the way I had found her on our most recent trip to Porto Alegre to visit Aunt Martha and Uncle Rodrigo. I had accidentally left her there on an earlier visit and I missed her terribly, so one day when I knew Dad was preparing for a trip to Porto Alegre, I asked him to look for Ruthie. He promised he would. But when he came back, he was empty handed.

"I looked, but she was not there, dear little General," he said.

It was another year before we visited again and I had the chance to look for Ruthie myself. It was my cousin Edison who showed me where she was—abandoned under their house, which was on stilts about one foot off the ground.

"Where?" I called desperately, crawling on my stomach in the darkness under the house.

"Farther in," Edison called back. "Just keep looking."

And that's when I saw her. Tears welled up in my eyes, even though I was too old to cry about a stupid doll. None of my friends in Coqueiros played with dolls. They didn't have any dolls to play with. Besides, I was seven years old by then, much too old for rubber babies, but the tears came anyway. Aunt Martha's house was near a river, and in the time since my last visit, when I'd left Ruthie behind, there had been a flood. And Ruthie had gotten caught in it. Now she lay washed up in the mud beneath the house. She'd lost an arm and her eyes were clouded over with rust. Her hollow body, once such a wonder of drinking and peeing, was filled with black mildew. She was ruined.

SENHOR AGOSTO doted on me. He was an old fisherman who lived with his son and their family in a one-story stucco house almost directly across the street from us. The house was painted a cheerful red, practically orange, with a window in the front where *Seu* Agosto spent his days. *"Seu"* is the abbreviation for Senhor, which means "Mr." The window had no glass, just shutters, like everyone else's windows, but all in all it was a very nice house. *Seu* Agosto's son was the local *sapateiro,* or shoemaker, and he earned a fine living for his family.

I never actually went inside *Seu* Agosto's house. I only talked to him from the street as he leaned out his window. As soon as *Seu* Agosto finished breakfast, he'd pull his hard-backed wooden chair up to the windowsill and drape his hands across it, or rest his elbows there, and settle in for the rest of the day. Every single morning it was the same. Housewives throughout the village, and others like *Seu* Agosto, who'd long since slowed down in life, hurried to finish the dishes or get the wash on the line so they could get back to their windows and watch the world go by.

Seu Agosto was ancient. A thin fringe of silky white hair hung from behind the old fisherman's ears to the nape of his neck. In the crumpled hollow of his mouth, not a single tooth was visible. But I wasn't afraid, not of his creviced skin or cloudy eyes, or even of the sour smell of his clothes. None of it bothered me. I talked to *Seu* Agosto almost every day, even if just a quick hello. I especially talked to him in the winter of 1942.

Dorothy teased me when she noticed where I was going. "Why do you hang around with the old man?" she demanded. "Is he your boyfriend?"

I ignored her and put on my *tamancos* anyway. *Seu* Agosto's house was perched just a hundred yards from the water's edge, and from his window he liked to stare out at the ocean. His observations fascinated me. Over time, I realized that my old friend could predict the weather with unerring precision, even days in advance.

"*Vento Sul,*" he'd say in his gravelly voice, and this would mean a special three-day period of south winds was on the way. If, in the far distance of clear blue sky, *Seu* Agosto saw signs of rain, he'd laugh and say, "More trouble for the bus."

Seu Agosto read the skies the way my parents read the Bible, with an understanding just as literal. He knew well the havoc rain wreaked on our soft dirt roads. In my first year of school in Brazil, a hard rain could mean a day off. I was in kindergarten and Dorothy was in fourth grade then, and the two of us rode the city bus five miles to the German Lutheran School in Florianópolis. In good weather, the trip took about half an hour, what with all the bumps and passenger stops. One memorable and frequent stop was about one quarter mile from our house, just before reaching the Lonesome Beach. It was the house of a local politician, João de Assis. Every morning his maid ran out to the street, stopped the bus, and we waited for his teenage son, Nereu, to come out of the house and catch the bus. Sometimes it took three to five minutes, but to me it seemed like hours. Mr. Assis was a very important man and neither the bus driver nor the passengers complained, at least not out loud. With rain, the going was even slower. When clouds broke open during the night, the ruts in the road were deep and slippery by morning. Often, the bus became stuck in the mud.

"Everybody off!" the driver would shout, and all the passengers would push the bus from behind. Dorothy and I loved those muddy adventures, especially when the bus broke down in the middle of the trip. That's when we would walk back home and skip school for the day.

That was before the war panic reached its full bore. Once the Brazilian government made it illegal to speak German, all of the German schools and churches were shut down, one by one. By the end of 1941, our German Lutheran School was closed. I had to change to the one-room schoolhouse in Coqueiros for first grade. Dorothy went to public school in Florianópolis and repeated fourth grade, because she was still scrambling to read and write in Portuguese.

Straight across the dirt road from us was a small Coqueiros neighborhood that was home to several families. Their cluster of homes wasn't visible from the road because of the hill that rose between us, and we were also separated by God: The kids in that neighborhood didn't go to our church, and therefore I seldom played with any of them. Mother and Dad didn't like me playing with nonbelievers. But several of those children did go to my school, and a group of us walked home together in the afternoons. Often, we encountered a very strange sight as we passed the crest of the hill. On our right, my house came into view. On our left, obscured by several high bushes on the side of the road, a man often hovered with his pants down around his ankles.

He was the father of one of the girls who walked home from school with us, and we all recognized him. But none of us wanted to acknowledge his presence, let alone his identity. We preferred to try to ignore the situation, for our classmate's sake as well as our own. Certainly, I didn't want to be the one to say anything! The man frightened us, the way he was always moving his hands and arms vigorously back and forth in front of his crotch, with a big grin on his face. The bushes where he stood were about fifty feet from the road where we walked. All of us walked faster when we saw him, trying to get past him as quickly as we could.

One of my friends, Vavau, would grab my hand and whisper fiercely, *"Não olha, Graça! É coisa feia,"* "Don't look, Grace! It is an ugly thing."

It was ugly. The sight of this man made me sick to my stomach, even though I didn't know why. My classmate was obviously mortified. She refused to give any sign that this man was her father, let alone greet him as we passed. Each time it happened, we simply hurried on to our respective homes without a word. But I have never forgotten the image of the man masturbating in front of his own daughter and her schoolmates.

In this same neighborhood lived a crazy lady. She liked to climb up to the crest of the hill overlooking our house, and there she crouched and screamed obscenities at the top of her lungs. She continued her nonsensical, furious diatribes for fifteen or twenty minutes, and then left the same way she'd come. We all ignored her and continued with our daily activities as if nothing were out of the ordinary. But my heart ached for this tormented woman. Surely she was possessed by the devil. What other explanation could there be for her behavior?

A frequent stop on my way to school, or after school, was *A venda do Zeca* (Zeca's store). It was a grocery store about a quarter mile from our house. Actually, the grocery was a collection of food items and dry goods shelved in the small living room of his house. Since Mr. Zeca had a young daughter my age, I'd been inside their house many times, and I knew that the family lived in two cramped rooms behind the store.

Other than Mr. Zeca's store, the nearest market was more than three miles away. Not surprisingly, Mr. Zeca ran a brisk and successful business for many years. His store was about twenty feet long with doors on either side. A large counter ran the length of the store, and in front of the counter all along the wall was a bench. Mr. Zeca kept a scale on the counter, and he used real weights to balance the scale, in the old-fashioned way. Mr. Zeca's customers didn't buy goods in large quantities. Instead, townsfolk purchased products in fractions of kilograms. Amounts such as 100 grams, 250 grams, or a half kilo were common, and the latter would be a large purchase. There were no paper bags to send away with customers. Mr. Zeca placed a paper sheet on the scale, scooped an individual's goods onto it, and balanced the weight on the other side. Then he folded the paper and, with the skill of a craftsman, turned the edges under with his fingers, so that nothing inside would spill out. Mr. Zeca sold basic staples like sugar, rice, beans, flour, coffee, candy, cigarettes, and *Cachaça*. Sometimes, as I poked through the storehouse in our own pantry, looking for a bit of cinnamon or some dried milk, I thought that with the way our family shopped, we could have our own store! The only things we would not have, of course, would be cigarettes and *Cachaça*.

Cachaça, also called *Pinga* or *Agua Ardente*, was an alcoholic drink made from sugar cane. The alcohol content of *Cachaça* is outrageous, and tricky to regulate. You could use *Cachaça* as starter fluid, you could use it as paint thinner, or you could use it as an explosive! I'm pretty sure you could use it to heat your house if necessary. If you pour some *Cachaça* in a dish and light it with a match, it can practically burn forever. In Brazil, *Cachaça* is often called "the poor man's blanket." It's one way that a poor, desperate man can forget his tragic life, and fall asleep in the warmth of intoxication.

Whenever I had a spare coin or two, I walked down our road to Mr. Zeca's store to buy sweets. Lined up on his counter were several large glass jars filled with colorful hard candy. I only made these candy runs by daylight, as by evening Mr. Zeca's store was no place for young girls or women. Even in broad daylight, young and old men alike sauntered into Mr. Zeca's store and ordered *Cachaça*. Mr. Zeca poured exactly an ounce from the bottle into a shot glass, and the men threw back their shots in single, pained gulps. Oh, how their faces contorted as the stuff went down! Judging by their grimaces and watering eyes, it must have tasted disgusting. It must have burned like acid, all the way down their throats and into their stomachs. I never figured out why anyone would want to buy and drink something that tasted so terrible.

Chapter Eleven

The Price of War

B Y 1941 AND 1942, intense anti-German sentiment swept through Brazil like wild fire. These effects took an especially heavy toll in the south of Brazil, where many German immigrants had settled before the war. In the five years from 1933 to 1938, Germany had doubled its imports of Brazilian products like coffee and cacao, but World War II brought what had been a fast-growing cooperation between the two nations to a screeching halt. When the United States entered World War II, most of Latin America followed. When Brazil broke diplomatic relations with Germany, German submarines began attacking and sinking Brazilian ships. In just three days during mid-August 1942, Germany sank five Brazilian ships and killed hundreds of Brazilians. Brazil formally declared war on Germany on August 22, 1942—and it was more than a paper declaration. Brazil sent 25,000 troops to Italy in 1944, and 451 Brazilian soldiers were killed. Brazil's airplanes and ships were actively engaged in protection of the South American coast.

Meanwhile, the effort to identify German spies reached zealous proportions among officials and even citizens. German factories and businesses in Porto Alegre were shut down. It became almost impossible to run a

German shop anywhere in Brazil. Sooner or later, someone in a German school or church or store was bound to slip and speak German—most of our teachers at the German Lutheran School had spoken German more fluently than Portuguese. But disobeying the law could get you sent to prison.

What I really hated, though, was when townsfolk taunted Dorothy and me. One day when Dorothy and I were returning from the German school on our way to catch the Coqueiros bus, this took on a sinister edge. We were followed by several kids who chanted softly, just loud enough for us to hear, *"Alemao Batata. Come Queijo com Barata."* It meant, "Stupid German, eats cheese with cockroaches." Nonsensical in English, but no more so than "It's raining, it's pouring" or "ring around the rosy" or "liar, liar, pants on fire." The idea was that it made a pleasant, easily remembered rhyme (in Portuguese anyway) for accusing anyone with fair skin and blue eyes.

Usually, I just put up with it, walking faster and clenching my teeth in anger. But this time the attacker was closer to my own age, and I wanted to fight back. "You eat cockroaches!" I yelled. "You eat dead snakes with rotten bananas! You eat maggots in your coffee!"

"Shut up," Dorothy said, when she heard me do this. "You'll just make it worse."

She had unusual fortitude when it was called for, considering how fiery a temper she had with Mother. Indeed, when it came to Mother, Dorothy applied her fortitude to provoking instead of avoiding conflict. Certainly this was true whenever Mr. Norbert came around.

Mother met Mr. Norbert shortly after we arrived in Coqueiros. He was the organist at the German Lutheran church and the music director of the German school Dorothy and I attended. He had helped Mother get a used piano for practically nothing. Mother couldn't believe her luck with such a bargain, and she was thrilled to have music in the house again. Often, Mr. Norbert came over to play duets.

"Mother!" Dorothy laughed whenever she saw Mr. Norbert coming up the walk. "Come quick! It's your boyfriend here to see you."

"Shush, Dorothy," Mother snapped back. "I've heard enough out of you."

But her cheeks flared red every time, revealing just how sensitive she actually was about this line of teasing. As a result, she never allowed herself to be alone with Mr. Norbert in the house, insisting that one of us girls was present whenever he came to visit.

The Lutheran church held its Christmas program for a full and festive congregation on Christmas Eve, 1941. Everyone was dressed in their best—men in suits and women in colorful skirts and hand-embroidered blouses. Candles along the altar illuminated the beautiful stained glass windows that the Germans had imported from their homeland. Before long, Mr. Norbert simply lost his head in the mood of celebration. He opened his mouth and sang, *"Stille nacht, heilige nacht . . . ."* Many of the people standing in the pews joined in, sweetly and joyfully.

The next morning, the police showed up to arrest Mr. Norbert. They took him and several of the school's teachers to prison. That was the end of Mother's duets. None of us ever saw Mr. Norbert again. Later, we heard from others that he died of pneumonia at the prison.

SOMETIMES, as *Seu* Agosto watched the world go by, he talked about the war and its effects on our lives and the lives of those around us.

He urged me, in his scratchy but firm voice, "Don't speak the English, Graça. Remember for me you don't speak it."

He knew that English—though not illegal—sounded enough like German to raise suspicion and get folks like my family into trouble.

It wasn't easy to be targeted and disgraced this way. It weighed on me because it weighed on my parents. Dad especially attracted attention. It was bad enough that he was German-born. Brazilians loved their country and hated their enemies in equal measure. So Dad's passport was a problem, since it showed Germany as his country of birth. It also showed his status as a naturalized American, but many Brazilian officials were ignorant of the nuances of American immigration law. From their perspective, it was simple: Dad was born in Germany and therefore probably a German spy.

It scared me when the soldiers stormed Coqueiros and searched our house. There were about a dozen of them, in full dark green uniforms posturing outside our front gate. One of the soldiers clapped his hands sharply, the local custom for announcing one's arrival. Doorbells were uncommon in Brazil.

The soldiers were looking for any type of spy equipment, especially two-way radios. Dad had a shortwave radio that he loved. He was fiercely attached to it, often using it to tune into the BBC to catch up on the latest world news. Many times, I drifted to sleep to the strange, squeaking sounds of that radio through the wall, the newscaster's voice blaring and then fading to nothing, then blaring again as the radio signal ebbed and flowed from places far away.

"It is for spying," the lead soldier accused, after examining the radio for several minutes with his comrades.

My mother moved slightly, almost imperceptibly, closer to my father. She stiffened her palms against the dark fabric of her dress. She looked petite, with her eyes sunken and her goiter protruding from her neck. One could also see red sores on her forehead. I felt sad and frightened as I looked at my parents.

"No, it is only for the news, for my work as a missionary," my father explained in his clipped way.

One of the soldiers pulled the radio out from the wall and turned it around. He tapped on the backboard and tugged at the electrical cord. "Hmmph." He was clearly dissatisfied, but eventually he and the others left without Dad's precious radio.

But they didn't stay away for long. Within the month, they were back, and from then on, they raided us often. Finally, my father had to give up the radio. The Brazilian authorities just wouldn't accept that it wasn't a two-way, and as long as it was in our house, Dad was attracting problems for us. Mother was relieved to see it go.

For her, giving up English was by far the greatest sacrifice of war. She learned the hard way how serious a matter it was. Returning by train from a week of missionary work in a nearby town, she was overheard reading aloud to Dorothy and me from a children's Bible—in English. When the train stopped at the next town, it didn't start up again on schedule, and just as the passengers started to squirm, a squadron of policemen came marching toward us, about twelve deep. They arrested my father and marched him off the train. I watched from the thick glass window as they escorted him into the center of town. I was sure something terrible was going to happen. At the same time, I was horribly embarrassed. What could he have done that was so bad?

They questioned Dad for two or three hours, forcing the train full of passengers to wait. Finally, the police chief was able to reach the American Consulate in Porto Alegre. Staff there offered assurances that my father was not a spy. The train was allowed to move on.

From then until the war ended, Mother didn't speak English again, not even at home. But she suffered for it, always feeling straitjacketed by a language with which she fought. She never was fully able to express herself in Portuguese.

Ultimately, though, the practical effects of the war had the greatest impact on our daily lives, especially the gasoline shortage. By the end of 1941, we couldn't get any gas at all for our car. And since the situation was not about to improve, Dad gave up and pulled the battery out of the Chevy. He took off the tires and stored the car on concrete blocks at a neighbor's house.

Sometimes we could still take the bus, but the bus had to contend with the gas shortage, too, and it was even less dependable than usual. It rumbled past randomly, never on any kind of schedule, and much of the time it never showed up at all. The only reliable way to get around was on foot. Walking, even for long distances, became our primary means of transportation. This slow-motion lifestyle didn't suit my father at all well. As a man under pressure to save as many souls as possible before the end of the world—due to arrive soon—he needed to move quickly!

IN JULY OF 1942, Dad bought a sailboat. He was delighted. "Well, my Little General," he crowed, "come for a ride with your daddy on the most beautiful boat in the world!" He gave me a tour of the large wooden vessel. "This mast is made of bamboo," he explained, "and this pretty white sail is canvas. She can hold at least twenty people safely if she can hold one."

From the day Dad bought his boat until spring of 1944, sailing became our main mode of transportation to Florianópolis or to the other villages on the island.

Dad was right; it was a pretty boat. And big, too, enough to hold twenty people, but as far as safety, I wasn't so sure. Had Dad been a sailor, maybe. But Dad had no experience with sailing or watercraft of any kind. And neither did my cousin John.

Still, I trusted Dad implicitly, whether or not he had ever tied a knot or manned a tiller. My father could do whatever he wanted. If what he wanted was to be captain of the sea, he was captain of the sea, no questions asked. I did not have this same feeling about my cousin John. And neither of them had a knack for sailing in bad weather.

Time after time, we were caught on Dad's boat in sudden tropical storms—or we'd get stuck out on the water for a long windless afternoon. The two small oars Dad kept on board were useless. The boat was too big and too heavy to maneuver through powerful ocean currents with Dad's little paddles.

I took to running down to *Seu* Agosto's house before setting off anywhere with Dad or my cousin John. If *Seu* Agosto said the weather was going to be dry and windy, then I was fine to sail. But if *Seu* Agosto predicted a still day or a storm, I'd run back to warn Dad. I soon learned my warnings were utterly useless. Dad brushed them off, even though *Seu* Agosto's predictions always came true. I gave up and started finding excuses to avoid outings whenever *Seu* Agosto's forecasts were foul.

One thing I couldn't be excused from, though, was Sunday services. After Dad finished building the chapel behind our house in Coqueiros, he held most weekly services there, including Sunday school, and this meant we only needed to go to the main church in Florianópolis once every Sunday for the evening service. But for special Sundays like Easter, or for important guest speakers, we'd sail to and from the main church in Florianópolis both morning and evening. With an average wind, the four-mile trip took about thirty minutes. With a light wind, it could take an hour or two, tacking slowly back and forth across the water, looking out for the rocks that lurked above and below the surface. Usually, the boat was loaded with people. Dad was willing to transport as many locals as he could to hear the message of God.

After Sunday school in the main church in Florianópolis, about twenty of us jostled onto the boat for the trip back to Coqueiros. Dad's sermon had been inspiring that morning, and everyone's spirits were high. The bright mood persisted out on the water, even as a gauzy, purplish layer of cloud cover began to pucker more densely above our heads. The chatter and laughter tapered off and died over the next ominous half hour, as the purple gauze turned to an angry tangle of deep gray. From there, the roiling cloudbank blackened the sky overhead. With the darkness came wind, first a low growl and then a scream.

Weather along our coast could go on unchanging for days and days, or whip itself around in just seconds from one condition to another. I'd watched storms build and break from a safe distance on the cliffs above our beach, but never had I experienced one on the water. Any bad weather I'd encountered on the boat before was nerve-wracking, but this was sinister.

I looked at Mother, who had her eyes closed and was praying softly, "Dear Jesus, protect your servants, keep us safe in this storm."

I started to pray too. We both knew that the one thing Dad never kept aboard his boat was life jackets. In fact, he owned none.

Moments after the wind started howling, the torrential rain smacked down in forceful continuous blasts. I couldn't tell which way it was pouring. Torrents of water hit us from all sides at once, as the rain mixed with the waves crashing over the sides of our boat. We were taking on water with astonishing speed.

"Bail!" shouted my father. I crawled across the flooded deck to find a container. Everyone scrambled, some crawling like me. Others grasped the boat's ropes and handholds to keep their footing. There wasn't much to bail with—only one proper bucket, a bottle, and our cupped hands.

Even with all of us bailing for our lives, we barely made a dent in the flooding. Every time I dumped one handful of water over, waves crashed several gallons more onto the deck. Meanwhile the canvas sail thrashed wickedly over my head. I kept low, sure that the boom would careen across the deck and knock me overboard if I stood up.

Then came the crack, almost like a gunshot. The mast had split in half.

Its top half dragged in the waves, drowning the sail, and the bottom half stood helplessly on board, still attached to the boat. The slip of dark land behind us grew more distant as ocean currents pulled us farther and farther out to sea.

"Pray!" Mother screamed, and everyone began to pray.

Dear Jesus, I sobbed. *Please help Daddy save us! Please help him bring our boat to shore. Don't let us drown, dear God. Please stop the rain, God, please stop the storm.*

My father and cousin John thrashed with those two useless oars.

Dear Jesus, please don't let us die! Please don't let us die!

My prayers had become a chant of pleadings to the Lord. But as far as I could tell, the Lord wasn't listening. I was sure we would die. And we might have, if the wind hadn't jettisoned us into a crag of land more substantial than a rock but not exactly an island. It barely shielded our boat from enough wind to make it possible for my father and the others to get it turned back in the right direction.

The storm mellowed gradually over the three hours it took for the waves to carry us back to shore. Dad's beleaguered boat washed up about ten miles north of our beach in Coqueiros. We filed onto the wet sand. Those miniscule grains of earth beneath my feet felt like a miracle.

For the entire ten-mile walk home, barely a word was spoken.

Chapter Twelve

Death and Birth

LIFE'S EDGES ARE MORE URGENT and alive than anywhere in the middle ground. Consider birth, marriage, sex, or death, and the truth of this is obvious. In the physical world, the lip of land—soft or jagged—as it meets the curve of sea may be the most primal boundary area of all. Stone is ground to dust here by the wind and waves, and the lives of those who dwell along the water's edge are etched by the ocean's unceasing motion. The sea and its surroundings, in ways that I am still discovering, made me the person I am today.

As a child, I loved the ocean in the same way I loved God and my parents. I loved it for all that it was: Its beauty, its moods, its abundance— even its danger. Like our daily lives in Brazil, the sea was rich with surprise, good and bad. The contrast could be breathtaking—like the natural beauty of Florianópolis next to its pervasive poverty and disease. Growing up with these contradictions made them invisible to me, yet intensely powerful.

Sometimes, good and bad are so intertwined it's difficult to distinguish one from the other. Some of my most cherished memories are of the things moving between the bitter and the sweet. *Vento Sul*, the south winds, were like that. And the arrival of these winds brought some of my favorite memories. The wind itself usually lasted for three days or so. The water would stir up and grow cloudy, gray, and very cold, and our bay during *vento sul* looked dirty and uninviting. It was terrible for swimming, and not especially good for boating, either. But it was fabulous for catching crabs.

At the first hint of *vento sul* I prepared my crabbing net, which consisted of a piece of netting tied across a wire circle about twelve inches across. For bait, I usually used something spoiled and pungent—decaying chicken pieces or some other rotting meat. I attached the net to a sturdy bamboo pole with a cord, and then I lowered the whole contraption to rest on the ocean floor. Meanwhile, *vento sul* did its work, blowing crabs to shore. After five or ten minutes, I raised the net to find one or two angry crabs flailing in its strands.

As quickly as I could, I threw my net down and caught the crab in my hands, careful not to get clawed. It was hard to catch a crab before it scuttled back into the sea. I became an expert at this game, because I loved eating the crabs. I boiled them, or, to my father's horror, simply dropped them on the iron cover of our kitchen stove. A crab subjected to this hot, dry death staggered forward once or twice and then stopped. A few minutes later, its shell turned bright red and its meat would be ready to eat.

My crab habit upset my father. "Gracie," he'd say, "that is a live animal. Do you not have a heart?"

Dorothy readily agreed. "She's a savage, didn't I tell you so?"

But to me, the combination of cruelty and satiation was just another of life's perpetual paradoxes.

In addition to preaching kindness toward the crabs, Dad always taught us that it was better to give than to receive. But the idea wasn't easy for Dorothy and me to grasp or apply, no matter how many examples our father set for us in the way he lived his daily life.

In Coqueiros, beggars wandered the streets every day. Our family was wealthy by local standards, and a continuous stream of beggars came to our door. They came looking for clothes, food, money, or whatever other handout might be had. When beggars came to our wooden gate, with Nero barking on the other side, they clapped their hands to announce their presence. One of us then ran to the gate to find out what the beggar needed. Often, the person was hungry and claimed not to have eaten in days. Mother generously cobbled together a heaping plate of warm food and a sack of bread, fruit, and whatever else she had in the pantry.

When Dad was home, he listened patiently and with real interest to the beggars' stories. He always sent them away with at least a small word of encouragement, some Bible literature, and a sermon. Sometimes, the stories the beggars told were easy to believe in the face of obvious need— toothless grins and skeletal sick bodies, dressed in rags, smelling of things rotten and unclean. But with some others, it was harder to know if they really needed help, or simply wanted more. Dad tried to be careful, but it was difficult. The stories the beggars told were often so vivid.

One day, a man showed up with a dirty cloth wrapped around the right side of his face; only part of his nose and the left side of his face was visible. I went to the gate with Dad, and the beggar asked us for money to help feed his family.

"Why don't you work? You look healthy enough to me," said Dad.

"If you want to see, I will show you why no one wants to hire me," the beggar replied.

"Yes, show me," said Dad.

The beggar removed the cloth from his face, and Dad and I both gasped. The right side of the man's face was completely gone. We could see his jaw, the inner side of his nose, and the eye socket, which barely held his eyeball in place.

"Please, cover it up," Dad said quietly, and the beggar did.

Dad asked Mother to prepare some food while he went to his study and came back with as much money as he could spare. Dad never asked the man what was wrong with him, but most likely it was leprosy or some other flesh-eating disease.

Another time, a middle-aged man came to our gate and talked with Dad for a long time. When Dad asked him why he wasn't working, the man explained that the torn shirt he was wearing was all that he had. "I can't get a job looking like this," he lamented. "Could you help me buy a shirt?"

Dad believed the man was sincere, but it was the end of the month and we were out of money. So, my father slowly unbuttoned his cotton shirt, took it off, and gave it to the beggar.

"Dorothy," he said, "get some food for this man to take with him."

"John," Mother scolded under her breath. She frowned deeply, her frustration obvious. The shirt had been one of Dad's best.

Vendors paid frequent visits to our door, as well. Every day, sun-baked fishermen strolled by with wheelbarrows full of their daily catches. As they pushed their wheelbarrows, the fishermen sounded their bull-tusk horns. The sound was distinct and musical, so unique to the fishermen, I associate it with fresh fish to this day. Dorothy loved to go out and bargain with the fishermen, who always cheerfully raised their prices for us, figuring that we could afford to pay more. Dorothy would spend several minutes getting the price down to something reasonable, and then she'd ask Dad for the money. Dad would step out of the house and hand the fisherman the amount of money he'd originally requested. Then he'd say with a grin, "Keep the change."

"Dad!" Dorothy would yell. "Why did you do that? I had talked them down to a better price!" She was furious at seeing her expert bargaining skills go to waste.

But Dad only laughed and said, "Dorothy, he is a hard working man with a large family to support. Let us pay him the price he asked."

MY NEIGHBORHOOD friends embodied life's harshest paradoxes, too. In their stark poverty and daily joy, they defied easy understanding. The dead babies I carried were only one example. All kinds of diseases were rampant in Coqueiros. Tuberculosis was a common and particularly ruthless killer in rural Brazil. Life in general was raw and often short in our village, where by contrast, my family lived in immeasurable luxury. No wonder my friends were so willing to haul wood for the privilege of my exotic company.

One friend, a village girl named Edesia, lived with her mother and brother in a two-room, dirt-floor shack. Edesia's father had died shortly after her brother's birth, and his absence only sharpened the edges of an already hard life for the rest of the family. Edesia loved to escape to our house. Together we lounged in the hammocks my father strung on our terrace, swinging beneath the blood-red blooms of the fragrant bougainvillea dripping from the overhead trellises.

One Saturday morning, on the third day of a lovely *vento sul*, I was swinging in a hammock on the terrace, sated with crab and quietly happy.

"Graça! Graça!" Edesia's voice rang out from the yard below, wild with fear.

I scrambled down the stairs and into our kitchen, where my Mother leapt up from the pie dough she had been gently rolling out. "What is it, child?" she asked, taking Edesia's narrow shoulders into her wide, capable hands. Mother's palms were still dusted with flour, white against my friend's brown cotton dress.

Edesia's body heaved with sobs. "Please help!" she cried. "It's my mother! Oh please, please help!"

Mother untied her apron and tossed it down at her feet. "Let's go," she said.

I ran behind them down the length of the road to Edesia's shack, drawing the humid air deep into my lungs. I didn't know if my mother meant for me to follow, but she didn't tell me to turn back, so I continued. We walked past the small cook stove and short table in Edesia's kitchen to the second room, a crowded living and sleeping area. Edesia's mother lay in a small metal bed. Blood trickled from her mouth, and beside her, on the dirt floor, were cast-iron cooking pots filled with bright red blood. Edesia's mother was hemorrhaging from her mouth, too weak to cough, and choking on her own blood. Mother knelt beside the dying woman as her breathing slowed. Within moments, a long death rattle wrenched itself from her lungs, and Edesia's mother was dead from a tuberculosis infection she didn't even know she had.

After her mother's death, Edesia and her brother disappeared, probably to live with relatives. I never heard from her again. But later that night, my mother told me the story of my own birth.

I think the loss of Edesia's mother brought out some nostalgic feelings about me and my birth and, without my asking, Mother recounted the whole story.

"IT WAS SEPTEMBER 1933," Mother said, "and the afternoons in Flint were still long and warm. Tinges of gold and burnt umber on the maples and elms along Bennet Avenue, where we lived, were the only marker of the change of seasons."

I knew this story by heart, and I knew that other changes hovered in the air that fall. It was on one of those early September afternoons that Mother first realized she was pregnant with me. Dorothy was five years old then, and my parents had given up every hope of having another child. Mother was overjoyed at the news. She let several weeks pass before she told my father, and when at last she did, he was overjoyed. He was convinced, as he'd been with Dorothy's birth, that it was simply the work of God in his life, and furthermore that my mother would give birth to a dearly hoped-for son, who they would name John David.

Instead, I showed up, in a bit of a spectacle.

"As soon as I realized my labor had begun," my mother said, "your father took me to settle in with a church member in Clio, about ten miles outside of Flint. Meanwhile, a hundred miles away, your Aunt Elizabeth was baking bread in her kitchen when her sister-in-law Ollie came to tell her that I was about to give birth."

It was the afternoon of April 21, 1934. Aunt Elizabeth wrapped her sinewy arm around the heavy bread bowl and ran to the car with Aunt Ollie on her heels. They drove together across the hundred mostly barren miles to Clio. As the pavement unrolled beneath their tires, the bread rose high and airy in the backseat, filling the car with the rich aroma of warm yeast. Several hours later, they arrived.

"And wouldn't you know," Mother laughed, "that Aunt Elizabeth ran straight from the car into the kitchen and popped the bread into the oven to bake it."

Mother had a midwife on hand to attend the birth, but that was just the beginning of the expertise available that day. Dad's sister-in-law, Aunt

Lydia, had just given birth to her tenth son, and Aunt Elizabeth had ten children of her own. Then there was Grandma Kolenda, mother of six, also more than happy to advise. After the many hours of requisite hot towels, female talk, and fresh-baked bread for all, I emerged, open-eyed and squalling with good health.

"Then your Grandma Kolenda shouted something about you having her nose!" Mother scoffed. "Can you imagine? Oh, how I flinched. I thought your Grandma's nose was the largest, flattest, and ugliest I'd ever seen."

My mother admitted that in the early weeks she examined me anxiously again and again to reassure herself that Grandma had been mistaken. Hardly a vain woman, my mother still couldn't help but scrutinize my profile for several years to come.

"You looked nothing like Grandma Kolenda," Mother repeated. "You were always my little Grace from God."

Chapter 1. Lansing Church.

Chapter 2. Age 5. I felt very
self-assured and a little smug.

Chapter 4. Del Valle, 1939.

Chapter 5. Mom and Dad marry, December 9, 1922.

Chapter 5. 1902, Ludwig Kolenda family was still in Germany.
The empty chair was reserved for Uncle Ernie who arrived in 1905.

Chapter 6. Road from Rio to Porto Alegre, 1939.

Chapter 6. Dad, Dorothy and me (middle) watching
cousin Albert changing "a flat", 1939.

Chapter 7. Florianópolis, circa 1941.

Chapter 7. Dorothy, Nero and me in 1941.

Chapter 8. Albert Widmer, a trusted preacher and pedophile.

Chapter 8. Rev. Albert Widmer in Palhoça jail for child rape.

Chapter 10: Coquiero Cemetery shed where bones
were kept in 1942, now a tool shed.

Chapter 11. Sailing to church in 1942.

Chapter 12. In school uniforms, 1942.

Chapter 13. The market where I saw a headless man reeling toward me.

Chapter 13. Kolenda family, 1943.

Chapter 14. Looking down on Urubici.

Chapter 16. Uncle Rodrigo enjoying chimaráo.

Chapter 17 and 18. Uncle Ernie and Aunt Goldie.

Chapter 19. 12 years old in Highland Park, Michigan, playing Hawaiian guitar, singing, and legally blind.

Chapter 22. Live "on the air" with Hawaiian guitar.

Chapter 22. Traveling in Brazil for one and a half years
with Dad, Mom, and Hawaiian guitar.

Chapter 22. Stella was completely irresistable.

Chapter 23. Lygia "offered a door to hell on a regular basis."

Chapter 24. Stella. "We found time to sin."

Chapter 24. Lourdes (right) and me on the far side of Florianópolis Island.

Chapter 24. Ancient fig tree where I played and sang
church songs to hundreds and felt embarrassed.

Chapter 25. Luiz Sabino.
"If Dad had met him, he'd be a goner."

Chapter 25. Luiz Sabino.
"With enough sex appeal for three men."

Chapter 27. Uncle Rodrigo and Aunt Martha.

Chapter 28. I ran down to my rocks, to my beach, one final time to say "goodbye."

Chapter Thirteen

My Mother, Myself

I WAS PROUD to be the daughter of a fine minister, so close to God. I thought of myself as special. I pitied the unbelievers, who didn't know Jesus as I did. I felt especially lucky on the July morning when Vadica took me to the market in Florianópolis. I loved going to the market with Vadica; in fact, I loved going anywhere with her. She was only ten years older than I was, and full of stories and excitement. I admired her greatly. We rose early to catch the five-thirty bus into town. When we stepped onto the cobblestone street, the air was cool, and there was a slight fog over the ocean. I was nine years old. The sun had barely risen.

Even that early, Florianópolis was already busy. The public market, built in 1898, was framed by two red stucco buildings, each the length of a football field. Between them was an expansive corridor, filled with stalls. Inside, vendors peddled meat, *bacalhau* (codfish, a Brazilian staple), and shrimp, as well as rich sweet egg breads and toasted manioc. Outside, produce sellers' carts spilled over with towers of lime, banana, coconut, mango, papaya, pineapple, peppers, potatoes, and corn. Vendors called out over the festive strains of live Brazilian samba.

I loved to go to the Florianópolis market. It still operates today, nearly unchanged, but I've avoided it ever since that July morning when Vadica and I heard screams coming from the far end of the corridor. We were twisting our way through the produce carts to see what was happening when a headless man reeled towards me. Blood spurted from the place where his head had recently been. He jerked blindly like the chickens I killed every Saturday for our Sunday dinners. Behind him, his assailant waved a bloody machete. I watched the dying man stagger for yards and yards—though really it could only have been four or five long steps—before his body crumpled to the ground. My throat buckled somewhere near my sternum and the bile from my empty stomach erupted.

No one seemed surprised or even the slightest bit shocked at this happening, and no one seemed concerned as to who did it. Violent fights were not uncommon in my town. Undoubtedly the victim had insulted his assailant, or a member of his family, and the result was inevitable. Vadica and I were gone before the police arrived, and we never knew whether they chose to investigate or not.

After the market beheading, I could no longer decapitate our chickens with a sharp axe, as I had done before. To see them jump about headless was too much for me. I searched for a faster, more merciful method of killing. The worst thing I tried was tying the chickens upside down to a tree branch and while they struggled, swayed and clucked, they twisted their own necks until they broke. Much better was to tie them to the tree and first pluck a few feathers from their necks. Then, I'd use a very sharp knife to quickly slice through the featherless patch of pale skin. This quieted the chickens in only seconds.

MY DAD'S WORK required a lot of travel. I missed him so much. I missed him at bedtime, when I tucked the quilt over my head. I missed him when Mother and Dorothy screamed at each other in the kitchen. And I missed him most of all when I got the *bicho de pe*. Dad was the only one who knew how to pull these little bugs out from the soles of my feet. The itching drove me crazy, no matter how feverishly I scratched.

"Leave it alone," snapped Dorothy. She looked up from the spot where she sat on the gray couch doing her homework, and she stared at me as I clawed away at the bottom of my left foot.

"That's disgusting," she yelled again. "Stop it!"

"I can't stop it," I argued. "It itches."

In the center of the fleshy pad of my foot was a disk of thick, calloused skin. And hidden beneath that disk was a plump and fragile sac of eggs. I scooted across the wood floor toward the kerosene lamp that shone from the desk. I needed the light in order to examine the infection more closely. Above me, my Mother pounded away on her trusty Remington manual typewriter. Always in the evenings, she read from the Bible or wrote letters, never written by hand. Mother had the world's worst handwriting. Tonight she was writing to Aunt Henrietta, but her thoughts were not flowing smoothly. She tapped her sturdy black leather shoe against the floor in a quick staccato rhythm whenever she stopped to think, which happened every few moments. Tap, tap, tap, went Mother's foot as I picked at the bottom of mine.

"Mother!" Dorothy shouted again. "Tell her to leave it alone! She's just making it worse and she knows it."

"Grace," said Mother, as she slammed her black shoe down hard on the floor, "leave your foot alone. How many times must we tell you not to go barefoot."

It was a statement, not a question. Everyone knew I ignored my parents' admonitions against going barefoot. My one concession to the *bicho de pe* was to wear wooden-soled *tamancos*. Held on by a single thin strap of leather, these rustic sandals were the only footwear my village friends could afford, and, even then, they ran barefoot most of the time. My friends reserved their *tamancos* for special occasions, while I acquiesced to wearing mine regularly. Except when I was in a hurry, or forgot, or missed the feeling of the earth under my feet. Then, I ran barefoot. As a result, I was constantly picking up the *bicho de pe*.

This time, the swelling on my foot was quite nasty. "Gracie," Mother repeated, "haven't we told you not to go barefoot?"

"But I didn't go barefoot," I said. "I wore my *tamancos*. I promise."

"*Tamancos* are not shoes," scoffed Dorothy. At fourteen, she considered herself vastly superior to me in every way. Dorothy always wore proper shoes.

"Yes they are!" I cried. "*Tamancos* are too shoes!"

"No, they're not, except for wild Indians, like you. Gracie, our little savage." Dorothy laughed heartily. Her taunts were the mean kind, sharp like the blade of my chicken hatchet.

Still, I knew I deserved what she gave me. Especially now, when Dad was gone. Dad's absences were so much harder on Dorothy than on me. At least Mother loved me. If Dad were home more often, everything would be better.

"Well," said Mother, tapping her foot again, "maybe Gracie doesn't wear her shoes because she likes to catch the *bicho de pe*."

Surely she couldn't mean this. Nobody liked to catch the *bicho de pe*! It was a parasitic infection that began mildly with an itchy round spot on the bottom of the foot that quickly grew larger and angrier. Soon it would get bigger than a marble, and very tender. At that stage, it hurt to stand or walk.

"Well, answer her," said Dorothy. "Do you like the *bicho de pe*, Grace? Because you wouldn't get it all the time if you didn't leave your shoes in the woods and on the side of the road and at the beach and wherever else you kick them off. You get exactly what you ask for."

"That's enough, Dorothy," scolded Mother. "Leave the child alone."

It didn't matter that both of them were right about my habits being the cause of my *bicho de pe*. Mother still couldn't stand to side with Dorothy. She got up from her typewriter and pushed her chair back. "I'm going to read my Bible in bed. Grace, it's time for you to go to bed, too. There's nothing to be done for your foot tonight."

If Dad were home, he'd know what to do, I thought. He'd sit me near the kerosene lamp and prop my foot up on his knee. Then he'd use a sharp, flat needle to loosen the toughened skin around the callous. He'd work gingerly, going very slowly.

"We must be mindful not to break the sac," he'd say. "If the sac breaks, a whole crop of new eggs will spill out and plant into your foot again, and we'll have to start all over."

Even with Dad's careful touch, I hated this procedure. But in his absence, I avoided it altogether. Mother was much too impatient to be trusted with the needle. For one thing, she was distracted with all of her own allergies and parasitic afflictions. When I stood to hug her goodnight, carefully keeping my weight off my sore foot, I could see that the scabs on her forearms were raw and cracked open. She had been trying a new cure for two days, restricting herself to a mineral water-only diet, but so far it wasn't working. Nothing seemed to work: the Epson salts, the herbal teas, the special diets.

Not even prayer.

But every night, I prayed for Mother anyway.

In my bed, my own private enclave of total safety, I burrowed myself down under the quilts. I allowed for only the smallest crack of an opening near my nose for fresh air. Safe from bats, cockroaches, and other flying bugs, I could also think and pray more clearly.

Dear Jesus, please help Mama's sores. Please let her have something other than mineral water to eat. Please bring Daddy home soon. Please make Dorothy happy. Please forgive me for not telling Mama I went barefoot with Ina and Iolanda. And please, please don't let the bicho de pe *sac break in my foot.*

Given her own troubles, which were so much worse than mine, it made sense that Mother didn't cry any rivers over my little case of foot bugs. It wasn't that she didn't care or feel sorry for me when I really needed it. Like when I had the boils, which was often. Boils were something Mother understood, since she too suffered from them regularly. We all did. And she'd been especially kind the time my whole bottom was so covered with boils that I couldn't sit down for two Sunday services in a row. We had no treatment to speak of, other than letting the boils enlarge slowly through the surface of the skin until they got big enough that Mother or I could try to squeeze out the "core" of infected material.

It made sense to me suddenly: Mother was just better at breaking open boils than she was at breaking open the *bicho de pe*. I sat up and opened my

eyes against the dark. I'd forgotten something in my prayers. *Dear Jesus,*
I started again. *Please make Daddy be home more. Please make him know I
have the* bicho de pe. *Please make him safe. Please make everyone safe.*

I knew my father would come if he knew how much I really needed
him—if he knew that I needed him enough, needed him more than his
church needed him. I imagined myself very, very ill. Maybe with *bicho
de pe* in both feet, or worse. Maybe all the way up my legs. Maybe inside
of me, in my bones, in my blood. I imagined this until I could feel the
infestation everywhere, in my veins, in my mouth, behind my eyeballs.

If only this were real, surely Dad would have to come home and stay
home. He would have to.

Dad tried to explain to me why he had to be gone so much. He said
that there were no Bible schools in Brazil to train new pastors. The Brazilian
churches were multiplying fast and there was a great need for new trained
leaders. His job was to go from town to town holding week-long Bible
instruction. There were usually twenty to thirty young men present, and
he taught from morning until night, five days a week. Then on Sundays
there were always church services where he preached both morning and
night. On Mondays he would leave for the next town.

When Dad came home, I could tell he was tired and often he had lost
a lot of weight. Mother took great care of him when he was home. She
cooked and baked everything he liked. Maybe she did this to try to keep
him home longer. But it never worked; after a week or two he was gone.

The sea lured me with its tangy smell and the rough sound of its action
behind our house. In times of distress and uncertainty, I yearned for the
sea itself, its cool darkness, and the expanse of our private beach, the warm
rocks glistening beneath shallow waves. The sea offered me such solace, a
comfort I searched for but could never find inside our house. Dad was so
often gone, and Mother was older than her years and utterly humorless.
Surely, her allergies were part of the problem of her disposition.

It was as if Mom's body recoiled and rejected the moist green air in
our village with every breath she took. Mostly, the allergic reactions festered beneath her skin, erupting in large, unsightly sores that itched and
burned. Mother's letters to Aunt Henrietta during those first six years in

the tropics overflowed with vivid descriptions of her open sores. She tried every folk remedy and treatment that was ever suggested to her.

But Mother carried on with her duties as the perfect missionary wife. She cooked elaborate meals for our household—a household that almost always included long-term houseguests and relatives, and she continued to make pies for Dad every day when he was home.

She also played the accordion and sang for church services every day, and she traveled by boat and on foot to the nearest out stations, where a native minister would have started a new church congregation. She was responsible for Sunday school, and for all of the Easter and Christmas programs. Mother also took charge of typing letters several times a week to report our progress to supporters in the United States.

Mom worked nonstop, and it wasn't easy on her. Plus, she had to make sure Dorothy and I followed every church rule to the letter of the law. No listening to the radio, no makeup, no movies, no associating with nonbelievers. She was constantly watching us to make sure we followed every edict. Often, I thought of Mother as more police officer than mother, and I know Dorothy felt the same, especially when we were teenagers. But all this policing was her moral responsibility.

The good thing about working so hard was that it gave Mother less time to dwell on her own miseries and less time to remember the woman she was before she became the perfect missionary wife. And the hard work paid off in other ways, too. She lost more than seventy pounds during her first year in Brazil, and she never gained it back during the first six years we lived there. The downside was that the weight loss revealed her large goiter, an unsightly, balloon-like swelling on her neck at the site of her thyroid gland. Despite her rejection of vanity in all its forms, the goiter bothered Mother at least as much as the extra weight had, and we all knew this. I always considered her a very old woman, in her old-lady shoes, long drab dresses, thin lips tightly closed, eyes sunken and stern, and dark braid hanging from her dour head. But nothing can compare to the way I idolized her before I turned eleven. I thought surely she was the greatest mother in the entire world. She loved me so much, and I knew it without question. She worried about me, and when I was sick she prayed and stayed up all night, if needed, taking care of me. However, Mother was not demonstrative in her love. She kissed me goodnight, but I do not remember sitting on her lap as I often did with Dad. She was not a hugger or coddler. I would hug her but she seldom volunteered hugs. Dad was the opposite, always open to hugs and kisses from both of his girls.

Her rage toward Dorothy was confusing. I'd hear them often, as I lay in bed daydreaming or reading or picking off scabs from the insect bites that ran the length of my brown legs. Their high-pitched shouts and arguments from the kitchen crashed through the thin plaster walls. This fighting scared me almost as much as the snakes that slithered through the cracks in our window screens in the night.

"You're just like your father!" Mother screamed at my sister.

This confused me even more. Shouldn't it have been a good thing to be like Dad? Wasn't Dad our hero? Whenever these fights erupted in my presence, I got out of the way as fast as I could.

But the fights erupted regularly, no matter how I tried to hide. Mother was always dead tired. Between her itching and extreme overwork she rarely got enough sleep, and her exhaustion undoubtedly contributed to her impatience with Dorothy. But Dorothy's personality was also starkly different from Mother's. Dorothy liked to tease and laugh and she was outgoing and friendly to everyone. Mother was just the opposite. To her, life was a serious matter and she had no time for play. The combination was combustive. I never understood why Dorothy didn't try harder to keep clear of Mother's path. But Dorothy didn't. Instead, she seemed to take pleasure from deliberately getting in her way. Sometimes, especially when Dad was away, the battles between my sister and mother became violent. Mother came at Dorothy often with a broom or a shovel or whatever else she could grab, and Dorothy either fended her off forcefully or tore through the house screaming.

It was hard not to be afraid of Mother in her rages. But as quickly as her temper flared, she could also be reduced to tears. She was very emotional and cried easily. If you told Mother your cat had died, her eyes would fill up and spill over. At church and at home, she wept through her own prayers. Though I felt ashamed to admit it, all this crying embarrassed me. Since I was Mom's favorite, I felt I should be grateful. Mom loved me so much.

But she didn't love Dorothy; and that was painfully obvious. "Oh, if only you would give yourself to the Lord!" Mom would shout in anger. "If only you would get saved!"

Dorothy never told Mother or Dad that she was "saved." Despite this she dutifully played the accordion and sang in church and did whatever she was asked to do for the Lord.

She refused to be baptized, and showed no desire to be a card-carrying member of the Assemblies of God. This may have been her defiance, because she knew Mother wanted her so badly to become a Christian. I always thought Dorothy was a Christian and I was always surprised to hear Mother talk that way. As I grew older, I understood why Dorothy had no desire to participate in the closed communion services in Brazil.

I couldn't understand why Mother disliked Dorothy so much. Sometimes when they fought Mom quoted Exodus, saying, "The sins of the Fathers will continue for generations."

I didn't know what she meant. But I did know that once Mother made a judgment, she never rethought a judgment, changed her mind, or shifted her position even by a hair's width.

She was a black and white person. You were either saved or a sinner. In order to be saved, you had to be Assemblies of God. Maybe a handful of Nazarenes or Baptists would wiggle their way into heaven, but to Mother this was regrettable since they did not know the whole truth. Often she'd say, "So-and-so seems to be such a nice person. Too bad she's Catholic."

Years later, I joked with Mother about how shocked she would someday be to get to heaven and see all those Catholics milling about. She threw me a stiff glance that said she knew better.

I felt very sorry for Dorothy. But I couldn't dwell on questions or fears about my mother. I believed in everything she believed in, and couldn't afford to doubt her. She was loving and attentive toward me. And I tried to please her by being good, praying, and reading the Bible. My skills in singing and accordion earned me compliments from Mother, too, but never in excess. She was careful not to say too much, lest she encourage me toward the terrible sin of vanity. Still, her modest praise was enough: I knew I was pleasing her.

Mother may not have praised much, but she had other ways of giving attention. For one, there were the daily delousing sessions. All of the village kids, including us, had chronic lice, and it drove Mother crazy. Right after lunch, she herded Dorothy and me into her bedroom. There, she required us to bend our heads over a sheet of white typing paper, while she meticulously worked through our hair with a very fine comb. As the critters from our heads fell onto the paper, louse by louse, Mother shouted: "Get it! Kill it!" And Dorothy and I scurried to crack the brown, sesame-seed offenders between our thumbnails.

These combing sessions took all the fun out of lice. Mother took it so very seriously, and with such vehemence. Her efforts interfered with my social life. One of our favorite neighborhood pastimes was to crouch down, one girl in front of the other, and grasp through each other's hair with our fingers, searching for lice and their eggs, called nits. Often there were four or five of us in a row, and the person in front would move to the back of the line every so often. When we found a louse, we'd crack it satisfyingly between our thumbnails. Nits were even better to crack, as they produced a loud popping sound that we loved. While combing our fingers through each other's hair, we told stories and sang and enjoyed each other's company.

Apparently, our childish games didn't make much of a dent in the problem, because Mother found plenty more each afternoon. And with every louse she killed, her passion to clear our scalps intensified. One afternoon she got so angry at our lice that she grabbed Dorothy and me and several of our friends and dunked our heads into a sink full of Lysol. Within hours, a parade of angry mothers pounded on our porch door and berated Mother for ruining their daughters' hair. By the end of the week, the lice were back anyway, since the infested siblings of our friends passed them right back to us.

If it wasn't lice, it was dysentery. And when it wasn't dysentery, it was something worse. Like the morning I woke to find a small, pale snake lying still upon my patchwork quilt. It was about twelve inches long, and had no head. I leapt from my bed and screamed my lungs out. Mother came running, and screamed along with me as soon as she saw the thing. I grabbed the snake and ran to the kitchen, where I stuffed it into a glass jar to save for our maid, Vadica.

When Vadica arrived, I ran to her, breathless. "Vadica," I cried. "Look! Look at the snake that crawled onto my bed in the night!"

I thrust the sealed jar toward her brown face, and when she looked into it her mouth widened in laughter. "It's only a roundworm," she crowed. "A roundworm from inside of you, Gracie."

Mom could hardly believe that this thing had crawled out of my intestines. But Vadica hurried to the drugstore and came home with a large can of castor oil. I wasn't allowed to eat anything after supper, and Mother woke before sunrise to administer the remedy: A large swig of castor oil followed by an orange juice chaser. After a few hours, the worms began to expel themselves from my body by the dozens, or maybe even hundreds. Ugly, round, white worms, squirming loose from my bowels.

All my friends had worms, but their mothers grew concerned only if their stomachs began to protrude or if they complained of dire pain. I, on the other hand, got a goodly dose of castor oil every three months whether I needed it or not. So I never mentioned the hordes of pinworms I saw whenever I used the toilet. I was too afraid of whatever treatment my mother might dream up for me.

The Brazilian children in our neighborhood were terribly weak. They had skinny little limbs, knobby knees, bulging tummies, and sores that didn't heal. Undoubtedly their health woes sprang from all sorts of disadvantages: Poor nutrition, lack of milk, inadequate prenatal care, and other ills of poverty. Ina, one of my best friends, was a good example of the way deprivation affected the kids around me. Ina was as wiry as a coat hanger, a year older than I, but much smaller. I liked playing with her and together we had loads of adventures. One day, as we were leaving my kitchen where we'd been having a snack together, Ina got distracted on her way down the steps. She missed the second step and fell to the ground, all of six inches. For a child like me, a little stumble like Ina's would have been nothing. It would have been less than nothing—like a sneeze, or a yawn, or a stubbed toe at worst. But when Ina tried to stop her fall with her hand, as anyone would do, the pressure resulted in a severe compound fracture of her right arm. Both bones, the radius and the ulna, shattered so badly that they protruded raggedly from the flesh of her arm. How unfair it was, I thought, that Ina was so fragile when I was so strong. Surely God had a reason for favoring me so kindly. I was grateful and guilty at the same time.

Meanwhile, Mother's battles against nature continued, including the *baratas* that overran our kitchen. Every evening, when we returned from church and turned on the sallow kitchen lights, the floor was momentarily brown, literally carpeted in roaches. They would run at the light, but always a few—perhaps the oldest or sickest—would trail behind the group. Mother immediately started stomping her feet, trying to crush them. Dorothy called this "Mother's *Barata* Dance." It didn't work very well. So Mom turned to poisons, especially DDT. This worked for a time, but eventually the roaches grew immune, and a new crop of larger, heartier roaches emerged in their wake.

It frightened Mother, the way these infestations took root, grew wild and out of control, and refused to respond to her efforts to destroy them. Her battles seemed to me a monumental waste of time, and I really could not feel safe under the wing of someone who was so terror-stricken. I was much happier when Dad was around, or at least when we had houseguests.

Chapter Fourteen

Sailing Away

U RUBICI was about one hundred miles straight west of Coqueiros, a picturesque town nestled into a lush valley with mountains rising above it on all sides. The residents were mainly Latvians who migrated to Brazil in the early part of the twentieth century. About half of them had settled in the state of São Paulo, near the town of São João da Boa Vista. These hopeful immigrants were following a charismatic leader, a Latvian immigrant himself, who predicted that the end of the world was imminent and preached a life of simplicity and disdain for material goods. The Latvians who didn't make their homes in São João da Boa Vista settled in the state of Santa Catarina, in and around Urubici.

My family first visited Urubici in February 1941. It was the first of many grueling, hundred-mile trips to that beautiful region. The main draw was the Latvian people who were kind, intelligent, and always anxious to make us feel welcome.

Our journey to Urubici meant leaving Coquieros at the crack of dawn, driving on the one-lane dirt road out of town. Soon, our way wended up foothills and then mountains. Traffic would be surprisingly thick, mainly trucks coming from Urubici loaded with lumber, and other trucks coming into the region with building materials, cloth, and other necessities of life. These trucks literally crawled along at five or ten miles an hour. It was impossible to pass them unless a particular driver was thoughtful enough to stop in a wider part of the road and let us edge by. This was scary enough for Dorothy and me, but there were other, more harrowing dangers along the route.

About twenty-five miles from Urubici we made a sharp left turn at the small village of Bom Retiro. There we found a gas station, motel, restaurant and a few houses. From Bom Retiro, in the near distance, we could see The Panelao, or the large pan, a land formation that resembled a skillet turned upside down. The Panelao was a prominent mountain jutting high above the rest and one that we had to cross in order to reach Urubici. It seemed like we often reached Bom Retiro around two or three in the afternoon, just in time for the daily tropical storm. I'd look from our car and see the clouds gathering and darkening as we got closer. Dad always pulled into this little village to fill the tank and get a little something to eat at the restaurant. "How's the mountain driving?" he asked the truckers who nursed their coffees in the same restaurant.

"*Não pode ir, é muito perigoso, espera até a chuva passar,*" they usually said, which meant, "You can't go. It is very dangerous, so wait until the rain passes."

A broad smile spread across Dad's handsome face. "Well, then," he responded with a shrug, "hurry up, Mother. Come, girls. Let's get going."

"John, listen to the truck drivers," Mother pleaded in a high-pitched whine. "They know best. Let's wait here a while, and have another coffee."

But inevitably Dad ushered us into the car and took off towards The Panelao. For the first eight miles out of Bom Retiro, the road was flat and curvy. It didn't start climbing noticeably until just before reaching the foot of the mountain. This, invariably, was when rain drops first started to splatter the car windows. Just as the steep climb began, the rain cascaded down in sheets. The one-lane road, with its fine red dust and dirt, became as slippery as soap. And in these conditions, trucks coming down the mountain left deep ruts in the sticky clay. The road had continuous hairpin curves. Eventually Dad was forced to stop the car and fish the heavy metal chains out of the trunk to wrap them around the rear tires. The chains helped a little with the traction, but we still slid from one side of the path to the other.

On one side of the road was the mountain: reassuring, solid, and protective. But on the other side was the precipice, beyond which was thin air that dropped straight down hundreds of yards to the earth below. There were no guardrails, no shoulders, no safety at all. Many trucks and cars slid over that precipice to meet their fate. The slim edge of the road was dotted with white crosses and faded paper flowers, to remind us of those who hadn't made it.

Mother prayed continuously. "Dear Lord, please protect your servants. Help Dad keep the car from falling down the precipice, and keep us safe in your arms."

I hunched in my seat and bit my nails, tasting the salt from my skin and the gristle of cuticle between my teeth. Dorothy didn't say a word. She sat straight up in the seat beside me, her eyes open wide, her lips pursed tightly. I could see and feel her silent fear, and it only magnified my own. The mountainous ascent took between thirty minutes and an hour, six miles that felt like sixty. Miraculously, we always reached the summit, from which we then had to inch slowly down for another five miles. During the descent, the rain had usually slowed or stopped, so the road wasn't quite so slick. But the moist clay caked our tires so thickly that Dad had to stop again and again to scrape it off in order to continue forward.

These mountain drives were truly as dangerous as they seemed back then—or more so. They weren't overstated due to a child's exaggerated fears. The risks were real, as evidenced by the makeshift grave markers along the pass. But Dad loved the adventure. He greeted it with a wry smile and an eager willingness, not once or twice but every time he got the chance. And why not? He was thoroughly convinced that God would take care of His servants. What was Dad if not a devoted servant of the Lord? And so, from his point of view, there was nothing to fear. Nothing at all.

THE VIEW from the mountain summit was truly breathtaking. The valley of Urubici spanned several miles, with rivers flowing in many directions and greenery so vivid it was almost blinding. It looked like Shangri-La. When we reached the bottom, we passed several farms, with the houses and yards full of colorful, blooming flowers.

The final adventure before entering Urubici was crossing the main river on the edge of town. There was no bridge, only a raft called a *balsa*. The raft could shuttle one vehicle at a time. The process was primitive, and worked like this: There was a cable that stretched from one side of the river to the other, usually anchored in a tree or stump on either side. The cable was attached to the raft by a thick rope. The cable operator stood on the raft together with the car and passengers. He then grasped the cable and pulled the raft from one side of the river to the other. The danger occurred when the river was high and the current was running strong. The rope securing the raft to the cable could snap and the raft would go floating down the river. There was no way, in such circumstances, that the operator could hold on to both the cable and the raft at the same time.

Mom, Dorothy, and I would step out onto the raft, the river spray dampening our feet and the smell of the valley filling our nostrils. Dad would drive the car aboard by way of two rough wooden boards that served as a bridge between the riverbank and the raft's surface. When the river was high, the whole ordeal was beyond precarious. Many cars and trucks toppled off the boards or the raft and sank in the river. Even when cars made it securely onto the raft, they often took an unwanted ride far downriver when the raft's rope or cable broke, as it frequently did. But in our case, we always made it safely across, if barely. And once on the other side, we were within a mile of Esquina, or the corner. This was the commercial area about two miles from the actual town of Urubici. Esquina was a thriving intersection with hotels, restaurants, brothels, stores, and churches. Lumber trucks usually turned at this intersection without ever actually entering the town.

Esquina and Urubici were like the American Wild West. Except for the occasional car and the lumber trucks rumbling through, folks got around by way of horseback or horse drawn carriage. Houses and stores were mostly one-story wooden structures like the ones on the set of a Western film. The local lumbermen were just like cowboys. They rode horses and dressed like American cowboys, with leather boots and straw hats with neck scarves or chin strings. On Saturday nights, they gathered at the Corner to drink, dance, fight, and look for girls in the bars and brothels. Dance hall brawls that ended in death were common occurrences, as was the sight of a horse galloping down the dusty street through Esquina with another horse in hot pursuit, its rider shooting madly at the rider he was chasing.

Mom and Dad did everything in their power to keep us away from Esquina on Saturday nights. Meanwhile Dorothy and I did everything in our power to stay overnight with friends who lived there. My parents' friends, the Karps, owned a fabric store and lived above it on the second story, and they always welcomed us. But we usually stayed about two miles from Esquina with the Karklis family, next door to another Latvian family, the Andermans. The Anderman farm was famous for the *Roda Grande,* a large wheel propelled by rushing water from the surrounding mountains. This large wheel turned many smaller wheels that worked in tandem to supply electricity to the Anderman household. Mr. Anderman also invented a steam-powered car that burned wood to generate the steam. When gas was in short supply during the war, we often rode the two miles to church in this car. Dorothy and I preferred the fun of riding horseback to Esquina. We stayed with the Karklis family and their daughter Ruth, who was the same age as Dorothy. Ruth always borrowed horses for us to ride whenever we needed to go anywhere.

ON ONE of these trips to Urubici, as usual, we stayed with the Karklis family. They grew their own vegetables and grains, and raised chickens, ducks, sheep, cattle, and, for transportation, horses. They spun wool with foot-driven spinning wheels, and wove their own blankets and sweaters. Urubici gets cold in winter, even snowy. So when we stayed there, Sister Karklis warmed our beds with stones she fired on the wood stove, and I burrowed in between two thick feather ticks. In the morning, the wood stove blazed in the kitchen, and from my bedroom, I could smell the coffee and hot rolls.

I loved to milk the cows with Brother Karklis and his son, Edvino. The barn was spotless, but still, there were the layered smells of tangy manure and fresh milk, and the sweet scent of the animals, their skin and sweat, and their moist breath. I loved the mooing. I was not afraid, only amazed at how gentle they were.

On this particular trip, after the market beheading I had seen in Florianópolis with Vadica, I took special comfort in feeding the newborn lambs whose mothers had been killed. Inevitably, I fell in love with one, and Mother took notice.

"John," she said to my father, "why don't we let Gracie have a lamb? It would be such a blessing for her to forget the bad experience she had at the market. She is such a dear girl."

My father considered. Whenever Dad spoke, he did so clearly and slowly, always authoritatively. He carefully chose every word he said. "Marguerite," he answered, finally, "I like that idea. Let's pray about it and decide tomorrow."

The next day, my father announced that the lamb would be my project. I was to feed her, care for her, get her fat, and then we'd have fresh lamb to eat. Even Dorothy was enthusiastic. We made a small box out of wood to haul my woolly baby on the bus trip back to Coqueiros. I named her Becky, for her beauty and girlishness. She was bright white, with intelligent black eyes. I knew she understood what I said to her, because she murmured back to me with soft baa-baas. Soon, I could tell if her baa-ing meant she was hungry or just happy. I held her on my lap and bottle-fed her several times a day. I loved to curl the tendrils of her wool around my fingers and bury my face in her softness. She nearly always stayed beside me. When we walked in the woods together, she became covered in burrs and dust. I bathed her and combed my fingers through her wet ringlets.

By December, Becky was thriving. She was almost seven months old, with a thick coat of wool. It was Brazilian summertime, so Mother decided to shear her. She used the wool for pillows, and was pleased. Meanwhile, Becky was becoming a nuisance. Neighbors complained that she ate their flowers and bushes and spoiled their yards with droppings. She ate our flowers and bushes, too, but I didn't mind. She was my girl, my best friend.

With my Becky, love was easy and uncomplicated as it could never be with my sister or my parents. If I could have given my life once for Brother Widmer, then I could have given my life ten times for Becky.

Mom and Dad were not happy with the one-room schoolhouse in Coqueiros, and by 1943, I was enrolled in a private school in Florianópolis, run by two sisters. I took the Coqueiros bus to and from school by myself. Becky knew when I came home from school and she was always waiting for me at the bus stop. Even so, I wasn't scared when I first skipped off the bus one day in May and found that Becky wasn't waiting there as she should have been. She was almost a year old, and was strong and healthy. Probably she was just on her way. I called for her as I ran down the dirt road towards home. The noontime sun blazed overhead.

When I arrived, I was sweating hard and my lungs burned from running. I pounded up the steps and through the front door. Dorothy was in the kitchen, sitting at the table, looking down at her cutting board. She was slicing tomatoes for *feijoada*.

"Dorothy," I panted, "have you seen Becky?"

My sister ignored me and continued slicing. Her knife made a smooth frictionless whish as she drew it against the worn board again and again.

I watched her and thought maybe I should wait until she was finished cutting tomatoes before asking again; perhaps then I could have her full attention, without interruption.

But then she spoke suddenly, almost absent-mindedly. "Grace," she said, "you should look in the refrigerator."

I obeyed Dorothy automatically, as usual. Our refrigerator was not much taller than I was, and heavy, with two large metal hinges on the right-hand side of the door and a large handle on the left, perfectly level with my chest. I had to pull hard on the handle with both hands, knowing too late what I would see. There on the middle shelf were mounds of ragged meat, with red blood pooling beneath them.

There was sudden darkness, and a ripping inside. I was screaming inside yet couldn't make a sound, pushing past the open refrigerator door, past Dorothy, into my bedroom, where I stayed for three days and nights. I lay motionless in my bed, waiting to die. Mother and even Dorothy tried to bring me food, and to comfort me with words. I refused everything.

Dad came to my room. He held my hand and said, "I'm so sorry, my little General. I thought you knew that someday we would have to kill Becky, but I should have warned you. Please forgive me. "

Nothing helped and I didn't believe a word Dad said.

But I didn't die. I lived with the pain, and with the questions it fertilized. Why would my father have slaughtered Becky without even letting me say goodbye?

I didn't plan my revenge, but I took it all the same. It was the Sunday after Becky's death and I knew from the moment I awoke that I would defy my father.

When I'd finished with my crime, I walked back to the house, greeting Nero on my way. Nero licked my hands and looked up at me with his big German Shepherd eyes, sad and loving. My father was waiting for me in the entryway.

It was God's will and a Biblical imperative for Dad to beat me, whether he wanted to or not. Beside him stood a baby-doll carriage that belonged to me, and from inside it he pulled a wooden coat hanger. He told me to bare myself and bend over. The beating hurt, and my skin welted and then split open. Blood ran down my legs and mixed with the dust and salt on my feet. I was sorry for the beating, and I was sorry for my father, who didn't want to do it. But I wasn't truly sorry for what I'd done that Sunday morning.

I could not be truly sorry. I'd meant to defy him, even if I hadn't yet known why. When I got up and out of bed, the sun was already hot and the water in our bay was still and calm. I knew it was unthinkable for me, the minister's daughter, to skip Sunday school. The church was right on our own property! All the same, after I ate breakfast, I went outside and made my way down the rocky cliff to our private beach. The stones there were dark and hot, and they were covered with oysters, my favorite snack. I used a sharp rock to crack them open, oyster after salty oyster, sucking the meat from their shells until my stomach strained with fullness.

I leaned my head back and stared up at the wide sky. It was not too late to go home and not too late to go to Sunday school. The water lapped over the rocks and covered my bare feet, brown from the sun. It soaked the hem of my dress, and was cool and inviting. The water was so still, so gentle. How wonderful it would feel to glide across the calm bay in a boat. I began walking down the beach toward my friend's house. She was playing outdoors, too. Together, we carefully hauled her father's boat, a white skiff with green trim and two wooden oars, to the water's edge. She climbed in first, and I pushed us off. The water was so clear we could see the rocky bottom even dozens of feet from shore.

We sang Portuguese school songs as we rowed, and we splashed each other with our oars. Blue sky pressed against blue water until time collapsed; there was no way to know how long we floated, two nine-year-old girls, happy.

But as we paddled and then drifted farther and farther from the beach, I heard Mother's voice, calling for me to turn around. Sunday school was about to begin. I splashed a high arc of water droplets toward a seagull overhead. My friend giggled.

Then I heard my father. "Graceann," he called, "come back here right now."

His voice was measured and certain, as always. I could picture him behind me, standing very erect, with a questioning look on his round face on the jagged rocks above the shore, and behind him were our house, the church, and what was left of Becky. In front of me, the shimmering waters of our bay rocked gently onward, spilling almost seamlessly into the darkness of the open sea. A rhyme came into my head, something we children often sang to decide who had to be "it" in tag, or to choose which game to play, or the better of two paths. Softly, I sang the rhyme out loud:

La em cima do piano
Tem um copo de veneno
Quem bebeu!
Moreu!
On top of the piano
Is a glass of poison
Who drank it!
Died!

"Graceann!" my father yelled, louder now. "Turn around!"

I slipped my oar into the water and paddled just a little farther toward the horizon.

Chapter Fifteen

Stoning

ALL CHILDREN FEAR DEATH, and I was no exception. I didn't dwell on it, robust and well-cared for as I was. But there were occasions—the baby funerals, the market beheading, the loss of Becky—when the boundary between this world and the next was palpable. At those times, I clung fiercely to this world. I knew I belonged in the land of the living.

Yet, as my father's daughter, I was also acutely aware of the glory of the afterlife, the golden moment of reckoning for the righteous at the gates of heaven. I knew the righteous had nothing to fear in death, and every reward to look forward to. My imagination was filled with colorful archetypes of those who had faced death with nobility and courage, and had died in the name of God. Even my own family's journey to Brazil—the ocean passage and the hair-raising drive along the surging ocean—was pervaded by my parents' willingness to risk all our lives for the sake of Jesus Christ and the Assemblies of God Church. I knew this made me special.

God knew it, too. I was closer to God than others were. How could I not be? Perhaps someday the Lord would send me a direct message, as he had my mother during her pneumonia. Or my father on his meeting with Aimee Semple McPherson. Or Albert Widmer. Or the Apostle Paul, with his vivid encounter with Jesus on the road to Damascus. Or Joan of Arc, the Maid of Orleans.

Would voices call to me, as they had to Joan, from the direction of the church bells? I wasn't sure, but one thing I knew: If I were ever to hear God directly, it would no doubt happen in the presence of my father.

If only I were in his presence more often! My praying (and scheming, in equal measures) from my bedroom did little to keep Dad near at hand. But he knew how much I missed him, and how much we needed him. And whenever he could, he took Dorothy and me along on his shorter trips, even if it meant we missed school.

One such trip took place in February 1944. I was almost ten years old. Summer vacation was drawing to a close, and day by day the wind off the ocean grew cooler as the surface of the water shifted ever so slightly from sapphire to something darker. Dad was heading off to preach in several small towns south of Florianópolis and also in the interior of the state of Santa Catarina.

"Hurry up, General," he commanded, tousling my hair and giving me an affectionate push toward my bedroom. "You've got packing to do. You, too, Dorothy. Fill your suitcases. We'll be spending a week or two on the road."

First, we stopped for a few days in Tubarão, where Dad held a week of Bible studies. He preached at night and Dorothy, Mom, and I sang. From Tubarão, we headed into the interior to the town of Orleans—the same name as the birthplace of Joan of Arc—and there we made our way to the home of the town's minister. His unpainted, three-room wooden house was near the center of town set into a hillside right next to the dirt road.

The house had no glass in the windows, only beveled shutters that the minister's wife pulled closed at night. The living room was about ten feet wide and eight feet long, and the bedroom was about the same. Mother and Dad slept in the bed and Dorothy and I slept on the bedroom floor on *esteiras,* or straw mats. The minister and his wife slept at a neighbor's home to accommodate our visit. The pastor was young, in his middle twenties. He was always smiling, even though one of his front teeth was missing. His straight brown hair, neatly combed and cut short, accentuated his dark brown sunken eyes. His wife, an attractive, petite woman in her early twenties or late teens, tried her best to make us feel at home. They were expecting their first child, and were bursting with pride over their home, the fact that they owned it, and were able to host our family.

The first night of our stay, Dad conducted church in the minister's small living room, furnished with just a few wooden chairs and a small table. Dorothy and Mother played the accordion, and all four of us sang familiar songs from the *Cantor Christao,* an Assemblies of God songbook. They were songs we all knew, songs that bonded all the members of Assemblies of God together. One of our favorites for reaching new converts was *"Vem Pecador":*

> For, Christ invites you, Come sinner!
> He gives eternal life; Come sinner!
> Today is so favorable
> Come sinner!
> The day is so acceptable
> Come sinner!

Another favorite went:

> Christ saves the sinner
> He washes the black heart
> To the contrite, with love
> He offers salvation.

The minister's windows were wide open, and hot, humid night air filled the room. Insects buzzed in the darkness. Curious neighbors gathered, and soon the whole house was shoulder to shoulder with people. The side yard also filled with onlookers.

Dad decided the next day that the church would have to be larger. He set his sights on the side yard, and spent the afternoon building benches from planks of pine, ten in all, and arranged them on either side of the yard space, facing down the hill, with an aisle down the center. The planks were cut of rough, raw wood, unpainted and teeming with splinters as thick and sharp as small nails. Up to six or maybe even eight adults could share one bench easily, so the makeshift church could accommodate up to eighty people.

The front, where Dad preached and we sang, was at the bottom of the hill facing the street. Dad and the minister strung two ropes of light bulbs—three or four sixty-watt bulbs on each rope—through the tree branches overhead, and awaited the arrival of the congregants.

The first to arrive were the insects. As soon as the lights came on, swarms of bugs attacked them. One Brazilian beetle has a hard shell, and is round, dark brown, smaller than a golf ball and about the diameter of a nickel wing to wing. These beetles were famous for flying into lanterns or light bulbs.

After the bugs came the people. As soon as Mother and Dorothy started the accordion music, townsfolk streamed into the side-yard church. Soon there were sixty, then eighty, then more than a hundred. People crammed the benches and wedged into every inch of standing room, then spilled into the streets outside the minister's house, straining to hear and see what was going on. Inevitably, the news of two American girls was also a major attraction.

On the third night, Dad was hoping for an even bigger crowd. And it seemed he would get his wish, going by the way people started streaming into the side yard before Mom and Dorothy even began playing. Then came the surprise.

Two Catholic priests led a large procession down the avenue to the minister's house to disrupt Dad's church service. *"Para com isto!"* they shouted. "Stop what you are doing!" *"É o diabo quem fala."* "It is the voice of the devil!" *"Não escuta o que eles estão dizendo."* "Don't listen to what they are saying!"

People scattered quickly from the benches in the wake of the priests' shouts. The local minister, his family, and about thirty congregants were all that remained.

Dad turned to his wife and daughters. I could see into his soul as he cast his gaze on me. "Start singing," he said. There was a smile and an excited look on his face, and his jaw was set in defiance.

Mother was still playing her accordion. Dorothy and I stood on either side of her. We sang in Portuguese, *"Saudade,"* as Dad had commanded:

> I am very far from my beautiful land. I am very sad
> I am very lonesome for Jesus
> When do you think I will go
> Birds and beautiful flowers, want to enchant me
> Oh terrestrial splendid birds, I don't want to stay here!

As the people's shouts continued over our singing, I felt the sweat of fear break out on my hairline. But I was too paralyzed to wipe it away. Then one of the light bulbs overhead shattered with a sharp pop.

It must have been a beetle, I thought, striking the hot bulb with just enough force. I hoped he was dead. And then a stone, about the size of my fist, hit the ground two feet from where I stood. Another rock flew past my shoulder. And another another nearly struck Dorothy. The rocks hit some of the congregants, and they scrambled toward the house to hide. I scrambled, too.

"Stop, Grace," my father called. "Dorothy, Mother, stand up and sing!" he shouted. Dad stood beside us, and the young minister and his wife filed out of the house to stand with us. Two or three more of the most faithful followed, and the four of us, Mom, Dad, Dorothy and I, warbled "The Old Rugged Cross," in English, to bolster our courage. This song wasn't translated into Portuguese yet, but we knew the English lyrics by heart.

> On a hill far away stood an old rugged cross
> The emblem of suffering and shame
> And I love that old cross where the dearest and best
> For a world of lost sinners was slain.

I looked out on the street and saw hundreds of people in the dark. I could see the whites of their eyes as the stones continued hurtling toward us. The crowd shouted, *"Vai embora!"* or, "Go away! Stop doing this!" They only grew angrier as we continued singing.

My mouth tasted funny, like metal, and I needed to use the bathroom. I pressed my legs together as we continued:

> So I'll cherish the old rugged cross
> Till my trophies at last I lay down.

My mother was not a beautiful woman, but her voice was lovely, and as we sang, I focused on the undulations of her notes, their softness and clarity. My father's voice emanated from deep in his chest, full of richness and vibration. I loved them more than anything on earth. Dorothy stood erect and sang as loud as she could. Why did Mother think Dorothy was not saved? Did Mother think that right then? I was proud of my sister and full of love for her at that moment. Salty water ran into my open mouth as I sang, and I recognized the taste of my own tears.

Another lightbulb shattered overhead, and it was not caused by a beetle. I hoped that all of the beetles in the world were alive and well.

> I will cling to the old rugged cross
> And exchange it some day for a crown.

THE SHOUTS IN THE STREETS rose in angry waves, and my bladder pounded in agony. The crowd was blood-thirsty, their mania swelling and rising up with the power of an ocean wave. Like the Christians before me, persecuted by Romans, killed by lions, stoned to death by unbelievers, I, too, would meet my end.

> In that old rugged cross, stained with blood so divine
> A wondrous beauty I see
> For 'twas on that old cross Jesus suffered and died
> To pardon and sanctify me.

I stopped crying. I lifted my head and set my chin. The side yard brightened around me, and I raised my voice and sang upward to the Southern Cross.

> Has a wondrous attraction for me
> For the dear Lamb of God left His glory above
> To bear it to dark Calvary.

Power surged through me and the heaviness inside was gone. Suddenly I no longer needed to pee. A light, floating feeling lifted me up, and all around me, tiny specks of light sparked and flickered. I sang so loud my throat burned. My father placed a firm hand on my shoulder, and his pride and love for me pulsed warmly through his fingers, through my blouse, through my small collarbone, which sloped gently toward my heart.

> Its shame and reproach gladly bear
> Then He'll call me some day to my home far away
> Where His glory forever I'll share.

THE THRONG OF PEOPLE in the street had quieted. The stones stopped. We hadn't run. We hadn't surrendered. In clumps of twos and threes, the street crowd began to trudge back toward the cathedral, toward the rich tones of the church bells. The church bells were the town's method of signifying a momentous event and heralding the locals to meet at the cathedral.

When had my father lifted his hand from my shoulder? When had my Mother stopped playing?

It was over. The crowd had retreated. A gauzy cloudbank passed slowly in front of the moon. The minister and his family shuffled down the center aisle of our makeshift pews and into the procession of townsfolk flowing through the street toward the cathedral. At my father's command, Mother, Dorothy, and I followed the minister's family.

There, alone in the crowd, it hit me: the emptiness of an unfulfilled anticipation, a noble calling unanswered, was as searing as any unrequited love. Sadness swelled in me as my understanding pulled into focus: tonight, after all, I would not die. I had welcomed the sweet nobility of death for my father's cause. I'd been prepared for a righteous transcendence. It couldn't be over, just like this.

Take me, Jesus! I prayed. *Take me for the sake of the unbelievers!*

But the Lord had other plans. There I stood, nine years old, damp with fear and excitement, but not dead. Tears burnt behind my eyes and the sharp taste of disappointment crept up my throat and filled my mouth. The weight of my misery over not dying pressed hard on me for many days to come.

Later that night, at the cathedral, the old priest condemned my father and his congregation before the townsfolk. "They are of the devil!" he admonished. "Not one of you should gather to hear him preach." He waved a robed arm at my father. "Reject him, reject the devil!"

We all walked together back to the minister's house and talked a while. Before we slept, we prayed.

The next night, my father held another church service, and this time an even larger crowd gathered. After the priest's warning, everyone wanted to hear what the Americans had to say that was so evil. My father commanded Dorothy and me to sing. My voice shook with the words as I waited for the first stone to fly. But nothing happened—except that many in the crowd were converted that night, and for several nights thereafter. Later, back in Coqueiros, Dad received a letter of apology from the Catholic bishop, who'd heard about the ruckus. Dad read the letter out loud to my mother.

As I listened, I knew without doubt that my father was the most powerful man in the world.

Chapter Sixteen

Vadica and Evita

In December of 1944, Vadica left our home and married a man named Agenor. I was happy for her, and excited. Finally, she had found a husband! But I was also heartbroken to see her go.

While I was still on vacation from school, I pined for Vadica something fierce. She came to visit toward the end of January, and I was ecstatic.

"Can I come home with you for a visit?" I begged.

Vadica laughed. "Of course, if your mother says so."

Mother was utterly baffled. Why would a ten-year-old girl want to tag along with Vadica and Agenor? But she said I could.

Mother packed sandwiches and lemonade for us, and Vadica, Agenor, and I left on foot. It took about six hours to get to their house, which was twenty-five miles south of Coqueiros. When we were within about two miles of the house, we came to a small store where we stopped for staples. Once a week, Vadica walked to this same store to do her shopping.

The young couple's house was a typical three-room shack, with a kitchen, bedroom and a small living room, where I slept on a straw mat. I planned to stay with them for two weeks. The house, near a river, was on stilts about two feet off the ground. Once a year the river overflowed its banks. They lived in the middle of nowhere, literally. No neighbors and no development, just total isolation. But Agenor owned the house and the two-acre farm that surrounded it. He grew sugar cane and sweet potatoes. I was never lonesome or bored. Vadica spun yarn the whole time, and I kept busy doing chores for her.

Making sugar cane juice was hard work. Agenor cut the sugar canes, dragged them one by one to the press, and then tied his ox to a long pole. As the ox circled the pole, the press operated. My job was to feed the press with sugar cane, one cane at a time. The cane went through the press, and the pulp ended up on the ground on the other side. The juice sloshed into a crockpot. We did this for several hours a day. Vadica told stories and we sang church songs together.

Agenor was a man of few words. He was several years older than Vadica, in his early thirties. He never stood erect, and usually kept his head lowered. He had brown eyes and brown, sun-bleached hair. Vadica made him smile and I could tell he loved her very much, as he always talked to her with respect, and made a point of complimenting her after each meal.

When I wasn't helping them with the sugar cane, I sat on the steps and watched the world. Vadica and Agenor had a large rooster who spent hours trying to catch chickens. This was high entertainment. The chickens usually got away, but occasionally the old guy would nab one and climb on top of her for sex, which I found fascinating.

One day while sitting on the steps, I watched a snake swallow a frog whole. Afterward, it lay in the sun for hours. As the frog slowly moved through its body, the lump became smaller and smaller until finally it disappeared. When I told Vadica what I saw, she came up with another one of her stories, this time of a man-eating snake. I was sure she was telling the truth.

Perhaps the most amazing thing was that Sunday came and went, and we never went to church. I couldn't ever remember not going to church on Sunday, except for skipping Sunday school after Becky was killed. Part of me felt guilty, for surely God knew, and surely this was a terrible sin.

But another part of me felt wild and free and glad not to be in church. I prayed to Jesus for forgiveness.

About ten days into my visit, Vadica asked me to go to the sugarcane field to call Agenor for dinner. I was hungry, and ran hard into the field. I yelled for Agenor but he didn't hear me or respond. I ran in the direction of where he should be, without looking down.

I stepped with my whole weight on a stump left after the cutting of the sugar cane. It was jagged and sharp, and pierced almost through my right foot. The pain was searing. I tried to scream, and I must have, because Vadica and Agenor both came crashing through the field and together they carried me to the house. Vadica washed my foot and wrapped it with a cloth. It continued to hurt, and the next day it was red, swollen, and throbbed with pain. Vadica soaked it in hot water and also used some local leaves to draw out the infection, but it did not improve. Agenor and Vadica loaded the ox cart with sugar cane juice, sweet potatoes, and sugar canes to take to the market, and prepared to take me back to Coquerios. They left enough room for me to sit in the cart, and we left early the next day. It took longer to get back by cart than it had taken to walk. Agenor led the ox and Vadica walked behind it, keeping a close watch on me.

Mother was surprised to see us, and glad that Vadica had brought me home. Mom immediately placed my foot in hot Epson salt water, treated my foot with some of her salves, and wrapped it in clean rags. I cried when I said goodbye to Vadica and Agenor. Mother looked on curiously. She never understood why I so enjoyed being in the middle of nowhere with these two people.

AROUND THE TIME Vadica left, Uncle Rodrigo moved into our house with Aunt Martha and their two youngest sons. I loved having them there with us. Aunt Martha was so wonderful—quiet, stern, and wise. She helped mother as much as possible, but her main job was taking care of Uncle Rodrigo. Each morning, Martha rose early, started the woodstove, heated water, and awakened Rodrigo. She served him *Chimarão,* or *mate* tea, that he was accustomed to drinking. It's a pure green tea placed in a natural gourd shell. Tradition called for drinking the *Chimarão* from a silver straw, and adding boiling water to the gourd after each sip before passing it on to the person at your side. Mother used to shudder at the thought of tuberculosis or other dread diseases whenever Dad drank *Chimarão* with others. But the belief was that the sterling silver straw with its gold tip killed all germs.

Aunt Martha was kind to Dorothy. When Mother and Dorothy argued, Aunt Martha took Dorothy's side. She often asked Mother to quit fighting with Dorothy. She also told Dad about the fighting, asking him to intervene on Dorothy's behalf.

OUR DOG NERO loved me with all his heart. He understood me. He was smart and communicative, and very attached to his people. He was also the most protective dog in the world. The whole time we lived in Coqueiros, we never once had an intruder enter our home or harm our property—or any of us. On the other hand, our guests were able to walk right past Nero, who knew they were welcome on our property. This was true even when guests were visiting for the first time. How Nero could tell, I never knew, but he seemed to have an unusual sense for human beings.

Most mornings, Nero greeted me as soon as I came outside. Sometimes I brought him a scrap or two from breakfast. Often I threw sticks for him or stroked his wiry fur. One Saturday, in late 1944, Nero didn't answer when I called for him. I looked in his house, and Nero was there, sleeping. I called to him again, and patted him. But he did not respond. I called to my cousin John, who came and pulled Nero out of his house.

Nero was dead.

We looked in his food dish and saw that its contents appeared strange.

"I think he's been poisoned, Gracie," said John.

John's suspicions were confirmed the next day. It was Sunday, and when we returned from church that evening, John discovered two burglars in his room. He ran them out of the house empty-handed—they scrambled out the same window they'd come in—but after that incident we had to be careful to lock our house tightly at night and whenever we went out. Without our faithful Nero watching over us, everything felt different, less certain. Before that day, I felt special. Protected. But after Nero was poisoned, I was too scared to stay home alone at night.

In 1945, the Brazilian press was totally enamored with the beautiful Argentinian, Evita, who married the debonair Juan Peron. Evita is the diminutive of Eva, and in English it means, "Little Eva" or "Beloved Eva." Eva was 15 years old when she moved from the interior of Argentina to Buenos Aires with dreams of becoming an actress. In 1944 she met the then Colonel Juan Peron, and they fell in love. They lived together for almost two years, as she worked in the background helping build his popularity. He soon became Secretary of Labor and Welfare, and in 1945 was elected president of Argentina. They were soon married, and Evita became popular all over the world. She was shunned by the social elite, but loved by the common people, the poor. In 1951, Peron was reelected as president and Evita was nominated for vice-president. Eva died in 1953, of uterine cancer, at the age of 33.

There were countless pictures of Eva in magazines and newspapers. And when Juan and Eva were married their wedding was all you could read about, anywhere. World War II was over, and the people were hungry for light and more exciting news. Brazilians loved a romance and they loved a beautiful woman, especially a blond one.

Dorothy became infatuated with this story. She started a scrapbook in which she meticulously pasted every published article and photograph of Evita and Juan. She did this in secret, but I knew all about it and understood completely why she would do it. Mother would never allow this type of celebrity worship.

Through careful spying, I discovered where Dorothy hid her book, and every chance I got, I sneaked into her room, went to the bottom drawer of her armoire and reached my hands under the layers of clothes until I felt the hard edges of the book. Then I pulled it out and looked for anything new that Dorothy had added. Over time, I too became enchanted by the beautiful "Argentinean Lady." I wished I could have my own scrapbook.

One day, Dorothy was in an especially foul mood, and she refused to let me tag along to the beach with her friends.

I decided to use my clout. "You better let me go," I taunted, "or I will tell Mother about your Eva book."

Dorothy's explosion exceeded my wildest imagination. She threatened me with my life and made me swear that I would never say a word. "NOT ONE WORD!" she screamed.

I promised Dorothy that I would not tell Mother, on the condition that she would let me see her book whenever I wanted. Having no other choice, Dorothy agreed. I never breathed a word to Mother, and Dorothy continued her admiration of Eva.

IN MARCH of that year, the new school year began. I had to change schools, since the school I'd been attending only went to the fourth grade. The only two choices were the public school in Florianópolis—poorly run and overcrowded—or the Catholic school, which provided a much better education. I was about to turn eleven, old enough to care a great deal about where I went to school. And I wanted to go to the Catholic school.

First, the Catholic school was much more prestigious, which I appreciated. Second, I really liked the school uniforms. The girls wore maroon pleated skirts with straps that crossed in the back, and white blouses, black shoes, and white stockings. For special days, they even wore white gloves.

"I suppose it won't hurt her," Dad said.

They knew I would get a better education there, so my parents allowed me to attend the Catholic school.

Fifth grade in Brazil was considered a preparatory year for entering high school. The nuns were strict and required us to act like ladies at all times. Though challenging, I was glad for my one year of school with the sisters. The work was difficult and I had a lot of homework. I no longer had much time for hanging out with my friends in Coqueiros; my days as "the General" were largely over.

I found, too, that I had less and less in common with the village kids. This hurt my old friends, and Mom and Dad weren't too happy with other changes they saw. My parents disapproved of any friend who wasn't a member of our church, and now, since most of my friends were

Catholic, I felt the sharp sting of my parents' disapproval. I made one special friend, Lygia Ferro. Lygia lived near our house in Coqueiros, and we spent time together in and out of school. Lygia's father, Mr. Ferro, was a pharmacist, and her mother was a gracious, lovely woman who tried hard to befriend Mother. Mother, unfortunately, could not abide having a Catholic friend, and tried to convert Mrs. Ferro, who eventually gave up on the friendship.

FOR SOME REASON, nationalism, the irrational love of a place delineated by boundaries as imaginary as folk tales and paper currency, seemed to run strongest in the places where life's struggles are most stubbornly entrenched.

Because of the fervent nationalism I grew up with in Brazil, I feel more patriotic about Brazil today than I do about America, though I've lived in the United States most of my life. In every Brazilian school I attended, my teachers zealously—and perhaps more important, joyfully—emphasized the utter importance of the Brazilian national symbols. In Brazil, no matter where you were or what you were doing, you stopped in your tracks at the first strain of the national anthem: You placed your hand over your heart, and, if there was a flag anywhere nearby, you turned toward it in reverence and respect as you heard the anthem:

> *Ouviram do Ypiranga as margens placidas*
> *De um povo heroico e brado retumbante*
> *E o sol da liberdade, em raios Fulgidos*
> *Brilhou no ceu da Patria nesse instante*

> "It was heard from the placid banks of the Ipiranga
> the resounding cry of a heroic people
> and the sun of liberty, in brilliant rays
> Shone in the skies of the homeland at that moment."

It may be difficult to fathom the absolute hero status enjoyed by a Brazilian who honors his country with some measure of success. Champion drivers such as Senna and Fitipaldi are worshipped by the entire population. Sports stars—soccer player Pelé, and tennis player Guga (from Florianópolis)—have celebrity status far beyond what one can imagine.

Brazilian politicians also enjoyed exalted celebrity status. When I was in grade school in Brazil, the president was a man by the name of Getulio Vargas. Vargas was born in 1882 in the state of Rio Grande do Sul, the same home state of my uncle Rodrigo Lemos. Like my Uncle Rodrigo, Vargas was born of cattle ranching parents.

Vargas assumed the provincial presidency in 1930, in the wake of a slew of political errors on the part of his predecessor, including having sent the Brazilian army to Rio de Janeiro to fight over a fraudulent election. In 1933, Vargas was elected president of the nation. His term ended in 1937, but through a coup d'état, he formed a new political party and held onto his office until 1945. Charming and outrageously charismatic, Vargas knew how to sway the people in his direction.

As a schoolgirl in the early 1940s, I was usually the teacher's pet. And as the teacher's pet, I was often selected to carry the Brazilian flag at the head of our frequent parades in honor of every national holiday, major and minor. In 1945, President Getulio Vargas actually came to Florianópolis, and we organized an enormous parade in his honor. As usual, I took up the front, carrying the flag only steps from Vargas's motorcade. I was dressed in my maroon Catholic school uniform, wearing white gloves and brightly shining patent-leather shoes. My long braids hung on either side of my face and were tied with white satin bows. I practically split open with pride. Like the rest of Brazil, we chanted, "Getulio! Getulio! We want Getulio!"

Vargas's "dictatorship" ended in 1946, when he became a senator for his home state of Rio Grande do Sul. Then in 1950, he was again elected national president. In 1954, the time came for Getulio's term to end. Once again, he refused to step down. The military threatened him and eventually he agreed, under duress, to leave. He retreated to his bedroom, wrote a long speech to his people, and shot himself in the heart.

Chapter Seventeen

Taking Leave

THAT SAME SPRING, Dad announced: "We have been in Brazil almost six years and it is time for a furlough. We will return to America at the end of this year, as soon as I finish the churches in Itajai and Blumenau."

I burst into tears at the news. What a horrible blow. I loved my school. I loved Brazil. I was Brazilian! Brazil was all I could remember, and I dreaded having to go to America. I could no longer understand spoken English, let alone read or write English. I was eleven and Dorothy was seventeen, and both of us felt sick at the thought of our impending move.

Soon, though, we had other news to grapple with. Just two months before we left for the States, my cousin Albert and his wife Lourdes came for Sunday dinner. I had also invited friends from the church for dinner and to spend the afternoon. After dinner, Lourdes said that she wanted to talk to me in private. We left my friends and went into the study.

Lourdes took my shoulders in her hands and pulled me in close. "Grace," she whispered, and I could feel her breath on my cheeks, "please do not tell these girls that Dorothy is not your sister."

What on earth was she talking about? I could hardly open my mouth to speak. I answered haltingly, "Of course. I won't say anything."

But in truth I had no idea what Lourdes meant. That night after we came home from the church in town, I asked Mother what Lourdes had meant by her comment.

"You will have to ask your father when he comes home next week. He can explain it to you."

I didn't know what to say or what to think. It didn't seem real. But I didn't say a word to Dorothy. Finally, Dad arrived. Within minutes, Mom told him what had happened. He asked me to come into his study and he'd tell me all about Dorothy.

"Why did Lourdes say Dorothy is not my sister?" I asked him. "Is it true?"

"Grace," my father said. The word hung in the air and then seemed to spiral to the floor, settling as slowly as dust motes falling from a shaft of light. "I can only tell you the truth."

My father sat in the plain oak chair and stared toward me, but not at me. He might have been looking out the window that yawned open behind me toward the sea, but it seemed more like he was looking through me, or past me, into a place only he could see.

What truth? I wanted to say, impatient as always. But it wasn't like Dad to just sit like this, staring, and something stopped me from pestering. I picked at the loose threads of my sleeve cuff and waited. I could feel my heart in my throat.

"Dorothy is your adopted sister," he finally said flatly. Still he stared intently past me, into that mysterious void.

A nasty lump rose in my throat, swelling it shut. But I blinked back the tears and waited until Dad cleared his throat and spoke again.

"She was such a charming baby," he said, more brightly. "A charming baby, and a good baby. I remember seeing her there in church on her grandmother's lap. She couldn't have been much past her first birthday."

"In Michigan?" I asked, realizing immediately it was a silly question. Of course it had to have been Michigan, I wasn't making any sense to wonder where Dorothy was born. But Dad didn't chide me at all.

"In Michigan," he repeated. "It wasn't a happy home for your sister, living with her grandmother. I knew they were trying to get her adopted. But I hadn't stepped forward, not yet. Not until that day in the church when she reached her little arms up to me." He stopped again, and his face softened. From outside the open window, the squeals of children were followed by peals of laughter and more squeals. Dad didn't seem to notice or react in any way to the noise. "She sat there," he continued, "on her grandmother's lap, reaching out to me. I was making my usual greetings after church. And she reached her arms straight toward me and she smiled. And I picked her up right then and there and put her into the arms of your mother."

Dad was looking straight into my eyes again. Wherever he'd been, the distant place behind the window evaporated. Even his voice changed. "So you see, Gracie, the moment we adopted Dorothy Mae, she became a part of our family, and she has been ever since."

He placed his hands on his knees and stood up, and it was clear the spell was broken. He tousled my hair as if to punctuate the end of his story, a story I accepted completely, even though I longed for a glimpse of whatever secret world he had visited while he remembered that long ago day in Michigan.

Mother, I now realized, made a point of reminding Dorothy of her sinful birth status every time they quarreled. Dorothy also knew, from Mother, what had happened during Lourdes' visit, and she knew now what Dad was telling me in his study.

"She wonders how you will take this news," Dad told me. "I hope you will accept and love your sister, as the Lord wills, Gracie."

A huge sob wracked my chest, and I buried my face in my father's shirt to cry. Then I went to Dorothy. She was standing outside the door, and had probably heard what we had been saying. I said, "Dorothy, you are my sister. The adoption doesn't change anything and I love you."

Dorothy teared up and came over to give me a hug. Later she said, "I wished you didn't have to know about this, Gracie, but then, everyone makes such a big deal out of it that I'm glad you finally found out."

Dorothy, I soon learned, had always known she was adopted. She had always known the story of how she came to be in our family. And little by little, between what Dorothy grudgingly shared with me and what I could press out of my parents, the story surfaced of what really happened in those early years in Flint.

Early in their marriage, my parents, like most of my father's siblings, had intended to have a large family. As years rolled past, it became clear that my mother was not going to become pregnant. Then, in the spring of 1927, God stepped in. A very young member of my parents' church in Flint became pregnant out of wedlock. A "great sin, a terrible shame," my mother wrote in her journal. The whole thing stirred up a terrific scandal in the church community. Finally, on December 31, 1927, the baby was born, a girl. The young mother called the child Dorothy.

Several weeks passed. As Dorothy's mother cloistered with her newborn in her parents' small home near the center of town, low whispers and clucking tongues rippled through my father's congregation. Some kindly older women discretely offered casseroles and crocheted blankets, pale yellow and pink. But there would be no festive baby shower for little Dorothy and her errant mother. The shame and judgment were much too thick.

Which is why it was so unthinkable, the thing my father announced to my mother. He did it one evening in mid-February, when it was very cold, and the Michigan snowdrifts piled four and five feet high along the roadsides. He arrived home from his evening prayer service and hung his brown wool coat in the front entry. He placed his overshoes neatly beside the radiator to dry. My mother set a cup of hot coffee and a slice of apple pie on the kitchen table. They sat together while my father ate. On the mantel above them, the pendulum clock ticked as his fork scraped his china plate. When he was finished, my mother wiped the table's surface, maple lightly etched from years of use, until it was clean of crumbs and stickiness. Then my father pushed his palms into the muscles of his thighs and leaned forward to look his wife in the eye.

"Maybe," he said, "that child was a gift from God."

"John," my mother said slowly, "what do you mean?"

"Her name is Dorothy," my father said. "The name is derived from the Greek. It means, literally, 'Gift of God.' I believe we are meant to adopt the child."

Despite grave reservations, Marguerite complied. She felt she had no choice—her singular mission was to serve God by serving her husband, and God was watching. On September 28, 1928, under the dark shadow of my mother's silent opposition, Dorothy Mae became a Kolenda, and my mother never forgave her for it.

I felt terrible for Dorothy, and guilty, too. I couldn't help feeling that somehow I had taken something from her. Mother loved me so much, and never tried to hide her partiality. It made others sad, too. My cousin, Lillie Brenda Gary, known as Lil, was twelve years old when I was born. She spent time living with my parents after my birth to help my mother with the care of her two young children. For several years during my infancy and early childhood, Lil had come to stay and help Mother and Dad during summer months. According to Lil, Dad took full responsibility for Dorothy, dressing her, feeding her, singing to her, playing with her. Meanwhile, Mother ignored Dorothy almost entirely and spent every moment lavishing me, her baby, with maternal affection.

BEFORE WE LEFT Brazil for the United States, Dad was determined to finish the building of two large churches in Santa Catarina. He sent a letter to all of his relatives asking them to sacrifice what they could for the cause, and meanwhile, he sold off everything we could spare—Mom's accordion, our furniture, the typewriter—to raise the needed funds. Within weeks of Dad's plea, the checks started trickling in by mail. Most were for five or ten dollars. Dad never received more than $200 in total contributions for a given month during our years in Brazil. That's why Uncle Ernest's envelope was such a shock.

Ernest was Dad's youngest brother, born in Brazil in 1905. During the first part of the war, Ernie had gone to work for my parents' dearest and best friends, Rollin and Henrietta Severance, at their tool and dye company. Until that time, Ernie had been a full-time minister, but during the war he saw the opportunity to make a lot of money, and in 1943 he left the Severances' company to start his own company, a direct competitor of the Severances, right in the same town.

"We trust he has not done you any harm," Mother wrote to the

Severances. "We never felt he would stay by you faithfully. As John says, 'Ernest never was a man of very much principle,' and maybe you found that out." Mother's opinion of Ernie was dismal. She couldn't stand the man.

According to my parents, Ernie was always trying to prove himself. This may have had something to do with Grandma Kolenda, who lived with Uncle Ernie and Aunt Goldie, who spoke only of my father, her favorite son. "When John comes, I go," she always said, meaning that when my father returned to the States, she would be ready to die. This must have hurt Uncle Ernest, who did his best for her, and yet, she only praised his brother John.

Uncle Ernie was a good salesman, charming, likeable to almost everyone except Mother, and before long, very successful. His company did very well. So well that the check he sent to Dad was for two thousand dollars. This, in 1945, was an enormous sum of money. It was enough to complete the two churches before our departure. Ernest had proved himself in a big way, and he had earned his brother's admiration.

Mother was harder to please. "We wonder how much he will continue to prosper," she wrote to the Severances after the arrival of Ernie's check. "That is why we accepted this special gift from him. True, it seemed like a gift from God sent to us, as without it we would have had to stop building. Then we also felt that if Ernie's business should fail, this two thousand dollars would be safely invested in God's cause for all eternity."

And Mother's prophecy came true. A few months later, Uncle Ernie's business began to fail due to the end of the war and less demand for his products. By the time we arrived in New York that September, Ernie had given up the tool and dye trade and returned to the pulpit full time. He and his wife Goldie, both beautifully dressed and smiling, were the ones who came to meet us at the Port Authority in New York City.

Part II

1945 to 1949
And Back Again: America

My mother's frequent Bible quotation to Dorothy and me:

Ephesians 6: 1, 2, and 3

Children, obey your parents in the Lord, for this is right.
Honor your father and your mother—which is the first
commandments with a promise—that it may go well with
you and that you may enjoy long life on the earth.

Chapter Eighteen

Above the Fruited Plains

I T WAS OBVIOUS to both Dorothy and me that Mom didn't approve of Uncle Ernie, but she seemed to like Aunt Goldie. When she saw them at a distance from aboard our ship in the New York harbor, she said, "There they are, John, there's Goldie! I don't see how that woman can stand being with that man."

"Shush, Marguerite," Dad said. "Don't talk that way in front of the girls."

"As if we haven't heard it a million times," said Dorothy. Mother cast her a hateful stare.

Dad loved his brother unconditionally, and was always able to overlook his faults. My parents were happy to see them, and grateful to them for insisting on meeting our ship in New York, but there was tension right beneath the surface. Maybe Mother was still holding a grudge against Ernie for betraying the Severances in business. For sure, she was disapproving of the way Ernest and Goldie looked. Uncle Ernie looked sharp, and Goldie was dressed to the nines. Next to Goldie, Mother looked about a hundred years old. I couldn't help but be in awe of my aunt and uncle, even though I felt guilty because I knew Mother and Dad wouldn't want me to be so admiring.

The Waldorf Astoria Hotel, where Ernie and Goldie brought us to stay the night, was a real palace. The hotel was originally built by William Waldorf Astor in 1893. The remodeling and present structure was completed in 1931 as an Art Deco landmark. Located on Park Avenue, it was originally the largest hotel in the U.S., with 47 stories. Dorothy and I were absolutely awed by the sweeping staircases, sparkling lights, and gold décor. I felt I was in a fairyland, the sort of place poor missionaries like us could never afford. For our evening meal, Uncle Ernie arranged a private dining room for the six of us. The sheer volume of silverware flanking my plate unnerved me. Which fork was I supposed to use? I kicked Dorothy under the table. She kicked me back. Under this kind of pressure, there was no way I could enjoy the meal. Several waiters hovered over us, trying to anticipate our every need. Mom looked dour, and Dad's face was strained with tension. They were tolerating the circumstances, but clearly, this was not their element.

After dinner, we all took a stroll through Times Square. I was enthralled with New York City on that warm September evening. All around us, bright colorful lights glowed and pulsed, and laughing people filled the streets. It was perfectly lovely. Especially fascinating was a billboard for Camel cigarettes. The smoker blew out real smoke with every puff! I was amazed.

But Mother disapproved of us even looking at the Camel sign. "That's how they get people to smoke, by making it look so good," she snapped.

Farther into Times Square, Dorothy spotted a hotdog stand. The smell made our mouths water and our stomachs rumble. We begged Dad to have one, and he handed us each a Coney Island, smothered in ketchup, mustard, and relish. It had been six years since we'd tasted anything quite like it.

Uncle Ernie laughed at our delight. "Here I spent a fortune on the best restaurant in town, and this is what they like!" he said.

America, I was discovering, was not nearly as bad as I had feared.

THE NEXT MORNING we left for Michigan. Nothing could have made me more proud than riding across the country in Uncle Ernie's flashy Cadillac, large and shiny and beautiful. How different this was from the death-defying drives across Brazil. When we pulled up at Aunt Elizabeth's farm, Grandma Kolenda was waiting for us in the yard.

She ran as fast as her spindly legs would carry her, both arms high in the air, crying, "Thank you Jesus for bringing my John home." Then she threw her arms around my father. "John is here!" she shouted. "Now I go!"

Aunt Elizabeth and Uncle Fred shushed her, Mom and Dad shushed her, Uncle Ernie and Aunt Goldie shushed her, but Grandma held her ground. "John is here, I go," she insisted.

The whole Kolenda family had gathered to greet us at Aunt Elizabeth's, and it was exciting but overwhelming. The overwhelming part was that I couldn't understand a word they were saying. My English had disappeared. A few days later, we drove again with Uncle Ernie and Aunt Goldie to their home in Saginaw, Michigan, which they shared with Grandma. I was especially glad to see their daughter Faith. She was very pretty with honey blond hair, like her mother Goldie, and beautiful blue eyes. Faith was my age, born one month after I was, and I was sure we'd be good friends. Somehow, this seemed to trouble Aunt Goldie, who tried to stop the two of us from being alone together. Whenever we were about to set off anywhere, she drummed up a reason why one or the other of us needed to stay behind. I wondered if Aunt Goldie didn't like me. I couldn't understand this and it hurt my feelings, until one day Goldie caught me on my own and warned me, pleaded with me, really, not to say anything to Faith about Dorothy. Whatever could she be talking about? Didn't Faith know Dorothy was adopted? After all, it seemed everyone else did. But this mattered little to me, so I had no trouble giving my solemn oath to Goldie that I would say nothing of my sister to Faith. This seemed to bring my aunt tremendous relief.

Meanwhile, Grandma took quickly to her bed and began to fail fast. Dad had meetings with church representatives in Springfield, Missouri, and left matters in Mother's capable hands. A week passed, and as Grandma worsened, Mother decided to kneel at Grandma's bedside and pray for her recovery.

In the middle of Mother's prayer Grandma commanded her to stop praying. "Stop that, Marguerite, I'm ready," she said. "I want to go."

Before the sun rose, Grandma died in her sleep.

DAD TRIED to find us a place to live as fast as he could after Grandma died, but it took a while. We went back to Farmington to stay with Aunt Elizabeth and her family on their farm, and remained there for at least two months. I started paying attention to how things worked in America. My cousin Albert was six years older than I, and already in high school. He was as handsome as could be. He had blond hair, and a fit, muscular body. Athletics were his passion, and in fact, years later, Albert traveled around the world participating in Masters World Championships and four times was the World's Senior Olympic Decathlon Champion. He took his workouts seriously. In the mornings, he'd do push-ups and recite some little poem or other that he'd concocted:

"Grace, Grace, dressed in lace, went upstairs to powder her face.
She belongs to the Brazilian race, and can't even tie her own shoe lace.
She doesn't even know how to wash her face."

I didn't really know if I was supposed to laugh or cry at Albert's teasing, but he'd go on with one terrible verse after another until I couldn't stand it. I tended to follow my cousin Lenore around instead. Lenore was three years older than I, and extremely beautiful. I studied her carefully—her hair, her stylish clothes, her graceful mannerisms. I wanted to be just like her.

I went to a one-room country school just outside of Farmington with my cousin David. My ability to speak and understand spoken English gradually improved, but my accent was thick and, to American children, comical. I couldn't read or write a word in English. My math skills were fine, but I could only do the multiplication tables in Portuguese. I was eleven years old, but I had to start school back in the first grade with six-year-olds. *Dear Jesus,* I prayed, *please help me learn English again. I promise to try my very hardest.* By the end of the two months, I moved up to fourth grade.

Finally, in late November, Dad found us a small place in Hamtramck, the Polish area of Detroit. The tiny house had a living room and kitchen on the main floor and two bedrooms upstairs. It's no wonder Dorothy chose to live with cousins in Lansing. Dad was gone most of the time, and Mother had no patience for her. For me, the new house was lonely, and school was lonely. I completed fifth grade at the local elementary school, where the children found me an easy laughing stock.

Dear Jesus, I prayed. *Please make it easier to be a missionary's daughter. Why do I have to be laughed at for not speaking English when it's all because of my faithfulness and saving souls? Also, could you please look after Dorothy? I miss her and am so very worried about her.*

Shortly after that beseeching prayer, I fell on my back on the neighborhood ice skating pond. Stars, bright pinpoints in the evening sky, sparkled above me as a white-hot agony seized through my back and legs. I wondered how I was going to manage to stand up. The rink was empty except for me, and the only sound was the occasional whoosh of a passing car and the eerie creaking of the December snow. Judging from the sound as I hit the ice, I was pretty sure I'd broken my tailbone. The stabbing pain shooting through my backside was another urgent clue.

Skates had been a surprise Christmas gift from Mother and Dad. Since we moved to Hamtramck and I first saw the ice skating rink, skating was all I could talk about. I'd been trying to teach myself how to ice skate. I wanted to twirl and turn like other girls I'd seen as I walked by the park each day. Those girls were graceful, like dancers, gliding across the frozen surface, their blades carrying them effortlessly forward and backward and through pirouettes and leaps high into the air and down again, without so much as a wobble. When I lurched out onto the ice, it felt different than what I was expecting based on how the other girls looked. First of all, there seemed to be a lot more gravity involved. The ice was stickier and slipperier than it ought to have been, so the sheer act of keeping my balance kept me in a constant state of panic. Finally, though, I got some wind under my feet. I placed one foot in front of the other, as I'd watched the other girls do, circling round the rink once, twice, and half of a third time before the tip of my blade caught recklessly into a bump in the ice. In a split second I was flat on my back. I hit the ice square and hard, like a hammer.

I don't know how long I lay there before I decided that I really had no choice but to get up, whether I was able to or not. I managed to stand, slowly, and the pain in my tailbone sharpened and shot down both legs. By the time I hobbled off the ice and took my skates off, I was beginning to worry about how I'd possibly survive the walk home. I did it one agonizing step at a time.

When finally I limped through the front door, Mother looked me over dubiously. Her eyes settled on the skates dangling from my left hand. "What happened to you?" she asked.

"I fell."

Mother said nothing.

"On the ice," I added quickly, in case that part wasn't painfully obvious.

"Put your skates away and sit down," Mother said, already on her way into the kitchen to start the teakettle for the hot water bottle. Mother was a big believer in hot water bottles. She was also, like all good Pentecostals, a big believer in prayer over medicine. "Ask the Lord for his healing," she told me as she handed over the red rubber bottle, wrapped loosely in a white muslin dishcloth. "And thank Him for His loving care."

I prayed as Mother suggested, and although the pain persisted, it did ebb very slowly day by day. Within a week, I could walk almost normally again. For weeks I found it excruciatingly painful to sit. I had cracked my tailbone a good one, most likely it was broken. Mother never did take me to a doctor. By the end of a month, the pain was wearing me down.

I started to wonder about Sister Beall, who led the divine healing service at church. Sister Beall's hands-on healing came immediately following every church service. Anyone who needed healing from the Lord could simply walk up to the altar and ask. Finally, I was desperate enough to muster the courage. I stepped gingerly along the red carpeted aisle toward the altar. Sister Beall, a tall, stately, and charismatic woman, stood before me and extended her hands. I could smell the earthy scent of the holy oil with which she'd generously anointed both of her palms. Sister Beall placed her palms on my forehead and then leaned back and closed her eyes. All at once I felt it: a sudden "click"—or a shift, in my tailbone. The pain disappeared, just like that. It was immediately replaced by a warm, tingly feeling. When Sister Beall opened her eyes, I looked into them and saw what I was convinced was real love.

Chapter Nineteen

Highland Park

FINALLY, IN APRIL of 1946, Dad was able to buy a house in Highland Park, Michigan. The house was a three-story on Midland Avenue. We lived on the first floor in a three-bedroom apartment. On the second floor there were two one-bedroom apartments and on the third floor a two-bedroom apartment with low dormer-like ceilings. These apartments were rented out, and with the rental income my parents were able to pay the mortgage easily—though the maintenance responsibilities were a handful for Mother, as Dad was gone most of the time. It would get even harder, because Dad was planning to return to Brazil for six months of Bible study.

Dorothy had been living with relatives for several months, but after we moved to Highland Park she came back to live with us. Dorothy's absence didn't help her relationship with Mother. With Dad gone most of the time, they fought more than ever.

"It's time you did something with your life," Mom yelled. "You're eighteen years old!"

So, before Dad left for Brazil, he took Dorothy to the local high school to inquire about her options.

"We can place her in the tenth grade," the administrator told Dad.

Dorothy was terribly upset to hear this.

Dad suggested secretarial school, instead. "This way," he explained to Dorothy, "you will learn English and typing and maybe even find a career, if God wills it."

Before he left, Dad sat me down and explained that he wanted me to learn an instrument. Music was such an important part of our worship services, and Dad understood that novelty was a powerful tool in Brazil. "Gracie," he told me, "I want you to learn something unknown in Brazil—something that will impress the local people when we return to Coqueiros in a few years."

He chose the electric Hawaiian guitar, a large and oddly rectangular contraption that was most appreciated for being the first reliable electric guitar on the market. It was black with colorful sparkles in the shining paint. It was a dreadful looking thing. Fortunately it had a black canvas case with thick straps, which made it less obvious when I carried it to and from my lessons.

Every week, I rode the city bus to my teacher's studio. And every day, I diligently practiced this awkward instrument. It was a heavy beast, and certainly no comparison to the lovely Spanish guitar. I was ashamed to lug it around. But I felt a resigned sense of duty to my father, especially since he was away for most of the time we lived in Detroit.

My father's absence obligated me all the further to that clunky Hawaiian guitar. In every letter he wrote to me from Brazil, he reminded me to practice, "so you will surprise all of them when you get here!"

For him, I persevered until I could read music fairly well and play nearly anything by ear. He also asked about my progress in his letters to Mother. I wasn't about to disappoint him. For my final recital in Detroit, I played "The Hawaiian War Chant," a very difficult piece.

Mother came to the program, and I was sure she was impressed, but it was difficult for her to say so. "It was fine," she admitted, "but you know in Brazil you will be playing for the Lord, and not those kinds of songs."

Dorothy enrolled in a business school in Detroit before Dad left. From the beginning, she found it very difficult to keep up. She came home frustrated and angry. She had missed most of the elementary schooling in the United States, and had never been to an American high school. Her English skills were marginal.

Mother didn't understand the problem. "God helps those who help themselves," she told Dorothy. "If you weren't so lazy, you could do the work. You must take responsibility for your actions."

Every night, Mother found fault with Dorothy's efforts. I tried to stay out of their fights, but the only way to avoid them was to run out of the house as soon as they started.

Once I asked Mother, "Why don't you like Dorothy?"

She looked at me with a shocked expression and said, "I love Dorothy, but Gracie, there's a lot you don't know!" Then she tightened her lips, turned around, and walked away.

At that moment, I realized there was nothing more that Mother would reveal.

After six months of Bible study in Brazil, Dad became anxious about the devastation of the war in his home country. He went to Germany to look up relatives and visit family homesteads. He took along Uncle Fred Brenda, his sister Elizabeth's husband, and they also visited the Brenda family in Germany. Dad never stopped talking about the destruction of his homeland and the sad stories Uncle Fred and Dad heard from their German relatives. Dad told me some of these stories and he always added, "Gracie, don't forget, war is a terrible thing; no one gains anything from it."

After that, he traveled the United States raising money for his latest passion: a commercial printing press. He was determined to start a successful publishing house in Brazil. Meanwhile, for the next two years back in America, we barely saw him.

The Assemblies of God was growing fast in Brazil and there was an urgent need for printed materials such as Sunday school papers, monthly church periodicals, Bibles, song books, and religious teaching materials for Bible studies. During those years, these materials were printed in various places, it was expensive, and demand could not be met. This became a passion for my Dad, and he traveled through the U.S. raising money to buy land in Rio de Janeiro, to build a structure, and buy an adequate printing press to handle the demand.

Mother and I continued attending Sister Beall's church, Bethesda Missionary Temple. Dorothy also went with us, when she lived in Highland Park. We were active in this church, in fact. We went twice on Sunday, morning and evening, and every Wednesday, and more often when there were revival meetings. Sister Beall was Pentecostal, but not associated with the Assemblies of God. Later she became associated with some new beliefs, which got her into some trouble with Assemblies of God leaders. Mother was not the least bothered by the controversy surrounding Sister Beall. Sister Beall was an unbelievably dynamic speaker and had built up a church membership of more than three thousand members. Later, she even started a Bible school. From Highland Park we took the street car and had to transfer two times. It usually took at least forty-five minutes each way, but we went every chance we got, and I never once complained. Sister Beall was reason enough to want to go.

But for Dorothy, Mother had only suspicion and judgments. After a while, she even took to dropping in at the secretarial school to check up on Dorothy's progress. She was determined to prove that Dorothy's failures were no one's fault but her own.

One afternoon, Dorothy was absolutely furious when she got home. "I can't believe you're spying on me!" she screamed.

"If you could be trusted, I wouldn't have to watch over you," Mother argued back.

This was basically the last straw for Dorothy, and not long after that, she dropped out of school altogether.

By November, Dorothy moved in with friends. Mom was furious at her ingratitude, and expressed her disapproval in letters to Dad, who wrote back promptly from Brazil.

"I do love our girls," he wrote, "I do love them. But to receive such pay, that is inconsideration, to have strangers being preferred before us . . . it is hard, very hard. But then the Lord knows and will not let our prayers go unanswered. I know, however, that our Gracie will never treat us that way, nor grieve our hearts like that."

Dorothy drifted in and out of living with Mother and me for the next year until she landed a job as a sales clerk with J.B. Hudson and Company in Detroit. Finally, she was able to get her own apartment and move out for good.

By the time I was thirteen, I was keenly aware of my mother's aged and stern appearance. Especially as I grew more aware of and interested in America's material culture, I became embarrassed to have my friends know my mother. She looked more like my grandmother!

This point was driven home one afternoon when Mother and Dad and I were shopping in Detroit. My mother was searching for a hat.

A stylish young clerk was assisting her. "Give this one a try," the red-lipped salesgirl urged my mother.

Mother arranged the hat atop her braided coifs, and stared unsmiling at her reflection in the oval mirror. It was a lovely grey felt hat, with thin light pink trim on its wide rim. I thought it looked beautiful on her.

"What do you think?" the salesgirl asked pertly, turning to my father. "Now doesn't that hat look sharp as a tack on your dear mother?"

I was mortified. Mother wore a dark dress, extra long, closed-laced shoes, and her braided hair was pinned back in a bun. She wore no makeup, and she still had a goiter. But did she really look that much older than Dad?

Mother's flat expression turned stony to mask her shock. She gently removed the hat, and placed it back in the salesgirl's hands. "I'm afraid it won't quite do," she announced. With that, she spun toward the shop's front door and opened it briskly.

My father put his arm around her shoulder, gave her a hurried squeeze, then grabbed her left upper arm and marched with her out the door, without saying a word. I quickly followed.

Whenever Dad was home he made a point of visiting my cousin Ben, who lived in Detroit. Ben became a Communist, and he did so with all of the passion of a true believer. Ben was one of Aunt Elizabeth and Uncle

Fred's sons, and the intensity of his commitment to Communist ideology was not unlike my father's commitment to his religious ideology. Ben's motivation to convert others to his cause was just as intense as my father's passion to convert sinners to Jesus.

This was, of course, terribly disturbing for dear Aunt Elizabeth and Uncle Fred. As with most embarrassments, Ben's little problem was hushed up as much as possible. I don't even remember becoming aware of it myself until 1947, after our family had moved to Detroit. But the fact was, Ben had been active in the Communist Party since before our return to the United States from Brazil in 1946. Dad took a special interest in the situation from the beginning. If he could help sinners find God, he could help Ben find common sense. Every chance Dad got, he'd call on Ben, stopping in to "talk things through." Even after we moved from Michigan to California, Dad made a special point to stop by Ben's house whenever his travels took him near Detroit, where Ben and his family made their home.

But Dad wasn't the only one who took a special interest in Ben's politics. Senator Joe McCarthy had just been elected to the U.S. Senate in 1946. Fear of Communist infiltration of the United States government was escalating steadily long before Senator McCarthy ratcheted up his anti-Communist cause seriously with his famous Congressional hearings starting in 1950. As early as 1946, the FBI was registering all known American Communists, monitoring and recording their activities. Dad became keenly aware of this since he often got stopped and questioned within a block or two of leaving Ben's house. FBI agents wanted to know the nature of Dad's relationship to Ben, and the topics of their conversations.

How amusing the agents might have found the exchanges between Dad and Ben, if only they'd really known. Two men, each fiercely convinced of the truth of his ways, smugly trying to convince the other to change his mind. Dad was sure he could bring Ben back to the religious upbringing of his early years. There he'd sit at the kitchen table, a Bible in his left hand and his right index finger pointing emphatically at passages of scripture. My father totally believed in the "inerrancy" of the scriptures, or the idea that everything in the Bible was literally true whether or not it was disproved or contradicted by scientific fact. Dad would argue the case of the Bible's inerrancy with anyone, tirelessly, because he knew the Bible was true. He'd argue, and he'd argue, and he'd argue. And often, he argued brilliantly. The only problem with these arguments was that Dad was unable to listen to the other speaker. He had all the answers, and he knew you were wrong if you didn't believe in inerrancy, and that was really all there was to it for him. It made for a rather one-sided debate.

Ben would smile, utterly relaxed, seeming for all the world as if he were enjoying every minute of the discussion. Neither man, however, would be listening to very much of what the other was saying. Perhaps they didn't really hear a word. Sometimes that's how it looked from my vantage point: Two stubborn men, talking and talking but not hearing a word. Ben's lack of listening didn't faze Dad a bit. He would proselytize undeterred, an all-knowing smirk fixed upon his face. Mother would sit near Dad's side, her head bent in prayer, eyes closed, beseeching God to help Ben listen to Uncle John and "see the Light." The scene always amazed me, no matter how many times I saw it, which was plenty, since Dad took up the same tack every time we visited their home.

Ben's wife Donna accepted all this without a word. She tolerated her husband's politics and the consequences, as well as the conversion lectures from Dad and other family members. I admired her soft-spoken ways, and her loving way of welcoming us into her home despite our differences.

Ben never let the inevitable lecturing keep him away from reunions and events. In fact, he loved his family and never missed a gathering. Maybe the extra attention was a bonus of sorts. Maybe it made him feel special, or important. But despite the family pressure to come back to the ideological flock, Ben never abandoned Communism. Even during the 1950s, when other kids ridiculed his two teenaged sons at school and thugs followed them home and threatened and even beat them up on account of their "Commie" father, Ben held his ground.

Maybe I admired my cousin Ben as much as I admired his wife Donna, but for different reasons. His rejection of our religion frightened me on the one hand, but his courage to stand up for his beliefs—even in the face of my father's insistence otherwise—was intriguing, and, in a way, brought me a certain kind of comfort.

Shortly after we moved to Highland Park, my eyesight failed. Actually, the first vague problems with my eyesight had begun to emerge during our last few months in Brazil. But during our first months in America, the problems grew worse until by the time we moved to Highland Park, I could barely see.

Mother took me to see an eye specialist in downtown Detroit. His offices were bright and comfortingly sterile. "Fungus," he said as he peeled my eyelid back and shined a light into my pupil. "Undoubtedly something she picked up in Brazil. It's covering both her eyes, and growing fast."

"What can we do?" Mother asked.

"Scrape it off," said the doctor.

My heart jumped into my mouth. This was obviously bad.

"I'll start today," he cautioned, "but that's just the beginning. She'll have to come back for weekly treatments until it's completely gone."

Week after week, this doctor dilated my eyes and gently scraped them to remove whatever it was that was supposedly growing on their surface. Meanwhile, I was legally blind. I had to go to a special school and attend a sight-saving class. This school occupied a large room in a nearby grade school. There were bookshelves around the room and several desks in the middle. I received individual attention from a trained teacher who taught about eight to ten children in grades one through six. She read all the texts out loud to us that were printed in normal print. Many books were in extra-large print, and I learned to use a typewriter with large print. In our integrated classes, the blind kids always sat in the very first row. Other kids would point and laugh at us. Combined with my accent and near inability to read or write, I was now socially hopeless. My only salvation was my singing voice. Once every two or three months the blind kids were invited to lunch at the Lion's Club, which sponsored the special school. I was always asked to sing a solo. I was also asked to sing at the grade school assemblies. This gave me at least a small dose of positive attention from other children in the school to offset the teasing and disdain my blindness attracted.

I continued to have my eyes scraped for almost two years, and it wasn't until the last three months of seventh grade that my sight improved enough for me to attend the school near my home, like a regular kid.

NANCY WALTMAN was a godsend for me in Highland Park. She was our next-door neighbor, and unlike most of the kids at school, she didn't make fun of me for my accent or my bad eyes. Nancy was my age and went to the school near our house. She had dark brown short hair, a stocky build, and wore long dark pants. I never saw her in a dress. She was in a "tomboy" stage. She loved baseball, and the two of us spent hours throwing a ball back and forth to each other in the evening.

Nancy even had a spare mitt for me. In back of our houses was a baseball field, and we loved to watch the boys play. Nancy knew everything about the game and tried to pass on her knowledge to me. Nancy also loved comics. She had a marvelous collection of Mary Marvel, Superman, Archie, Spiderman, and more. "Take what you want," she'd offer, as we sprawled across her bed pouring over the colorful pictures. I was forbidden to read them, of course, so I could never bring one home. But I couldn't resist looking at the pictures. In most cases, the print was large and I could make out the letters. I think most of my progress in English came from Nancy's comics.

For a time, in junior high, Mother enrolled me in voice lessons. She attended with me. "She will sing only religious songs," Mother declared to my teacher.

"What about semi-classical?" asked the teacher.

"No," said Mother, "I think not."

I was embarrassed, but resigned. Occasionally, my teacher would say, "This is a perfect song for your voice." Then she would glance at Mother and add, "But your mother wouldn't like it."

I received a lot of attention at school for my singing, and was given the solo part in every chorus. At one citywide concert, I sang the main solo —"The Donkey Serenade"—and I was so proud I was bursting. I chose a colorful dress, and my hair was curled and pulled back with a fancy bobby pin. I stood up straight and couldn't help but smile, I was so happy. The auditorium was packed with hundreds of people, and I scanned the crowd until finally I spotted Mother. I sang perfectly. Afterward, person after person complimented and praised me. We were at a special school farther from our house, and as we walked home Mother looked straight ahead.

Neither of us said a word for a long time. I finally got up my courage to ask her how she had liked "The Donkey Serenade."

"Gracie," she said, staring straight ahead, "I don't approve of such a sinful song. I think you know that."

Chapter Twenty

Lost in the Peach Grove

MY PORK CHOP sat like a chunk of brick in my gut when Mother broke the awful news from across the dinner table one evening. It was the summer of 1947. All I could think to say, as my throat tightened against tears, was, "But where will I go to have fun?"

Time at Aunt Elizabeth's farm on the outskirts of Detroit was my antidote to the isolation of our new life in America. Time spent there made up for hard times at school and loneliness at home. I loved the way Aunt Elizabeth's farmhouse was always loaded with children—the ten of their own—as well as their children's friends. It was a place to play and blend into a group, a place where the whole family seemed warm and loving. Aunt Elizabeth and Uncle Fred's big clan was happy in a boisterous and chaotic way that I reveled in. To think of my auntie and uncle moving away was impossible.

"Pray for your dear auntie and uncle, Gracie, and ask the Lord to help you think of others, instead of yourself," my mother counseled.

But I could see that Mom felt a pang of heartbreak, too. When Aunt Elizabeth's family was gone, Mother and I walked in quiet tension through our empty house. Mom had looked forward to weekends on the farm just as much as I did.

Before long, my parents realized that the gaping hole left by the absence of Aunt Elizabeth and her family was simply too gaping to fill. We would have to follow them to California. We sold our house in Highland Park, and by December, we had found a small, upstairs rental apartment for Mother and me in the town of Turlock, California. Dad was gone almost full time, first in Germany with Uncle Fred and then raising funds for his publishing house. Mother missed him terribly, and we spent lots of time at Aunt Elizabeth's. Our apartment was only about ten miles from the peach ranch in Ceres where she and Uncle Fred lived.

Not long after we settled in Turlock came the biggest surprise of all. Dad decided he wanted to bring Mother along with him on his travels. For so long, things had always worked the same way: When Dad traveled, Mother looked after the home front, including me. This new plan of Dad's was quite a shift. Back in Highland Park, Dad wanted Mother to accompany him on his travels, but only in the summer, when I was able to join them on their trek through a series of towns and cities raising money for the publishing house in Brazil. All through June, July, and August, we had traveled through the United States spending a night or two in each city, visiting churches, and stirring up support for Dad's dream.

But now it was January in Turlock, and Mother and Dad insisted that I enroll in the local school. How could Mother travel with Dad if I was to be in school? Who would look after me? The logical thing, my parents agreed, was to have me live with Aunt Elizabeth in Ceres and enroll in the Ceres Grade School. I was fourteen years old, and placed in the eighth grade. I could read well enough, but I still struggled with spelling. Being in eighth grade meant that my cousin David, Aunt Elizabeth's son, would be in the same grade with me at Ceres Grade School.

David was something of a rising sports star, very popular with the girls, and I was very proud to be his cousin. In fact, I secretly hoped his status and popularity with the girls would help me make friends and gain acceptance. I made sure to introduce myself as David's cousin to all the kids I met. David was horrified. He had no interest in girls and was terribly embarrassed by me in general, a curse further exacerbated by the fact that we were forced to ride together on the school bus each day.

AUNT ELIZABETH was a typical German wife—strong, practical, and very much in charge of her brood of ten children. Auntie's kids liked to call her "the General," and it made me very proud to think that I shared a nickname with such a fine, kind, Christian woman. Aunt Elizabeth was one of my most tenderhearted relatives. She would never have turned down my parents' request to have me stay with her during their travels. What my parents didn't know, though, was that it was a very dark time for Aunt Elizabeth's family. My parents had no way of knowing this, because it was a secret no one ever spoke of, by unspoken agreement. Aunt Elizabeth would never have shared the problem plaguing her family, because its source was utterly taboo: One of Aunt Elizabeth's daughters, Ann, was having a nervous breakdown.

Ann was five years older than I was, about nineteen at the time. Her breakdown had come on like a sudden and virulent infection during her first year of college, and it quickly became so severe that she had to return home to Ceres. The whole household was thrown into unbearable tension and upheaval by Ann's erratic behavior. Worst of all, no one ever knew when an outburst was coming. Everybody walked on eggshells. None of us wanted Ann to explode, and even more, none of us wanted to be the one to set her off. Especially me.

I learned to watch Ann very, very carefully for signs of agitation. She was a pretty girl, with light brown hair and a slight build. She normally had a very quiet disposition, and seldom spoke. The most obvious warning was her throat clearing. It would begin as a single soft grunt. Then eventually, she'd grunt again. And again. If an attack was imminent, the grunts would become increasingly frequent—and more violent—until Ann flew into a total physical rage.

Like other members of the family, I learned without being told that I had to hide knives and scissors and even sewing needles. When Ann lost control, it would take several strong men to hold her down. Sometimes she tried to flee. On at least one occasion, she escaped and was gone for several days. The peace of her absence was ruined by the horrific worry we all shared about where she had gone and what would become of her.

Aunt Elizabeth prayed morning and night, and dabbed at her moist eyes throughout the day. A thick silence fell over the house.

Shortly after her disappearance, Ann was found. Local police escorted her home in a straitjacket. Aunt Elizabeth wept openly at the sight of her daughter's black and blue body, all tied up and still fighting. I was relieved that Ann was found and returned alive, and at the same time, I was deeply frightened by the vacant anger in her eyes.

Aunt Elizabeth spent many afternoons taking Ann to one doctor's appointment after the next. Though no one spoke directly about the problem, neighbors and people at church politely made suggestions and offered recommendations of physicians with specialties in "certain ailments." Aunt Elizabeth took Ann to every practitioner anyone recommended. Nothing helped. Well-meaning folks whispered that it might be time to think about an institution, but Aunt Elizabeth refused to even consider it. Instead, she prayed day and night.

I, too, prayed day and night, especially at night, because I slept in the same room with Ann. The farmhouse had three bedrooms, one for Auntie and Uncle, one for the boys, and one for the girls, so everyone shared a bed with someone. Before Ann disappeared we slept together, but after her return I slept with my cousin Lenore in a double bed across the room. Sharing a bed in itself was something I was used to, and I didn't normally mind. It's just that sleeping in the same room with Ann meant very little sleep and a lot of silent, fearful prayer. I lay stiff as a board and wide awake through most of the night, staring into the darkness, clinging to the edge of the narrow bed, holding as still as I possibly could. Sometimes I couldn't help but cry, and at those times, I prayed harder that my crying would not wake Ann, if by chance she was asleep. Often, I couldn't tell whether she slept or not. She tossed and turned both in her wakefulness and in her sleep. Sometimes, she cleared her throat, and my heart would jump into my mouth.

Please, Dear Jesus, I begged with all my heart. Hot tears streamed down my cheeks onto the thin cotton pillowcase. *Please make her go to sleep. Please help her stay asleep. Please help Ann get better, Jesus. And please, please don't let her hurt me!*

There were some nights when sleeping so close to Ann was more than I could handle. I had to get out of that bedroom. Out on the land behind Aunt Elizabeth's house, there was an apartment where Uncle Fred's brother lived. There was also a one-bedroom house trailer, where my parents stayed when they came to visit. I started sneaking out to the trailer to stay by myself instead of sleeping in the house with Ann. It was lonely in the trailer, but anything was better than the stiff-backed fear I felt in that narrow bed with my tormented cousin. I couldn't tell Aunt Elizabeth—or anyone else—how I felt, because none of us discussed or acknowledged Ann's condition in any way.

I could think of only one solution. Mother and Dad simply had to come home. Surely if they knew how things really were for Aunt Elizabeth, dealing with Ann's breakdown, they would know that she was in no position to take care of me. Surely they would not want me—a fourteen-year-old girl in eighth grade—hiding out by myself in a house trailer or sleeping beside a dangerously ill young woman.

I wrote my parents long, soulful letters, describing Ann's outbursts and Aunt Elizabeth's strain, and pleading with them to come home as fast as they could. Every day, when the school bus rolled to a stop at the end of the road leading to Aunt Elizabeth's house, I'd hurry off as fast as I could. I had come to hate the bus ride, since my cousin David refused to talk to me or acknowledge that I was his cousin. If we happened to run into each other during the school day, he looked the other way. His disdain hurt, but I couldn't blame him for being embarrassed by his awkward cousin with the Brazilian accent. All I wanted was for my parents to come home, and any day I knew their letter would arrive. So from the bus stop I ran the length of the road to Aunt Elizabeth's mailbox with the most urgent sense of anticipation in the world.

Finally, one afternoon, the envelope arrived. It was from Mother—her scrawled penmanship was immediately obvious. I hurried to the house and sat on the front steps to rip it open. Inside was a neatly typed, one-page letter.

"Gracie, you know how difficult it is for your Aunt Elizabeth. Pray for her, be patient, ask God to help you, and I know you will be all right," my mother wrote.

Hot tears spilled down my cheeks before I finished the first paragraph. My parents must have misunderstood my letters. But how could they have? I had described everything so clearly—Ann's outbursts, the throat-clearing, the running away, and then the straitjacket and the bruises. I had even told them I was sleeping in the trailer, alone.

As weeks passed, and Ann grew worse and more violent, Aunt Elizabeth and her whole family were focused on the girl's care. I understood the necessity of this all-consuming attention, but it also made me feel burdensome and horribly in the way. On the one hand I wasn't much help, especially since I wasn't a member of the immediate family. On the other hand, I didn't dare say a word about needing anything from anyone, whether it was help with a school writing assignment or just someone with whom to talk. More and more, I tried to be invisible.

On the opposite end of Aunt Elizabeth's peach orchard, my cousin Lillie and her husband Ralph had a small place. Lillie was one of Elizabeth and Fred's older daughters, the same Lillie who lived with us when I was a baby. She and Ralph had two young children. They had plenty of responsibilities to handle. Nonetheless, Lillie made me feel welcome when I strolled across the orchard to see her. Even her husband Ralph greeted me with a smile. He'd pull up a chair and chat for a bit. I invented any excuse I could to visit them.

When I wasn't at Lil's house, I cried. And I prayed. *Dear Jesus, I can't stay here, please make Mother and Dad come and get me. And Dear Jesus, please make Mother and Dad believe what I am writing to them. Help me to be patient and understanding. Help me not get in the way of Aunt Elizabeth or her family.*

Despite my prayers, I felt more burdensome and unwanted with each passing day. I was convinced that everyone in the family wished I was not there, and I'm quite sure I was right.

Depression settled over me like a fog. The only answer was to run away. If I were to run away, surely everyone would miss me, and feel terrible.

They'd contact Mother and Dad, who would feel even more terrible. They would have to come home. I waited for the first warm spring day, and then I started walking. As I walked, I pictured myself, alone, trudging down the road. I could see myself in silhouette, as if from above. And it made such a sorry picture, I wept. The more I walked, the sorrier I felt for myself. The sorrier I felt, the harder I cried.

After two hours of walking and crying and making step-by-dragging-step toward the city of Modesto, I reached Ceres. It was growing dark, and I was hungry. And thirsty. And that's when it dawned on me: What if no one misses me? After all, why would they? I was a burden in the first place, just a person in the way of a family with bigger things to worry about. I started back home, and walked until I reached the trailer. No one ever mentioned my absence, and neither did I. More than anything, I was ashamed of myself for trying to run away in the first place.

There had to be some better way to get my parent's attention and force them, especially my dad, to stop and notice me. I was sitting alone in the trailer behind my aunt and uncle's house, hiding from the world. I didn't want, couldn't stand, staying in the big house where I would have to be around my relatives. The trailer was small and lonely, but the house was worse. I wanted my parents and needed them desperately. Why couldn't they understand that from my letters? The need was like a wound inside of me, like my flesh pulling away from my bones, and it was worsening each day.

And all this hurting was squeezing out my ability to think straight. If I shut my eyes and concentrated on the pain, I could almost convince myself that it was a disease or a tumor growing somewhere deep in my chest, pulling me apart and spreading like a dark purple bruise from the inside out. It was hard to breathe with such a pressure trapped under my ribs. I had to make it stop. I had to find a way to get my parents to come. No, getting them to come was not enough. I had to get them to come and stay. What, what, what could I do?

I wracked my brain for one single thing that would make my parents notice me. It had to be something dramatic that would put me ahead of everything else. It had to be big, shocking, unforgettable enough to make my dad momentarily drop every other concern, even the church.

And that's when it hit me. The realization came with such force that the room spun a little. I would commit suicide.

It was so obvious, I was surprised I hadn't thought of it before. Suicide was the best and the only answer. It would make the ache inside me stop; that was a given. And it was permanent. If I killed myself, my father would never be able to put me out of his mind again.

I knew suicide was a sin, but that made it almost better. Plus it seemed so easy. All I had to do was turn on the gas on the stove and crawl under the two thin quilts that covered my twin bed. I would curl up on my side and press my cheek into the lumpy feather pillow—making sure to keep my nose and mouth clear—and then I would slowly drift to sleep. There would be no mess, no pain, no regrets. I would just fall peacefully to sleep and never wake up. I pictured myself lying in the bed, quietly dying. And I realized then that as I drifted into the blackness of deadly sleep, I would look back over my life, and carefully remember happier images of my parents at their best. I could so easily picture my mother baking in the kitchen in Coqueiros, or typing on her small typewriter in the evening. I could see her broad shoulders moving side to side as she played her beloved piano. Even the thought of her picking the nits from my hair filled my heart with love and gratitude for her attention. And Dad. I could see him on the sailboat, captaining us across the wide blue bay, or steering us to a precarious landing through that terrible storm. And most of all, I could see him striding through our picket gate and into our yard, a smile lighting up his face as Nero barked in greeting. Tears trickled silently down my cheeks and pooled into the corners of my mouth, their saltiness a surprising sensation.

I turned slowly toward the kitchen. The stove in the trailer was an old porcelain apartment-sized contraption with four square burners on top, each with a heavy, black cast iron rack covering the silver gas ring. The red control knobs ran across the front. I turned one of the knobs to the right and listened as the low hiss signaled the release of gas from the front burner. If I lit a match, the burner would ignite instantly. I turned the knob back to "off." Again, I pictured myself in the small bed. I perched on the side of the bed, as gingerly as I could. Still, the springs squeaked under my weight. I would be dead by the time anyone found me. Someone would have to contact Mom and Dad to deliver the bad news. I tried to imagine their reaction. Would they scream "No!" and drop the phone in disbelief? No matter how they reacted, they would have to realize I had been telling the truth in my letters, that I had been sincere when I begged them to come home. And they'd be very sad that it was now too late, as I was gone forever.

The more I considered the consequences of killing myself, the better I felt, and the more convinced I was of the wisdom of my plan. I stood up from the bed and went back to the kitchen, where I fiddled with the knob on the stove again, and took a sniff. I wondered how long it would take for the gas to fill the trailer. I tried to picture my parents' faces when they arrived. Would my body still be lying in the bed, cold and lifeless? Or would I already be—where did dead people go? The morgue? Would I already be at the morgue, lying in a coffin? It was all so confusing. But one thing for certain was that I would be dead. And Mother and Dad would have to face the sad consequences of having ignored me.

But what if they thought the gas poisoning had been an accident? I would have to write them a letter. Why hadn't I realized that sooner? I would have to make it clear that I'd turned on the gas on purpose, and that I'd done it because I was alone and ignored. I sat on the edge of the bed again, and ran through the things I wanted to say to my parents. "Dear Mother and Father, Please forgive me for what I have done. I tried to tell you . . ." Tell them what? That I needed them so much my only choice was to kill myself? What if they didn't believe my motive? What if even after I was dead, they just thought I was exaggerating and feeling sorry for myself? They'd never believe I could do such a thing!

I needed to lie down and think this through. It was so much more complicated than I originally thought. I didn't want to cry, but the shaking that rose up from my chest took hold and wouldn't stop, a long silent heaving with only the stingiest spurting of tears. I cried and cried this way, without knowing how long. The golden light of afternoon turned to dusk and the insects outside buzzed with the energy of spring. I don't remember noticing when darkness fell. I just remember how my crying turned eventually to praying. I prayed my heart out, begging for forgiveness: *Dear Jesus, please forgive me for being such a spoiled brat, and for thinking only of myself. Please don't let these thoughts come again. Please help me, Jesus, and bring my parents home. Please save me from my selfish heart, Please . . . please . . . please . . .*

When I next opened my eyes, I lay fully clothed on top of my bed. Strong sun shone through the window and sweat beaded my forehead. Birds chirped loudly in the trees, so loudly they didn't sound real. I cannot say that I was happy, but I was grateful to be alive.

SHORTLY AFTER that bleak night in the trailer twiddling the gas knob, a miracle took place. My choir teacher picked me to sing a solo at the spring music concert. Amazingly, the song she wanted me to sing was called, "I Love Life." This energetic young teacher worked diligently with me for the next month. I sang "I Love Life" every second of every day. It felt like God had written the lyrics just for me:

I love life and I want to live
And drink of life's fullness take all it can give
I love life, every moment must count
To revel in its sunshine, revel in its fount
I love life, I want to live, I love life.

I sang with all my heart. Every time I sang, the song grew more and more beautiful to me. By the time of the spring concert, it truly was beautiful. I was proud and happy that evening. I wore a long jersey gown with a white skirt and purple and pink flowery top. I had never had such a beautiful dress. My cousin Lil and her younger sister Lenore helped me find it. Mother and Dad were not there, but Lillie and Ralph came to hear me, and even David came, embarrassed though he was. Somewhere in the audience, despite her maternal heartache, was Aunt Elizabeth, and that perhaps meant the most to me of all.

Chapter Twenty-One

The Reappearance

FINALLY, in the middle of June, Mother and Dad returned. The first thing Dad did was find us a place to live. In July, the three of us moved back to Turlock. It was an indescribable relief to get away from Aunt Elizabeth's house. Finally, things could return to normal. The place we moved to was a small house Dad had rented. It was next door to the Smith family, who were members of the Turlock Assemblies of God Church. Dad left again for more fundraising, and in no time, Mrs. Smith struck up a friendship with my mother.

Something unusual happened to me shortly after the move; a throbbing pain developed in my lower abdomen. It wasn't anything I had ever quite felt before. No menstrual cramp or intestinal parasite or even food poisoning had ever felt quite like this. The pain intensified over the next two days until I was so incapacitated that even Mother was worried enough to think a doctor might be in order. Dad was visiting churches in Northern California for at least three weeks. So Mother asked Sister Smith if she knew a good doctor. Sister Smith mentioned that Turlock had a doctor who was not only a good Christian, but also a former missionary. Mother took me to his office immediately. Upon examination,

Dr. Johnson discovered that my white blood cell count was elevated, along with my temperature.

"She has a serious appendix infection," he told Mother. "We're going to have to operate."

My ears started buzzing with fear as soon as I heard the word "operate," and little flecks of white swam before my eyes. Mother must have held herself together, though, because she scheduled me for surgery the following morning at Turlock Emanuel Hospital.

Turlock Emanuel was an old hospital, built in 1918. Thirty beds were tucked into small shared rooms separated by a long linoleum tiled hallway. Nurses in white dresses and white hats hurried up and down the hallway, their hard-soled shoes clicking against the polished floor. There was a crisp and sterile veneer to the hospital that I found comforting. Plus, Dr. Johnson gave me a dose of something strong for my abdominal pain, and I was feeling much better than I had the day before.

For surgery, though, I needed to be put all the way under. The anesthetic of choice in 1948 was ether. By mid-morning, I was wheeled into the operating room, where a nurse placed a mask over my mouth and nose. I could hear the sound of my own breathing, amplified in my ears. The odor of the ether was sharp and unpleasant. Instinctively, I held my breath.

"Gracie, please breathe deeply and count backwards," said a voice. "Start at ten and count down to one."

"Ten, nine, eight," I droned, hearing my voice from a distance. "Seven, six . . . five . . . four."

When I awoke, a wave of nausea rolled over me so powerfully that I vomited in my bed.

"There now," said the nurse whose blurry face hovered above me, "try not to do that again. You're doing fine now, all fixed up."

Somehow, Mother had been able to reach Dad, and on my second day in the hospital, he arrived to see me. I was awake when I heard his footsteps outside the door; I closed my eyes almost all the way, but not quite. This, I realized, was my chance to get even with him for not coming home when I had needed him so desperately in Ceres. Through the dark haze of my lashes, I watched him walk to my bed.

He leaned forward and took one of my hands in his. Then he kissed me on the forehead, saying, "Here's Daddy."

I opened one eye slightly, and mumbled in the foggiest, groggiest voice I could muster: "Who are you? I don't have a father."

My father's face collapsed in pain at my words, and for one fleeting moment, before I felt terrible, I was completely satisfied with myself.

For the rest of the summer we were able to travel with Dad. Every summer, Dad took the pulpit at Christian camp meetings. These camps, owned by large church districts, served as a place where Evangelicals could vacation with their families and other like-minded Christians for weeks at a time. In America, we usually went to the Michigan campground. Later, after our second return to America in 1946, we also explored a German camp in Bridgeman, Michigan, and the Northern California camp near Santa Cruz.

I loved camp! Or at least I did in the early years. I enjoyed being the preacher's daughter, and I experienced no difficulty at all in living up to my father's expectations of me. Camp was a special place in many ways, not the least of which being that Dad was usually one of two main speakers. This made him special, and it made me special, too. The morning speaker tended to focus his sermons on various Bible study topics for believers. Pretty tame stuff, for the most part. But in the evening, things heated up considerably. The evening speaker got down to business with a fire and brimstone sermon meant to get people to give themselves up to the Lord right away, and consecrate themselves to serving Jesus. The evening service usually ended with an altar call, and most of the congregation responded by filing up to the front of the church to pray fervently to the Lord. Many spoke in tongues and others broke down emotionally, weeping and sobbing in the face of the Lord's power. Altar call was a place where those who had never had this experience—whether speaking in tongues or being reduced to divinely inspired tears—were coached on the methods of receiving the Holy Spirit.

In the mornings, while the adults were having Bible Study, we kids gathered in a separate chapel or in a larger tent. We spent the mornings singing lively church songs, praying avidly, speaking in tongues, and generally expressing our faith however we saw fit. The ministers assigned to us were usually young and energetic. They went to great lengths to make worship fun, and most of the kids loved camp as much as I did.

Besides the preaching, our ministers also led discussion groups just for us kids. We would speak in great earnestness about how to live a Christian life in a non-Christian world. Of great interest to us were the evils of dancing, makeup, and movies. Since we knew—from being told again and again—that eschewing these sins made us superior to and more holy than our non-believing peers, it helped to remind us of the benefits of our sacrifices.

Once in a while, though, someone dared to ask a question. I remember Charles, especially, a redheaded boy, maybe ten years old, with a face so covered in freckles there was barely any pale skin showing through. Charles had the guts to ask what the rest of us were thinking. "What about movies that ain't sinful?" he wanted to know, a mild twang accentuating his point. "What about movies that show loving folk, respecting the Lord?"

But Charles couldn't stump our minister. He didn't miss a beat. "Charles," he said, "that's just the kind of trick the Devil loves to play on us," he said. "But the Lord doesn't work that way. If you look in your alleys, you will find many garbage cans that are full of the stench of rotten food, but occasionally, buried in the stench, might be a bit of fresh food that's been thrown away. Now, a loving father would never ask you to go to your alley, dig through the garbage cans, and look for the good food that might be there. Yes, there are some movies that may not be harmful, but in the same way, your loving heavenly Father would never want you to go to an evil, filthy, sinful theatre to see the one movie that might not condemn your soul."

We all clapped wildly at this explanation. The devil couldn't trick us so easily! At camp, the line between good and evil was clear as day, and ministers seemed infallible in their ready answers to any challenge. Of course, we never discussed complex topics such as abortion. In fact, no one ever discussed abortion—it was as if it didn't exist. But if you wanted to know why God disapproved of mascara, camp offered assurances.

For the children of Evangelicals, camp was an opportunity to "fit in" in a way that was impossible in the outside world. Most of us found it exhilarating to meet so many other Evangelicals our own age. Inevitably, there was a great deal of flirtation and match-making. Within the first few days of camp, boys and girls began to pair up, and soon you would see couples sitting together, walking together, and even being obvious in their inseparability. I experienced my first romance at a Christian camp. Daniel Stern was a German boy from Cleveland, Ohio, and I was sure I was madly in love. This particular summer, we were at German camp, and since the morning meeting was in German, Dad didn't make me go. Instead, many of us spent our late mornings and afternoons on the beach of Lake Michigan. The romance with Daniel faded within the first two or three letters after camp ended, but that didn't seem to matter a bit. Another one would emerge the following summer, whether with Daniel or a new boy.

The Christian camps were usually in a rustic setting. Some rooms were in separate cabins, often owned by individual families, and there was also lodging in large dormitories. Since Dad was a speaker, we were generally assigned to a very comfortable cabin. Meals were served in the camp cafeteria, and everyone ate together at long tables. As a speaker's daughter, I was always busy helping with virtually everything. I set tables, served meals, washed dishes, and swept floors.

But afternoons were usually free, and many families planned a special time together to fish, swim, or take a hike and have a picnic. Often, a group of families would plan to share an activity together. Since Dad and Mother were always busy getting ready for the next church service, I usually joined friends and their families for afternoon outings.

Back when I was young, Pentecostals were most often poor, working poor, or, at best, middle class. Very few were what we would have considered "rich." This was even more evident in Brazil, where the converts we attracted tended to be incredibly poor and downtrodden peasants who were attracted to our church's message of prosperity on the other side.

The closest I recall coming to the real-life world of the rich and famous here on Earth was the incident of the "half-millionaires" coming to Christian camp the summer I was fourteen years old. I can only imagine the riot that may have broken out if a full millionaire would have come our way, considering the uproar caused when the rumor about the half-millionaire spread through the camp. Everyone was talking about the rich folks, waiting to get a peek at the real-life moneybags. So when they showed up, looking like any other ordinary couple, with their two teenaged children—one girl and one boy—I was a little disappointed. And when I found out they were only staying for a weekend, I nearly lost interest all together. But Dad was undeterred by their ordinary appearance and short stay. He dedicated a lot of time and energy trying to get the half-millionaire interested in his Brazilian publishing house. Every sermon Dad gave that weekend was just another plea for help to support printing the literature needed to convert the heathens of Brazil. He even spoke to the half-millionaire directly. Dad never said whether he talked the fellow into a donation or not.

By the time I was fourteen or fifteen, my feelings about camp began to change, which was hard to accept. I was more socially conscious, for one thing, and I felt some confusion about my place in the larger world. There was one part of me that felt very comfortable being with people who were Evangelicals and believed as I did, and there was another part of me that resented having to perform in the role of "the preacher's daughter." In that role I had to work extra hard to serve people, sing solos or duets with Mother in Portuguese when asked, be on my best behavior at all times, and be careful not to question anything, especially during youth discussions! After the evening service, I was expected to be part of the altar call, and to help others by praying for them and with them until late at night. Eventually, I resented that responsibility, too.

But these conflicted feelings were my deepest secret. I couldn't speak of them to anyone, and, in fact, I refused even to think about them or admit them to myself. To feel this way could only be a terrible sin, worthy of a huge dose of guilt. It was easier to shove the feelings aside, or deeper down, and do what was expected of me, all the while smiling and believing, always believing.

BEFORE WE MOVED to California in early 1947, Dorothy lived in Detroit, and dated a young man named Jim Parinello. Although Highland Park was a close suburb of Detroit, Dorothy rarely contacted us after she moved out. We only met Jim on one occasion, and Mother and I almost never saw Dorothy. Dad tried to visit her every chance he got, but once we left for California, even his contact with her diminished.

Then, on May 14, 1949, Dorothy and Jim married. Mother and Dad found out after the fact, when Dorothy sent a telegram. Dad was terribly upset by the whole situation. He had wanted a respectable, traditional wedding for his daughter, not what was essentially an elopement.

"I sent a telegram to Mr. and Mrs. Parinello," he wrote to Mother. "It was delivered to them last evening. I could not help but shed some tears, as that is not the way a daddy would have it, just a telegram, and not being present on a day so important in the life of his daughter. But then God knows all about it and I must leave it in His hands. I just trust and pray it will not happen that way with our other daughter."

Mother said she was sure Dorothy was pregnant and "had to get married."

Dorothy and Jim had taken an apartment above Jim's parents' place, in the Parinello's Italian community in Detroit. Dorothy learned Italian surprisingly quickly, since it's similar to Portuguese, and she was soon fluent. All in all, she seemed to be doing well. To Mother's surprise, Dorothy did not have a child in nine months. More than a year and a half later she gave birth, on September 4, 1950, to a healthy baby girl, Marlene.

I started attending Turlock High School and loved it. I came down with a wonderful case of school spirit. My Brazilian accent was finally gone and I felt like a real American. I landed my first real boyfriend, Buzzy Smith. Buzzy had short brown hair, was very good looking, and any one of my friends would have loved to be his girl (some had already). He lived next door and drove a Model A Ford. To my great delight, Buzzy took me on driving dates, mostly to church and church-related activities.

I was allowed to drive, as long as Mother was in the car with me. The state of California granted special driver's licenses to anyone with a legitimate necessity. Since Mother didn't drive and Dad was gone so much, I was allowed to enroll early in the driver's education class at Turlock High, and I passed the behind-the-wheel test. I loved the feeling it gave me to sit at the wheel of our car as we wended our way along the streets of our town. It seemed that overnight there was nothing I couldn't do.

I wanted desperately to try out for the school musical. Everyone said that with my singing voice, I would probably get a part. But when the time came, I felt sick to my stomach at the thought of having to sing in front of my parents in a romantic musical. I knew well how upset they would be. There was no way I could survive that, so I didn't try out. My music teacher didn't understand and was deeply disappointed, and as much as it hurt to lose her approval, it was nothing next to the fear of losing my father's. Fortunately for me, they decided not to do the musical that year because of budget concerns. This kept me from having to explain to everyone why I was not in it.

When I was fifteen, Mother and Dad took me on a trip to Los Angeles. It was the summer before we went back to Brazil. First, we'd be spending a few weeks in Michigan, at the Christian camps. But before leaving California, Dad had some very important business to take care of in the big city. Apparently, he had been given the name of a rich man, and he'd been tipped off that this particular rich man might be interested in supporting the Assemblies of God cause.

The drive from Turlock to Los Angeles whizzed by quickly enough, and it was mid-afternoon when we pulled up in front of the rich man's address. We couldn't see his house from the street, but there was a large and impressive metal gate guarding the driveway.

"Mother, Gracie, you will wait in the car," Dad said. He opened the driver's side door and stepped out. He adjusted his hat and disappeared through the big gate.

Mother and I stayed inside the car and prayed out loud for most of the time we waited for Dad to come back. Praying out loud was something we did as naturally as breathing. Our spoken prayers usually began with "Dear Heavenly Father" and continued with a litany of requests. When praying out loud was not direct requests of God, it was usually a not-so-subtle vehicle for a sermon. These sermons-masquerading-as-prayer were "for the good of those here on Earth," who were eavesdropping on what was purported to be a conversation with God. A good example of a prayer as a request was the heartfelt series of prayers I sent off hoping to find my doll Ruthie. Examples of prayers-as-sermons included the way Dad would pray out loud at a family gathering, asking God to save some errant relative, like my Communist cousin Ben. The advantage to the prayer-as-sermon technique was that no one, even Ben, would dare interrupt my father in his conversation with God.

Whenever Dad was home, he tended to read the Bible, usually the New Testament, after breakfast. Then we'd all kneel down by our chairs and each person would take a turn praying out loud. This was another good time for any one of us to sneak in a prayer-sermon for someone else. For instance, asking God to forgive Dorothy for fighting with Mom, or asking God to give Gracie wisdom in her choice of friends, etc. When Dad was gone, Mother tried to carry on with this daily devotion, but she was often too busy to follow through with it, to the relief of Dorothy and me.

As Mom and I sat in the hot car that afternoon, waiting for Dad to emerge from the rich man's house, we prayed a litany of requests in Dad's favor. "Dear Lord," Mother prayed, "please place the Brazilian publishing house on the heart of this wealthy man."

Dear Jesus, I prayed, *please let this man help Daddy help the people in Brazil.*

After about an hour, Dad reappeared and came back through the metal gate. His face was drawn and his shoulders sagged as he approached the car. His mouth was pursed as he opened the car door. "No, Marguerite," Dad said as he settled into the front seat. "I think this trip was in vain, as he did not seem the least bit interested."

A great and terrible sadness welled up in me. I could literally feel the pain across my chest, squeezing my heart. What an awful disappointment for Dad! And how embarrassing for my father, who was such a proud man, to have to beg for money, to have to lower himself to this rich man who had so much power over him and over us.

DESPITE NOT BEING IN THE MUSICAL, I had a great time in the spring of my freshman year at Turlock. I was fifteen years old, the California spring was in full bloom, I had a boyfriend named Buzzy with a car, and everything was finally going my way.

Until one summer evening at dinner, my father said, "Gracie, it's time to go back to Brazil."

Part III

1949 to 1952
With Fresh Eyes: Brazil

My favorite Bible verse:

I Corinthians 10:13

No temptation has overtaken you, that is not common to man. God is faithful, and He will not let you be tempted beyond your strength. But with the temptation will provide a way of escape, so that you may be able to endure it.

Chapter Twenty-Two

Fish Out of Everything

OUR SHIP, *THE S.S. BRAZIL,* sailed in late October, and since there were only two classes of staterooms to choose from, first and second, we sailed second-class. From the moment Dad announced our impending departure, I was in a state of mild shock, ensconced in an almost pleasant numbness that protected me from the other alternative, which was to have my heart break. But one night, late at night, as Dad walked by my cabin, he paused to listen. Inside, I was lying on my bed, sobbing. I could barely speak, I was crying so hard.

"What is it, Gracie?" my father wanted to know.

"I-i-i-m so-o—o lone-some," I hiccoughed through my tears.

Dad did his best to comfort me. He placed his hand on my shoulder and said, "Gracie, everything is going to be fine. We are doing the Lord's work; He will help you and heal your sorrow."

But this time his words did not help one bit.

On November 2, we arrived in Rio de Janeiro. A large national church convention was taking place over the next two weeks in Rio, so we stayed on to participate. Brazilians love music of any kind. Most of the Assemblies of God Churches had large bands and large choruses. I caused an immediate sensation with my electric Hawaiian guitar. This strange instrument I played was a magnet for bringing in "sinners" to hear me play, then to hear Dad's sermons. I may as well have been Elvis, judging by the enthusiasm of the audiences I drew. Obviously, Dad had chosen the right musical instrument for me to wow the crowds. Dad did his share of crowd pleasing, as well. With each passing year as a missionary, my father's charisma and people power grew stronger. There was a scuffle during the convention between a group of ministers and the church leaders, and it grew so heated that eventually tempers flared in both groups. A lunch break brought a temporary halt to the battle, but Dad spent the hour in his room instead of eating. When the meeting reconvened, Dad took the stage and preached for almost an hour. When Dad was finished, these same men who sixty minutes earlier had been at each other's throats were now hugging each other and begging tearfully for forgiveness.

When the convention ended, we continued on to Coqueiros, where Aunt Martha and Uncle Rodrigo were living in our house with their sons Edison and Rudolfo. Rodrigo had removed the screens—they made the air "unhealthy"—and we never were able to convince him to put them back on. Since he and Martha remained with us for the rest of our time in Brazil, I was forced to accept this new screenless reality. Meanwhile, electricity was now available twenty-four hours a day, a major improvement from four years earlier.

Demand was high, and we still had to supplement with candles and lanterns, but for the most part, the current was vastly more available than when we lived there before. The biggest challenge was my electric guitar, which required a large transformer that we carried everywhere.

The worst change, though, was the one I saw in my childhood friends. One was already married, and the rest were desperately searching for husbands. None had gone to high school. I was definitely not in any position to be their "General" anymore, nor did they want me to be. With nothing in common except our age, we found a void where friendship had once been.

Over the course of December and January, I received about five letters from various American friends, including one from Daniel Stern, my first boyfriend, met during summer camp. With each letter, I grew more morose and despondent.

"Poor Grace has had such a lonesome day for America, crying constantly," my mother wrote to Aunt Esther. "She has received letters from America, but it makes her even worse. Things are so different here that it is pitiful. But she is such a good girl and so helpful at the meetings; everyone just loves her."

Making my isolation that much bleaker, I didn't go to school the first year and a half after returning to Brazil. Instead, I traveled the country with my parents, playing that electric Hawaiian guitar and singing solos, duets and trios with Mother and Dad. I loved being with them, and the travel was fun and stimulating. Sometimes, it was literally stimulating. Our transformer was a bit glitchy, and it gave me continuous electric shocks as I played on the cold, damp floors during church services. The shocks weren't terribly severe—usually—but they were constant and annoying. I begged Mother to let me stop when the shocks got unbearable. She said I should pray to God to help me. So I prayed, and I'd make it through the service.

We consistently drew crowds. The Pentecostal movement was already huge in 1950, and many of the congregations we visited had between two hundred and two thousand members. One church in Rio de Janeiro had more than twenty thousand members. When we weren't performing in live services, our music was playing on Brazilian Christian radio. Dad had made sure that before we left the United States, Mother and I made several recordings with her on accordion, me on guitar, and the two of us singing solos and duets. Our recordings were some of the earliest Christian recordings available in Brazil, and they were instantly popular.

ONE OF OUR EARLIEST TRIPS during this time in Brazil was to Urubici, where I'd been given my pet lamb Becky all those years ago by our dear friends, Brother and Sister Karklis. The area was still remote and comparatively undeveloped, and as soon as we arrived, word spread about our strange musical instrument. We announced a meeting for the following Sunday evening, to be held at the local Assemblies of God Church. The next thing we heard was that several trucks were coming to the meeting from the city of Urubici and the surrounding countryside. Rumor had it that the plan was to disrupt our meeting.

I was terrified. This uncivilized area was not unlike the American Wild West in the late 1800s, with weekly shootings and a general sense of lawlessness. Mother and I were in the middle of a song when the trucks rumbled up outside the church. The earth shook beneath their tires. The shaking stopped and the growl of the truck engines fell silent. A large group of rough and tumble men barged into the church and stomped to the front rows. They filled every last seat in the church. Out of the corner of my eye, I peered at the intruders. They wore bright colorful shirts, black pants, and leather boots. Most carried large, wide-brimmed straw and felt hats.

I wanted to run, and Dad could sense this. "Keep playing, and keep singing," he said.

And so we continued, as if nothing was happening. Dad cut his sermon short, stopping after only thirty minutes instead of his usual forty-five to an hour. When the service was over, no one moved.

"More music!" insisted our visitors.

Mother and I began to play again, and for at least the next hour, we played on and on. We finally excused ourselves, and the men gestured their permission for us to leave. We promised our return soon. The next day, we left the area as scheduled.

Dad was thrilled. "I really picked the right instrument for you, Gracie," he said. "It's a real crowd getter!"

I MET STELLA ANDERMAN on that same trip to Urubici. Stella's family owned a hotel and restaurant next to the Karps' fabric store, at Esquina. Sister Karp was related to Stella's family, and she told me that the Andermans had a daughter my age who was anxious to meet me. One day when I was visiting the Karps I spotted a girl standing outside the restaurant next door. She was irresistible in the most charming, girlish way. She had short curly blond hair and the most animated smile I'd ever seen. I was sure she must be the girl Sister Karp had told me about. I immediately went over and introduced myself. That was the beginning of a lifelong friendship.

Stella's parents were Latvians, and Stella's father, Emilio Anderman, was a highly intelligent and well-educated man who was also terribly bitter against his parents' generation. The elder Andermans had been part of the Latvian group that followed a charismatic leader, who preached the end of the world. In response, the preacher's supporters, including the elder Andermans, had sold everything or given most of it away and waited for a judgment day that never came. The angry Emilio escaped from Brazil to America as soon as he finished high school. He received a scholarship to the University of Pittsburgh, where he earned a degree, and, in the meanwhile, took up fanatical Communism. After graduation, he came back to Brazil to convert others to his Communist cause. He visited Urubici, fell in love with Stella's mother, and settled down for the long haul.

The Andermans had two daughters and two sons; Stella was the older girl—and in spite of or because of our strange blend of polarities and similarities, we became the best of friends. My father, of course, intensely disapproved of Stella's father and was leery of me spending time in their home. Mr. Anderman had a way of leaving his magazines around his restaurant and hotel—magazines from Russia, full of photographs of beautiful people beaming from ear to ear. No matter what the people were doing in the photos—from toiling in the fields to working in factories to sitting in parks—they were ebullient. But even at age fifteen, I knew it was propaganda, and Stella and I enjoyed laughing at the pictures. In the end, my father's disapproval of Stella was the very incentive I needed to reach out to her and get to know her better. Every time we came back to Urubici, I made sure to visit her. She visited us in Coquerios many times, too, whenever we were back home for a few weeks at a stretch. I was enamored with Stella, and our friendship flourished. I saw something in her that completed an empty spot in myself. And since I was looking hard for any safe way to simply be me—whoever that was—Stella was completely irresistible.

AFTER URUBICI, we headed to other nearby Santa Catarina cities: Itaji, Blemenau, Joinville, and Tubarão. We held services in other states, stopping in São Paulo, Rio de Janeiro, Minas Gerais and Rio Grande do Sul. All along the way we stopped to visit American and Swedish missionaries, and at every stop I drew hordes of attention with my new and novel guitar. I made new friendships, many of which were longlasting, since we revisited many churches every few months or so during our rounds. I never had a boyfriend, but I had many secret crushes. My girlfriends and I loved to gossip about boys we admired and thought were cute. We did this in secret, of course, or at least that's what we thought.

We stayed almost a month in Minas Gerais, where Dad's missionary friend Laurence Olson had a daughter Carolyn, about my age. During our time there, Carolyn and I completed a sewing course. By the end of it, we could look at a picture of any dress, take measurements of the person we were sewing for, and draw up an accurate pattern. I also sang on the radio every morning.

"Grace is so busy here," Mother wrote. "She goes to a sewing school every morning at eight, and then goes to the radio station at ten o'clock, then back for lunch, before returning to school at noon. She is such a good girl; everywhere we go people appreciate her so much. She loves to sing for the Lord and wants to be a blessing."

I did try to be a good girl and a blessing, and make my parents proud. It was easy enough to do, as long as we stuck together and kept the rest of the world at bay.

After departing Lavras, we went onward to visit the Missionaries Johnson. The Johnsons lived in the state of Minas Gerais, in the city of Varginha. They kept a bulldog as a pet, and this dog was quite ugly with her wrinkles, flat nose, and weepy eyes. But at the same time she was irresistible. I didn't even mind the pungent smell of the animal, or the way it sneezed and passed gas every other minute. Upon this particular visit, the bulldog had just given birth to puppies, whose father was, oddly enough, a German Shepherd. Oh, how I wanted a dog for Florianópolis! We still had not found a good watchdog to replace Nero. Since we were on our way home, with only a few stops to go before reaching Coquieros, Mother and Dad let me take one of the puppies. I named him Tigre. He was a scary-looking thing, with his bulldog head and his German Shepherd's body. He resembled some sort of medieval monster. And he was mine. I loved him, and Mother and Father thought Tigre was just what we needed to guard our house in Coqueiros.

We loaded Tigre into the car with us and left the Johnsons' home headed toward São Paulo. Our destination for the night was a town called Queluz, or "What Light!" It was situated in a near-coastal valley on the other side of a large mountain pass. Darkness fell long before we reached the highest part of the mountain, and from there we had only to travel about twenty-five miles to the town. That's when Dad noticed that the brakes were failing. He also noticed that the discharge light was on, and we were almost without electric power. At the mountaintop, Dad cut the engine and got out to inspect the car more closely. Suddenly a streak of bright light shot through the air followed by a deafening crash. I could have sworn a meteorite had just pounded the earth less than a hundred yards from our car. I was scared stiff! I was afraid it might be the end of the world! Maybe Jesus was coming! Maybe we would never make it to the next town and would die! Mother and Dad were silent, and this added to my fear.

It was a clear night and the moon was still shining brightly in the dark sky. There was no way the streak could have been lightning. We were on a narrow, winding dirt road with no ambient light for miles in any direction. And Dad was trying to conserve the car's battery by using the headlights as little as possible. We eased along the road in the pitch dark until eventually it forked off in two directions. None of us could tell which direction would keep us on the main road.

"I think it's this way," Dad said, veering slowly to the right.

After only a short distance, Mother cried out, "Stop, John!"

Dad hit the brakes and cut the engine again. We all got out of the car.

About a foot ahead of us was a precipice, a place where in the past there had been a narrow bridge, but now there was nothing but open air over a steep ravine. This was not the main road after all, but an old deserted route. Mother and Dad knelt down right there in the dirt.

"Thank you, dear Lord in heaven and Dear Jesus above, for sparing our lives this night," Mother prayed, tears wetting her cheeks.

Dad backed up and found the road we should have taken. Still, we didn't have any car lights. We lurched painstakingly along for several miles until we saw a dim light in the distance. By following that light, we eventually arrived in Queluz, a town that simply didn't live up to its name, "What Light!" It hardly had any lights, just the dimmest of bulbs on a few lampposts. By the time we rolled in, midnight was almost upon us.

We were all ravenously hungry but there was nothing open. Even the town's only gas station was closed. Miraculously, we found on the main street an unpainted wooden building with an old wooden sign that said, "Hotel." It looked like it had about six rooms. We were able to wake the owner with a bout of loud knocking, and it turned out that he had one vacancy.

"We'll take it," Dad said, no questions asked.

I helped Tigre get nestled into a cardboard box by my side. The poor dog was at least as hungry as I was. I gave him water and prayed that he would fall asleep quietly. Unfortunately, my prayers were not granted. Tigre did not sleep one wink the entire night. Instead, he started throwing up. Then he began to whimper and cry. Soon after he was seized by a bout of gut-wrenching diarrhea, during which he expelled an unbelievable number of worms. Even when he wasn't crying or heaving, Tigre's little body shook pitifully. I patted his damp head and wept myself. Poor, poor little dog. I was awake with Tigre all night, convinced (and terrified) that he would die before daybreak. Morning finally came, and while Dad went out to find a gas station, I cleaned up the awful mess that Tigre had made. Finally, after finding some coffee and bread for breakfast, we were on our way.

Mother enjoyed recalling the trials and travails of our many journeys. She loved filling in Aunt Henrietta on the challenges we overcame, the terrible roads, the relentless bumps. "You should have seen our trunk fly open," she'd say, "even though it was shut with a key!"

That was the trip during which we lost my electric guitar, which flew out of the trunk on the same dramatic bump, and to go back over those roads was simply impossible with their ruts and crevices. Besides, given the number of people constantly walking that road, it would be a miracle to have found it even if going back had been possible. Mother was just thankful we had another one in the car. "The Lord has helped us arrange something so Grace can play this instrument and continue doing much good," Mother insisted.

In April 1950, Mother wrote to Aunt Henrietta that, "We have made such long hard trips preaching almost every night someplace. The roads are often under construction and the bridges temporary and almost falling apart. On Monday night we almost went into a deep creek. The boards had fallen through a bridge, and we had to go out and fish for them in the creek. There were not enough of them to cover the bridge, so we had to carefully cross on two beams or else we would be in the creek. But the Lord undertook. We are thankful for a daddy with such a steady hand, for we must go over many dangerous places. We could not begin to tell you!"

What Mother didn't make a point of describing to Aunt Henrietta was just how much Dad loved these risky adventures, every minute of them. I can still see his face, flushed with excitement and smiling broadly in utter confidence that God would protect us. I, on the other hand, did not have that faith and was in complete terror when we traveled.

The next day, on the same trip that Mother described to Aunt Henrietta, we had barely started out when the support that holds the car's back springs broke on the road. We were far from any city or house but men were working on the road. Dad got an ax from them and chopped a tree in half, putting the pieces under the car and fastening them by chains. We went on our way in the lopsided car with one side propped up high. Of course people laughed and looked as we went by.

"It broke on us four times," Mother told Aunt Henrietta, "but the last time we were able to buy a two by four in a lumber yard and we got to our destination with three flat tires."

Dad was undeniably resourceful. No matter how broken down the car, no matter how impossible it seemed to repair it, he always found a way. It truly did seem as if God was on his side.

But there were some hardships even Mother could not endure for him. One spring we went to a city in the state of Minas Gerais, just for a Sunday evening service. The minister had a large family and no room for us to stay with him, so he found a hotel for us. Mother entered the room and gasped out loud. A rank odor filled the room, and the beds were haphazardly made with crumpled, dirty sheets—obviously used. When Mother stepped in closer to the bed and pulled back the bottom sheet, revealing the mattress, a swarm of black bugs scurried on its soiled surface. I still remember rows of dark, shiny bugs, scurrying along the mattress seams, one on top of the other.

"John!" Mother yelled. "Look at this! We can't stay here!"

Dad came and looked, raising an eyebrow and then setting his suitcase down with a matter-of-fact thud. "Marguerite," he said, "we can't hurt the pastor's feelings by leaving."

Mother was quick with a reply, quiet and firm. "This is the limit, John. You stay here and Grace and I will move."

I could sense the anger in her voice, and it was the first and only time I recall Mother standing her ground. Dad found us another hotel. He slept that night and the following with the bedbugs, while Mother and I enjoyed our clean and bug-free beds in peace.

Chapter Twenty-Three

A Letter from Virgil Smith

ALL MY LIFE I SUFFERED FROM GUILT. I knew the best guilt verses word for word: "For the wages of sin is death" (Romans, 6:23), or, "Children, obey your parents in everything for this pleases the Lord (Colossians, 3:20). A thing as simple as letting out the braids of my brown hair made me feel horrible. My abdomen would clutch up in fear as I bobbed my head from left to right trying to make sure that no one from church caught a glimpse of my sinful, loose tresses.

Still, no matter how much I suffered for it, I couldn't seem to stop myself from sinning. This was especially true whenever I was in the company of friends. If I wasn't talking to unbelievers, then I was giggling with my girlfriends about boys we liked. And if it wasn't that, it was some other taboo indulgence, like dabbing my cheeks with blusher, or, for that matter, even thinking about dabbing my cheeks with blusher. Vanity itself was sinful whether or not I followed through on the idea. And my social sinning was not limited to the things I did with the friends I made during our travels from town to town.

I found a special friend from Florianópolis to sin with whenever we spent time back in Coqueiros. She was my childhood friend from the

Catholic school, Lygia Ferro. Lygia offered an open door to hell on a regular basis. Lygia's mother sometimes came to our church, but her attendance was irregular and she never became a church member. Lygia and her family were Catholic. While we were living in the United States, her parents had "separated," a euphemistic term that skirted Brazil's legal prohibitions against divorce. This fact also made Mother disapprove of our friendship.

Lygia was tons of fun, and I adored being with her. She had dark brown straight hair, cut short to the shoulders. Her brown eyes and fair complexion added to her beauty. She talked incessantly and always came up with fun things to do. She lived at the very end of the Praia da Saudades, in front of the Catholic Church. She took me often to their private yacht club, which was only a few yards behind her house. We would take one of the small sailboats and cruised the Praia da Saudades. She was an excellent sailor, yet I insisted we stay close to land. We swam at the beach near her house. This was against my parents' rules, since it was a public beach, but I was careful to never mention it. Lygia and I spent time with some of her other friends, who soon became my friends, and none of them were members of the Assemblies of God Church. Again, I hid this detail from my parents. At the same time, I lived in fear that church members were lurking behind every corner, which often turned out to be true. I knew that watchful members were always ready to observe my sinful ways and report my crimes to the congregation—and my parents—at the next communion.

Communion services were monthly events held right before the Sunday night service. Communion was "closed," which meant it was for members only, and even then, only for members in good standing. Before communion was delivered, the communion leader asked if there was anyone present who had something to confess, or if there was a member who felt that another member should not be allowed to partake. Most often, this unleashed a fiery session of accusation and judgment. And generally speaking, members, especially those who felt certain that they were in good standing, seemed to enjoy the process. This was their chance to spill the beans on anyone who happened to be spotted heading into a movie theater, or talking to a nonmember, or—worst of all—talking to a member of the opposite sex for the sake of courtship or flirtation. Courtship rules were very strict and even when both members were of the same faith, they could not be alone; their courtship had to be chaperoned at all times.

These sessions took on the air of a courtroom, with the accused defending themselves against their accusers and trying to plead their innocence to the congregation at large. Church leaders explained with pride that this was how the early Christian church conducted itself and safeguarded the souls of followers. I hated these sessions, and did everything I could to avoid them. I lived in dread of being accused, since I was so often engaged in sinning.

Dear Jesus, I prayed, *please forgive me for all of my sinning. I know it is wrong and I am trying to do better. Sort of. It might take me a while to learn how to stop being friends with unbelievers. Please be patient with me. Please don't let Mother and Dad find out.* I prayed constantly. No amount of prayer or guilt, however, kept me from repeating my sins.

In May of 1950, right after I had turned sixteen, I received a warning letter from an American missionary named Virgil Smith. Missionary Smith was at least as charismatic as my father. He was known as a handsome man, forty-six years old, and highly intelligent. He'd trained as a dentist in the United States before becoming an Assemblies of God missionary. Missionary Smith's wife, Ramona, was as beautiful as he was handsome, but was tragically crippled by a long and deadly battle with Parkinson's disease. Missionary Smith had moved to the town of Joinville in Santa Catarina in June of 1941 and was a highly respected and very successful preacher, with a church membership of more than a thousand.

How this very busy preacher found time to single out one sixteen-year-old girl in another town, I couldn't fathom.

Missionary Smith's letter to me was apparently prompted by a complaint he had received from one of his church members about a young girl named Dulcinea. It seemed that Dulcinea was having a relationship with a boy who was not a member of the church. The tattletale member and Missionary Smith both remembered that Dulcinea and I had been good friends during my stays in Joinville. Undoubtedly, they said, I was the one who had influenced Dulcinea to sin. Virgil Smith's long letter was a stern warning about how I must immediately change my ways and denounce the "wickedness of flesh" that I was promoting among my peers.

"Have nothing to do with 'puppy love'!" he wrote. "It is not of God. No good comes out of it, but much evil. We do not permit it in Santa Catarina. It is considered sin by the leaders of this work." He warned me against trying to change the practice of the Brazilian churches, and reminded me that I really wasn't "old enough to take on such a responsible job." He cautioned me to let all my influence be for obedience, and to "not tell the young people about different customs in U.S. churches. They will not understand, and it will only leave them confused."

He then kindly enumerated, just in case I was unclear, the Official Instructions of the Churches in Santa Catarina:

- Courtship and dates are permissible for those who intend to get married and are of sufficient age. All courtship just for pastime is sinful.
- All dating must be in the presence of chaperones.
- All "petting" is considered carnal and sinful.
- All love affairs with unbelievers are considered sinful, and tantamount to forsaking God.
- Those who practice these things are considered rebellious and therefore subject to exclusion from the church.
- None of this prohibits friendly conversation between the young people of both sexes. There is clearly a difference between wholesome conversation and courtship. Wholesome conversations need not be in secret. There need not be dates set for wholesome conversation.

These rules were getting harder and harder for me to swallow. I tried, and sometimes I really believed the rules were just and true, but then, before I knew it, I'd be fighting again to reconcile the image of a loving God with the threat of a punitive one. I tried to talk to Dad about it. I could tell from his hedging that he didn't fully buy into Missionary Smith's admonitions, but he wouldn't come right out and say so.

Dad and I seldom spoke to each other in English and we had this conversation in Portuguese. I said, "Dad, what do you think of this letter from Brother Virgil? I didn't do anything wrong."

Dad did not look at me, but kept his head lowered and said, "Gracie, you know Brother Virgil means well. He is concerned about your friend, Dulcinea."

I replied, "But Daddy, she lied. I never talked to her about America."

His reply was, "Well, Gracie, I think you should answer him, don't make excuses, but thank him for caring about you."

I was furious at Dad's suggestion, and said, "I won't write to him. I have nothing to feel sorry for, and I know he won't believe me, so why bother to write? Besides, if I did something wrong I should ask Jesus to forgive me."

I stormed out of the room and we never talked about it again. However, knowing my dad, I am sure he wrote a letter to Missionary Smith apologizing for me.

His foremost obligation was to ally himself with the church he served, and no amount of probing from his distraught daughter could convince him otherwise.

Chapter Twenty-Four

Stella

I N BRAZIL there was a one year course of study called *Curso 91* that replaced a high school education. Students applied their efforts to thirteen academic subjects, and at the end of the year, they took rigorous oral and written exams. Those who passed were qualified to enter the university. Thanks to *Curso 91,* my cousin John Lemos was able to attend Bible school in America. Dad had promised John while he lived with us in 1945 that if he passed *Curso 91,* he'd send him to an American Bible school, and John met the challenge.

I hadn't attended school since our return to Brazil in December of 1949, and by 1951, I was feeling some urgency to resume my studies. I wanted to go to college, and I knew I needed more schooling to make that happen. My parents, on the other hand, were largely unconcerned with my educational status. They figured I might eventually marry a minister or a missionary, and that a college education just wasn't all that important for my future. What they really wanted me to do was to go to Bible school back in Springfield, Missouri, at the Assemblies of God headquarters. That's where I'd be most likely to meet a good missionary husband.

But I wanted nothing of the sort. I had dreams of a career of my own, and even more, I had a secret hope of becoming a doctor. Stella had a Brazilian cousin who was a successful woman doctor, and the mere thought of it filled me with admiration and a touch of envy. I desperately wanted to do the same.

Stella faced her own educational challenges. In Urubici, there was no high school. Latvians in the area and wealthy ranchers and lumber lords had the tradition of sending their children to other cities for high school. Education was very important for these Brazilians, and Stella's parents definitely wanted her to continue her studies. All they needed was to decide on a school and a living arrangement for her. It didn't take me long to come up with the idea of Stella living with us for a year to attend *Curso 91* with me. Since the classes were at night, Mother and Dad agreed that it would actually be safer if I had someone with me for the bus ride home. So in February of 1951, with my parents' reluctant consent, Stella moved in with us and we registered for *Curso 91*. By March, we were attending our classes.

In my mind, nothing could have been a better solution for either of us. Stella was everything I wanted to be—beautiful, gregarious, independent, and outrageously fun. She filled our shared bedroom with the smell of lemons and salt and desire, and she readily encouraged my late night whispers of uncertainty. Before long, I called her my Stellóca, and she called me her Graçóca; we loved each other dearly. These endings to our names do not have a direct translation to English, but it is a way of adding endearment to a name.

Stella loved to read poetry, philosophy, novels, indeed, any literature she could find. She shared a lot of this with me. I was only allowed to read my school books and church papers, and, of course, the Bible. So Stella's contraband reading material opened all kinds of ideas and questions for me.

Our academic schedule was truly demanding. We studied all day long for our evening courses. Five nights a week we sat through long and difficult classes. On Saturdays, we worked with a private tutors for help with the most arduous subjects.

Somehow we still found time to sin. With Stella, I congregated with unbelievers in restaurants and clubs. I made up my face and flirted with boys. In Brazil flirting is a common social game. It involved holding a gaze, eye to eye, longer than usual. Often the flirting was carried out in restaurants, at school, at church, or with passersby. And I listened to fiery Brazilian music, especially the sinful samba. We even managed to do much of our studying on our private beach. This habit brought out a stubborn constellation of freckles on Stella's face, the one aspect of her appearance that she didn't like. She was desperate to get rid of the freckles, and her theory was that with more sun, her face would tan completely, and the freckles would merge together and disappear. It was a theory proved dramatically wrong. The more time we spent in the sun, the larger and more distinct Stella's freckles became. She tried any new treatment she could get her hands on to lighten the freckles, but most of the creams just burnt her face without improving the freckles one iota.

"Stellóca," I said, "your freckles are beauty marks."

"Yes," she answered, "because they are mine and not on your face."

Stella convinced me once to take a trip with her to the other side of Florianópolis—the undeveloped side. It was December 1951, just before Christmas, and we took a bus to the scarcely inhabited beaches of the far side. We stayed with Lourdes, my friend from the Florianópolis church. Her family's home was a simple shack, made of wood siding with gaps so large that the sun shone in cheerful stripes across the dirt floor. I took along my accordion, because I was expected to lead services, which I dutifully did. The first night, as soon as I started to play, the house filled with people. I began to sing, and Stella sang with me in her lovely soprano voice. Eventually, the congregants sang the chorus:

My heart is full of Your great love
My heart overflows with Your praise
My heart I consecrate only to my Master
For His praise, for His praise.

I read from the Bible and said a few words, and then sang again. The people enjoyed these simple services, and I was happy to offer them each night of our stay. But I was a little embarrassed that I had to do it.

"Your services are better than the ones in town," Stella offered generously.

During the day, Stella and I went to the beach and swam in the ocean, with not another soul in sight. We ate hard manioc biscuits and *pirão de farinha* (a manioc root flour similar to sawdust that is made into a paste) and fresh fish. By the end of the week, we were starving, literally. With the only money we had—ten cents that I had brought—we bought a large bunch of fresh cut bananas from a local vendor and sat on the beach to devour them one by one. Stella's freckles were a dark brown; both of us were tanned and salty-skinned from constant swimming and walking the beach. A wind blew across the water from the west, and the sun was just brushing the edge of the horizon. Perfect, unspoiled happiness was mine, for that one endless moment.

Stella and I found other ways to get away together. Whenever we had a holiday from school, we went to Urubici and stayed with Stella's parents. Often our friend Yvonne came along—another beautiful girl, who was tall and slender, with straight blond hair and sparkling blue eyes. Sometimes I couldn't understand how I, with my plain face and "big bones," my long braids and my dark dresses, overweight, and with no makeup, could fit in with such pretty friends. Yvonne's father owned a trucking company, and he was always willing to let us hitch a ride to Urubici with one of his drivers. Often, Yvonne tagged along with us for as long as her Catholic school schedule allowed. Our winter breaks that year fell at the same time, and we spent three weeks together in Urubici. It was a vacation soaked in sin. First off, Yvonne was Catholic, and being in her company was in itself an endangerment to my soul. The situation was irresistible. We stayed at a truly glorious ranch with horseback riding and picnics every afternoon. When it rained, we listened to music in the house. We even danced. This would have been an absolute scandal if anyone had seen us and reported it to the church.

Often in Urubici, I woke up to the sound of some young man outside our window, playing the guitar and singing a love song. Serenades were often for Thalia, Stella's young sister. She was beautiful, with dishwater blond curly hair, blue eyes, and a raspy, sexy sounding voice when she spoke. Many of the local young men were interested in her. It was fun to hear the singing, with so much sincerity. One of the songs commonly sung was *"Cada vez te quero mais"* or in English, "Each time I want you more."

> I want to confess softly
> Near your ear my dear woman
> Although I suffer for wanting you
> I will cultivate your love my whole life
> In love I had suffering
> And sometimes it transforms itself in an ideal adventure
> For this reason my love
> I swear with fervor
> Each time I want you more.

Everyone knew about these serenades, and local church members were horrified by the practice. Every time my friends and I ventured into Urubici, the local minister's wife stopped me in the street, wagged her finger and let me know she'd heard this or that about our shenanigans on the ranch. When she'd finished listing the latest gossip about all of my possible sins, she'd say, "I'm warning you! You stay away from that Stella and her sister Thalia. And all of their friends, for that matter."

The truth was, more than anything, I wanted to fit in with Stella and her friends. I felt left out enough, simply by virtue of my church obligations.

Stella grew up attending the Baptist church in Urubici with her mother, and while she believed in God, she had no patience for the dogma—the "thou shall nots" of her own Baptist church, let alone the much more restrictive Assemblies of God. Once she moved into our house, Stella and I spent hours talking about what we really believed about God. Those whispered conversations, in the darkness of our bedroom, were important to me—and more sinful—than all of the socializing and swimming and dancing and flirting we ever did. Those conversations gave me the courage to ask questions that scared me to death.

"Stella," I asked, "do you think God is loving and forgiving or punishing?" It was the one question to which I most needed an answer.

Stella was silent for a few minutes and then she said, "Graçóca, I believe we are the ones that punish ourselves. I think God is a loving God and wants the best for us. For instance, in the Bible it says: 'The wages of sin is death, but the gift of God is eternal Life through Jesus Christ our Lord (Romans 6:23).' I think that if we sin, for instance, and do not take care of our bodies, which God says is His temple, we will suffer pain, even death."

"What do you mean?" I asked.

Stella continued. "Like not eating the right foods, eating too much and becoming fat, getting drunk, not getting enough sleep, not taking care of our bodies, then if we become sick or even die, that is our fault, not God's."

I thought about this for a long time, and then said, "I agree with you, if someone is hateful, beats his children, is unkind to others, lies, cheats, that will also come back to haunt him. His life will be miserable, or some will say, 'a hell on earth.'"

"Yes, that's it; I don't believe there is a white-bearded old man with a lightning rod ready to strike you every time you do something wrong," Stella said.

"And what does it mean to be a Christian? Do you think our friends are doomed to hell because they are Catholic?" I asked.

"I don't believe it for a minute," Stella said. "I think being a Christian is a very personal thing. Our friends are not doomed to hell because they may think differently than we do. We can not tell what is really in their hearts, only God can."

For the first time, I was admitting, out loud, my thoughts and doubts about my parents' teaching. Stella didn't have the answers, but she was always willing to listen and respond to my questions, and that was enough at the time. In one way, my father was right when he warned me over and over about associating with "unbelievers." There was a problem with having friends who didn't believe as he did. It caused doubts, and having doubts caused me to seriously question all of Dad's teachings. Stella cheerfully encouraged my questions and defiance of the Assemblies of God dogma.

Stella was always polite and respectful toward my parents, but she didn't call them Sister and Brother. Instead, she called my mother *Dona Margarida* and my father *Seu Kolenda*. They were willing to accept this since they knew Stella was Baptist. *Dona* means Mrs. in Portuguese; it is proper to call any person by their first name, and *Seu* is short for *Senhor* or Mister in English. I don't know why everyone called Dad by his last name. Perhaps it was because John is so common and Kolenda was an easy name for Brazilians to pronounce. No one ever called him *Seu* João, which would have been socially proper.

Stella was tolerant of Mother's preaching, despite her disagreements with Assemblies of God dogma. Mother did her best to show Stella love in her own way, especially for her physical ailments. Stella had a disturbing tendency to turn black and blue at the slightest bump. Worse, she would hemorrhage every month when she got her period. The hemorrhaging was like nothing I had ever seen. After four or five days of massive bleeding each month, Stella would be left weak and pale as milk. Mom forced her to consume huge quantities of green vegetables and anything else she believed contained iron. Stella obeyed dutifully.

As determined as Mother was to save Stella's health, she was equally determined to save Stella's soul. "Stella," Mother would say, "you should go to church more; it would make me so happy if you gave your heart to the Lord. You know He is coming soon, and I want you to be ready."

Stella couldn't bring herself to do it. She excused herself from services during the week, to study, and she spent most weekends with our friend Yvonne, or any one of her other seemingly endless supply of friends. We could not walk a block in Florianópolis without being stopped to talk to a friend of Stella's. I envied her gregarious personality. Stella attracted friends like moths to a flame. She knew many people our age that came from Urubici to study in Florianópolis, or for dental or medical needs. At school, she made friends much faster than I did. I felt jealous of them all, and especially jealous of Yvonne. I was sure Stella liked her better than she liked me. Every month at communion, Stella's name would be brought up as one of my many sinful friends. Even her curly hair was a problem. Everyone knew she had acquired it scandalously through the use of a permanent wave. That was enough to damn her to hell.

My Sunday obligations started at nine and lasted until noon at the chapel on our property, and picked up again at five in the afternoon, for outdoor service at the main park in Florianópolis. It was a stately park, with a huge century-old fig tree in its center. The tree's branches arched out overhead for fifteen feet in each direction, and were supported by tall wooden posts. Beneath these branches were scattered benches. On Sunday afternoons, the whole park filled with people. I played the accordion for these services since there were no electrical outlets for my guitar, and I would also sing. A Brazilian minister or one of my cousins would give a short talk and encourage people to attend our church service that evening. All the while, part of me felt embarrassed doing this. My friends at school often asked me about it and sometimes promised to come and see me, which I secretly dreaded. It just made me feel more like an outsider.

Chapter Twenty-Five

The Last Samba

NEVER IN MY LIFE had I been allowed to listen to the radio, except for BBC news as it filtered through my bedroom wall from Dad's shortwave radio. We never owned a record player and the entire concept of music other than church songs was strictly taboo. I was as surprised as anyone when I fell in love with Brazilian music.

Whenever I went into town, I reveled in the strong Latin beat of the music that played in the stores. I surreptitiously swayed my hips, just for the thrill of it. During Carnival, four days every year before Ash Wednesday, the delicious current of the samba dominated the local music scene. In fact, Carnival in Brazil was such a major holiday that the music usually started on New Year's Eve, which the locals called, *O Grito de Carnaval,* the "Yell of Carnival." During this time in the town—the stores, the streets, the parks—music was loud and constant. I couldn't help but get swept up in it. Everyone danced through the streets to the rhythmic beat of those infectious melodies. Given all the time I spent in Florianópolis, I heard this music plenty. Between my classes, tutoring, and church, I went to town every day. And then I had my social life with Stella, Yvonne and our other friends. During the year Stella and I spent in *Curso 91,* she and I spent countless hours listening to the radio at Yvonne's house, and dancing the samba around her living room.

"Such a disgrace," Mother warned whenever she sensed my enjoyment of music in Florianópolis. "It breaks my heart that your friends are such sinners. I pray every night that you will find friends who are believers."

"The devil's music won't lift you up," my father reminded me. "Close your ears to it and lock your heart against temptation."

But no matter how I tried, I couldn't manage to feel sinful when I listened to the samba. All I felt was joy. Was all joy sinful?

LUIZ LOVED SAMBA, too. He loved excitement, women, and all things American. Stella and I met Luiz Fernando Sabino through our friend Alda Jacinto, a night club singer who performed on the radio every week. Alda's father, Mr. Jacinto, was a teller at the Florianópolis post office, where we went to pick up our mail.

"My daughter, she is studying English," he told me one day, "and she would love to meet you if you would agree to it."

I did agree, happily, and soon Stella and I became fast friends with the lovely Alda, who was a willowy and beautiful girl of mixed French and African descent. She was eighteen years old and quite famous around our parts, although of course I'd never heard of her, since I was not allowed to listen to the radio. Alda even sang American songs, which made her all the more glamorous. She was full of energy and enthusiasm and we liked to be with her. She invited us one day to go to the radio station where she sang, and we instantly agreed.

Luiz was the leader of Alda's band—a darkly handsome charmer with enough sex appeal for at least three men. Luiz was eighteen going on thirty when it came to sophistication. He dreamed of one day living in America, and was obsessed with movies, fashion, cowboys, and especially American music. His band played songs like, "Dance Ballerina, Dance," and "When They Begin the Beguine," and "I'm in the Mood for Love" and kept the girls transfixed. Luiz was an incredible musician. He played the piano for each singer as if there were no other singer in the world, and no voice more beautiful.

Stella and I went to Luiz's house most Saturday afternoons, and it was always full of other kids, including Paulo—Luiz's younger brother—and loads of amateur musicians. Luiz's parents, *Dona* Orita and *Seu* Arnoldo, were warm and inviting and made everyone feel welcome. Sometimes Luiz took his father's car and we'd go to our church to pick up my Hawaiian guitar. I knew where the key to the church's front door was hidden, and was more than willing to sneak into the church when it made Luiz so happy. My guitar fascinated him because it was so different. Later on, when the afternoon wound down, Luiz brought me back to the church and I used the hidden key to sneak back in with my guitar. Mother never said a word about it, and I prayed it was because she didn't know.

Luiz was definitely "the man about town." Everyone knew Luiz because of his radio shows and his presence at the local dances. No one was more outgoing than Luiz, with his big smile and fast talk. Whenever I bumped into him in Florianópolis, he was surrounded by young people—boys and lots and lots of girls.

I would have loved to be one of Luiz's girlfriends. But it was absolutely outside the realm of possibility. Luiz was a sinner in every sense of my parents' beliefs. A dance band leader was bad enough, but he also smoked, drank beer, was not religious in any way, and had Catholic parents. There was no chance. On his side of the fence, I now realize I was equally out of the question.

"Grace," he said to me, years later, "do you remember what you looked like, with no makeup, *trancinhas* (braids), and all those long dark dresses? I liked you as a friend but could never have imagined romance."

I could have been broken hearted that I wasn't considered one of Luiz's pretty girls, but I chose instead to revel in friendship and excitement. I almost considered Luiz like the brother I never had.

Some days, I'd invite Luiz back to our house. This was risky given his smoking. That was one thing my parents simply could not know, not ever. I explained to Luiz that if my parents found out he smoked, I would be forbidden to have anything further to do with him. He was surprisingly careful, and as far as I could tell, my parents never did find out. Or at least, Mother never found out. Dad was gone so much that he never even met Luiz. If he had, he would surely have made Luiz a goner. Dad would have immediately seen right through Luiz's gentlemanly ways to the fiery young man about town. Mother, on the other hand, found Luiz perplexing. He was the epitome of politeness and manners, and he enjoyed playing Mother's piano. Stella and I sang along. But never when Mother was around.

"He's such a nice boy," she would say. "And yet, he's such a sinner." She said this with the most pained expression. "Grace," she'd lament, "it just breaks my heart to see you with such sinful friends."

Luiz treated Mother respectfully, so while she wished I wouldn't spend time with him, she never outright forbade it.

Often, Luiz threatened to serenade Stella and me late at night. "I'll come to your front door," he'd say, "and play for you, just three or four songs. I'll bring the whole band with me. Please, this once."

I made Luiz swear on his life not to do this foolish thing. I knew it would be a horrible embarrassment to my parents, the end of my membership in their church, and maybe worst of all, the absolute death knell for my friendship with Luiz. This was all very difficult for him to understand, but out of sympathy for me, he didn't follow through on his serenade threat.

Stella and I spent countless afternoons with Luiz at the radio station and at his house. I never lied to Mom—I always told her where we were going. I couldn't see the first thing wrong with this friendship. What I did see was how exciting it was, how blessedly different from just studying and going to church.

I FELT JUST as defensive about my friendship with Stella. Although Mother raised her eyebrows and grunted disapprovingly whenever the topic of Stella's hair, religion, or social life came up—and Mother made sure it came up often—I didn't believe that there was an ounce of wickedness in my sunny friend. To the contrary, I always envied Stella for her friendliness and constant warmth. I struggled against my own reserved nature, and hated the way I seldom was the first person to initiate a conversation, whereas Stella could easily talk with people from all walks of life. Stella, unlike Mother, seemed immune to the human inclination to judge others. For example, when we rode home from school at night, there was often a very beautiful young lady on board, always sitting alone. Soon it became clear that this woman was being intentionally shunned by the other passengers, none of whom would so much as speak to her. Finally one day Stella plopped down in the open seat next to the woman and struck up a conversation. The woman's name was Maria, Stella later told me, and she was the mother of two little boys. Her husband had abandoned her a few months back but since divorce was illegal, she was still married. Prostitution, on the other hand, was legal. "That's how that poor lady is feeding herself and her boys," Stella told me, shaking her short curls in frustration.

I was shocked to hear about Maria, because she was so young and so respectable looking. She dressed nicely in simple, homemade clothes that were modest, not provocative. She was not overly made up, and her demeanor was shy, not flamboyant. She just didn't match the profile of the usual Florianópolis prostitute. Probably she worked the day shift at one of the local brothels, and tried to hide her line of work by dressing like an everyday professional. But keeping a secret was no more possible for Maria than for me, or anyone else in Florianópolis. The people of Coqueiros knew her story, and no one wanted to be seen with her. Prostitution was legal, but dirty. Stella single-mindedly ignored this unwritten social code and made a point of befriending Maria and letting everyone know it. Her respect for the humanity of another looked to me like courage, not sin. Mother, of course, would vehemently disagree.

Chapter Twenty-Six

Meeting Dr. Jair

S TELLA AND I were returning from our classes—in our usual bubble of girl talk and giggles—when we ran into our dentist's son. What a sight for sore eyes he was! We adored Sylvio. But we were surprised to see him in town in the middle of the school year, since he was attending his first year of dental school in Curitiba, in the neighboring state of Parana. Stella and I waved our arms above our heads and called, "Sylvio! Sylvio!" until he broke into a laugh and ran the rest of the distance to meet us.

"Graça," he said as he fell into a walk beside us, "there's someone I am anxious for you to meet. He just got here from New York."

"How mysterious," teased Stella, tossing her curly hair. Stella always knew just how to be playful and harmlessly flirtatious.

"We would love to meet your friend," I said without a moment's hesitation. "How about tomorrow evening before we go to our school, about six o'clock?"

Quickly it was settled. We'd meet on the central park, under the ancient, massive fig tree. The tree was a prominent, easy to find landmark, and its branches provided shelter and shade for the town's most common meeting place.

Stella and I arrived ten minutes early. I smoothed my skirt and pushed my hair behind my ears. "Don't fidget, Grace," Stella scolded. "You don't want to look nervous." She sat down on a bench near the tree's base and motioned for me to sit beside her. I perched on the very edge of the bench and looked upward at the fig leaves gently rustling above us.

And then at exactly six o'clock, Sylvio strode into view. Walking beside him was a very handsome man. At least six feet tall and slender, this gentleman was well dressed in tan slacks and an elegant, multicolored silk shirt. His back was straight and broad, and everything about him exuded confidence and status.

"Here they are," Sylvio said brightly as we stood to greet him. "Grace, Stella, I would like you to meet the friend I spoke to you about."

I extended my hand and said, "Pleased to meet you, I'm Graça Kolenda."

Sylvio's friend accepted my hand and shook it firmly. "*Igualmente,* Dr. Jair Cardoso," he said, which means simply, "Same for me, Dr. Jair Cardoso." Brazilian custom demands a formal greeting, always in this manner, with each individual offering his or her name and a handshake. Dr. Jair and Stella repeated the ritual.

Dr. Jair, as it turned out, was a dentist. He had graduated from dental school two years earlier and was sharing an office with his father, who was also a dentist. He had earned a six-month internship in a well-respected New York clinic, but had abandoned the internship three months early.

When Stella and I asked why, the pleasantries faded away and Dr. Jair took the conversation abruptly in another direction. "I don't want to insult you personally, Graça, but I hate America and the people of New York. I have never had such terrible treatment in my life."

"But why? What happened?" I asked, embarrassed suddenly for my nation of origin.

"It's a long story, but it started the minute I arrived at the hotel I had booked well in advance," Dr. Jair said, his face contracting with anger.

"When I went to check in, they claimed to have lost my booking, and insisted they were full. They sent me to an inferior hotel where all the other guests were black, and all of the staff, as well. Not another white person was to be seen anywhere. Finally, I understood. They were treating me as if I were black. And so did everyone else, throughout my stay. Restaurant hosts seated me in the darkest, farthest corners, if they seated me at all. Everyone I met was distant and scornful. It was the worst experience of my life."

What could I say? I couldn't think of a thing that would make things right. Stella looked gray. "I'm sorry that happened to you," she said, "but I'm sure all Americans, even all New Yorkers, are not like that."

"I wish that were true," Dr. Jair said quietly, his eyes flashing. "But you are wrong. I didn't meet a single person who proved different. You don't know what it is like to be so humiliated."

Nothing was going to set this meeting right, and Sylvio looked as mortified as I felt. "So sorry," he said, taking his friend by the elbow. "Unless we leave now, Dr. Jair and I will be late for our appointment." With another series of handshakes, they were gone.

I couldn't shake off the shame and embarrassment of Dr. Jair's humiliation in America, and later that evening, after class, Stella and I lay in the dark, reliving the awkward meeting and analyzing what happened. "What I don't understand," I told Stella, "is how can Dr. Jair be considered black? Would you ever in a million years have considered him black?"

"Of course not," said Stella. "But I've never lived in America. You tell me, from what you know. How could Dr. Jair be mistaken for black?"

I was mystified. In Coquerios, most of my friends were of mixed race. Some had dark skin and some had lighter skin, like mine. Most had brown eyes, but some had blue or green. The color and texture of hair, even in the same family, varied from straight and dark brown to blond, and some had course kinky hair, as well. Especially in the South of Brazil, where there were large numbers of European immigrants, there was even more variety in colors of hair and skin. But at the end of the day, Brazilians considered all these people white—every last one of them. And so it never entered my mind that my childhood friends, or someone like Dr. Jair, would be considered black.

This all-encompassing attitude toward what constituted "white" was rooted in the enormity of the slave trade in Brazil—one of the largest importers of slaves in the world. Depending on which historian you believe, anywhere from 3.6 million to 4.5 million slaves flowed into Brazil from about 1550 on, and these newcomers changed the very nature of Brazil forever.

Unlike in the United States, slaves in Brazil were allowed and even encouraged to speak their native African languages and carry on with other cultural traditions including religion, food, arts, drums and music. They were also encouraged to intermarry with the Indians, Portuguese and other settlers. All of this led to the birth of some extremely unique cultural events known only in Brazil. For instance, the religion *"Condomble"* combines African beliefs and the Roman Catholic religion. Known by several other names (*Macumba, Quimbanda, Umbanda,* etc.) in various other regions, *Condomble* is popular in the large cities, like Recife, Salvador, and Rio de Janeiro. Even in Florianópolis, the Macumba congregation took to the sea on New Year's Eve, dressed all in white and hauling make-shift boats filled with flowers to the rocky beaches, where they were then pushed out into the ocean. People also threw flowers on the ocean, in honor of *"Iemanja,"* the goddess of the sea. And *"Capoeira"* is a joyful celebration of dance, sports, play, all set to the rhythms of African music. Even Brazil's beloved samba dance and samba music come from Africa.

The Brazilian slaves were freed in 1888, but the years of constant import left Brazil with the second largest black population in the world, second only to Nigeria. Brazilian leaders became concerned about bolstering the white minority, and from 1880 until the 1920s they encouraged the immigration of Europeans in an effort to "whiten" the population. About five million Europeans immigrated to Brazil, mainly to the south. My grandfather and father were among those who settled in Rio Grande do Sul. Today's Brazilians are a mixture of Portuguese, Italian, German, Spanish, Japanese, Arab, African and indigenous people.

Modern Brazilians, when asked about racism in Brazil, insist that there is none. Ask a Brazilian if he's prejudiced, and he'll tell you no, ninety-eight percent of the time. Ask if he knows someone who's prejudiced, though, and he'll tell you yes, ninety-eight percent of the time. Whatever the case, prejudice in Brazil is different from American racism.

In the United States, one drop of black blood makes you black, and therefore subject to racism. But Brazilians experience their cultural identity differently. Brazilian sociologist and writer Gilberto Frayre described Brazilians in his 1936 novel, *Casa Grande de Senzala*, this way:

"Every Brazilian, even the light skinned, fair-haired one, carries about with him in his soul, when in the soul and body alike, the shadow, or even birth mark, of the aborigine or the negro, the influence of the African."

The reality is that "brown" is Brazil's dominant race, and there's little or no tension between blacks, browns, and whites based on color. Brazilian prejudice is mostly based on social and cultural standing—which is where the "catch 22" lies. Blacks live mostly in the slums with inferior schools, and they often don't complete their education because they have to help the family make a living. They tend to fail the entrance exams for universities and come in last in the competition for higher paying jobs. And generation after generation, they pass along the legacy of poverty with its poor jobs, poor health, and poor housing in the slums on the outskirts of large cities.

Dr. Jair came from Florianópolis's upper middle class. As the son of a dentist, he attended the city's best schools and then the best dental school in the neighboring state. As far as Stella and I could figure, the only African characteristic Dr. Jair had was his course, kinky hair. I guess in the United States that was enough to define him as an inferior being.

In the dark of our room on that humid night, Stella and I drifted to sleep on the fitful energy of dismay for a world in which the right to dignity can be so easily withdrawn, on a basis as frivolous as the texture of your hair.

Chapter Twenty-Seven

Divine Betrayal

DURING OUR LAST THREE YEARS in Brazil, Aunt Martha and Uncle Rodrigo lived with us along with their two youngest sons, Rudolfo and Edison. Neither of these boys went to school. Edison spent a lot of time going from place to place, visiting and staying long periods of time with his other siblings and their families. When he was home with us, he helped his parents with their various chores. Edison and I were friendly but in some ways our lives had too little in common for us to really spend much time together. For my part, I had Stella and a constant focus on my studies to keep me busy.

But once in a while, Edison and I worked together in the garden. I loved having a flower garden, and our house in Coqueiros had a beautiful one that was started by Albert Widmer. The garden was designed as a large rectangle, surrounded by a three-foot wide path. Outside the path there was another small area with shrubs and flowers. The shrubs were tropical plants, low to the ground palm-tree like plants. The flowers were multi colored: red, pink, purple and white. There were also large rose bushes. It was truly a beautiful garden, but it also took a lot of work. Dorothy and I did our best to keep it flourishing. Dorothy was a much better gardener than I ever was. But when I came back to Brazil the second time, I found myself in charge of the flowers. Since I did love them so, I certainly didn't want to let them down through neglect or ineptitude. I was afraid to work in the garden alone because of the snakes. Often, as I entered the garden gate, I'd see snakes slithering away through the underbrush. So whenever they were around, Edison and Rudolfo helped me. When my cousins weren't available, I'd hire a neighbor boy to help me.

One sweaty afternoon when the air was more still than usual and the quiet settled around our yard like a blanket, Edison and I were working together in the front garden, trimming a large flowering plant similar to a poinsettia. The plant was quite neglected and badly overgrown, spreading into the small veranda of our house. It was becoming a nuisance for Dad, who liked to hang a hammock across the veranda whenever he was home. There, suspended above the porch in a sling of mesh fabric, he could relax and enjoy a peaceful, open-air nap after lunch. But now, the veranda was half covered with this bright red flowering tree. Edison and I worked hard, cutting branches several at a time and carrying them away.

We were almost finished when all at once I spotted it. High up toward the top of the tree, buried in the foliage, it appeared.

"Edison!" I yelled. "Jump fast! Don't ask questions!"

Edison leapt backward, and just as he snatched his hand away, a large coral snake attacked. The viper came within inches of striking my cousin's hand. Edison started shaking the branch, and the snake tumbled through the air onto the wooden floorboards of the veranda. The only way from the yard where we stood onto the veranda was through the house, so Edison sped as fast as he could, flailing his hoe, from the garden and through the house out onto the veranda where he mercilessly killed his attacker.

But both Edison and I knew that coral snakes often came in pairs. Warily, we made our way back to the garden. I was not as brave as Edison. He went near the tree first, and I reluctantly followed him. We both started at the top, examining every single branch. My heart beat wildly and the sweat on my brow and under my arms was not just due to the heat. Finally, Edison spotted the second snake. It was in the same area we had trimmed, coiling its way down the tree. We stepped back and waited for it to get to the ground, and then Edison killed it with the same hoe he'd used to strike the first one. It took so long for them to die, or at least it seemed that way. So pretty, they were, even wounded, their colorful stripes glistened in the sun as they wiggled along before finally they stopped and were very, very still.

"Dead," said Edison. "Totally dead."

RUDOLFO was around a lot more than Edison, especially during our last two years in Brazil. Dad let Rudolfo use our car to make money providing taxi services in Florianópolis. By this time, Dad tended to do his traveling by airplane outside the state of Santa Catarina. Within the state of Santa Catarina, Dad took the train and sometimes the bus. Driving Dad's car as a taxi provided a wonderful way for Rodulfo to make a living, and also to support his parents financially. Offering up his car was a sacrifice Dad didn't mind making; he was always willing to forego personal comfort and convenience to help his family. Besides, traveling by car in Brazil was still not easy because of the lack of paved highways. Traversing the region's network of terrible dirt and gravel roads was a hassle that even Dad didn't relish, even if he did enjoy the adventure of risk.

Rudolfo was always ready to help in the garden, and one afternoon when he was trimming a cactus-like plant we had a good scare. "I felt a snake in there," he said, jumping back. He grabbed a shovel and started poking under the plant, and sure enough, out slid a coral snake. Rudolfo swung the shovel, his biceps tensing under his brown skin, and brought the metal down on the snake, killing it immediately. Carefully, alertly, electric with fear, we looked for a second snake. Somewhere in the shadows it must be lurking, just waiting to avenge the death of its partner. And soon enough it emerged, only to meet the ruthless end of Rudolfo's shovel.

One Saturday Rudolfo was rotating the tires of our car, and had the whole vehicle raised up on the jack stand. Someone came tearing down our road yelling for help. "I've been bitten by a jararaca! I've been bitten by a snake!" Within seconds Rudolfo had the car on the ground and the hysterical neighbor loaded into the front seat. They went speeding off to the hospital, a huge cloud of dust rising on the road behind them. I stood and watched, thinking of the poor man's leg, bloated to twice its normal size. Would he live? Rudolfo returned in a couple of hours and said the man would be okay, as they'd given him the antidote in time.

Rudolfo and I became close friends. He was protective and looked out for Stella and me whenever he could. I specifically remember one occasion when I mentioned to Rudolfo that I thought Richard La Martini was very handsome. Richard lived with his sister and brother-in-law at the end of our bus route and often was on our bus. He was very friendly, smiling and talking to everyone, especially Stella.

Rudolfo became very angry and said, "Don't have anything to do with that boy; he is not a good person."

I thought that comment was strange, but I also knew that Rudolfo knew everyone in town. Being a taxi driver, he learned a lot about the people in our town, from experience and also by talking to other taxi drivers. About two weeks passed, and on a Saturday morning as Stella and I were going to our tutoring lessons, we saw Richard being dragged by two of his friends, one on either side, down the main street of Florianópolis. He was totally inebriated and hardly recognizable with a distorted pale face and wild hair.

Rudolfo often made a point of driving Stella and me home from our night classes in the evenings, when he wasn't busy driving taxi fares. We would also make a point of looking for him to see if he happened to be heading home at the same time we were. I liked having Rudolfo living with us. I felt safe when he was around, and both Stella and I enjoyed his company.

DURING THIS TIME, Uncle Rodrigo and Aunt Martha also lived with us. Uncle Rodrigo approached grooming—like everything else—with great gusto. After his chores, he usually took his "bathroom time." We never understood exactly what he did in there. Surely it involved brushing teeth, shaving, washing up, and the like. But it also involved a great deal of wild splashing, loud singing, and heated conversations with himself. When he finished, Uncle Rodrigo left the bathroom drenched—walls, ceiling, and floor. My father called him "The Duck."

Uncle Rodrigo said the evening meal prayer with unusual aplomb. He stood up and thanked God for everything: Good health, love, the wonderful food, and, of course, each and every beloved person at the table, individually, and at length. When he came to me, he might say, "Dear God, here is a wonderful niece, your anointed servant, Graça. You have given her so much talent, reading, writing, singing, playing the guitar, candle-making, bread-baking, etc, and you have given her health, beauty, kindness, and honesty. We surely are thankful for Graça, yes, we thank you with all our hearts for Graça!"

He went on for five minutes or more on behalf of every person around the table. Uncle Rodrigo did this loudly, with both arms flinging widely as if he were preaching before a crowd of hundreds. When he came to his wife, Aunt Martha, Uncle Rodrigo often worked himself up to tears. It was hard not to laugh or at least smile, but we would never want to hurt this man, who meant every word he said. Often, by the time he finished, the food sat chilly on the table. If Mother knew it was Uncle Rodrigo's turn to pray she would keep the food in the oven until the end of his prayer. I loved these blessings, and I loved Uncle Rodrigo.

Stella had great respect for Uncle Rodrigo. She made a point of admiring the poetry he busily wrote in his ornate longhand script. One after another, Stella read his poems out loud in front of him, with great feeling. "Graçóca," she'd say, "your uncle is a talented writer, a real poet." Every chance Uncle Rodrigo had, he brought a new poem for Stella to read. She was the only person in the household that made him feel important.

My dad had little time for Uncle Rodrigo. It must have hurt Aunt Martha to see the lack of attention my dad gave him. He was treated like a person you tolerated for Aunt Martha's sake. Uncle Rodrigo was eccentric, and did things his own way, but he deserved respect. Also, most heartbreakingly, his seven sons would seek my father's council more often than that of their father. I noticed that little by little they even stopped using their last names, Lemos, and chose to be called Kolenda, after my dad. This was unheard of in the Latin culture and I know it hurt Uncle Rodrigo deeply. On Uncle Rodrigo's deathbed a few years later, he asked my dad to see him. Dad was in Brazil at the time. Dad told me this account, with some degree of pride, that Uncle Rodrigo had asked him to come close to him so no one would hear what he said and he whispered in my dad's ear: "You not only stole my dignity, but you took away my name."

This made me cry, as I finally understood how this proud man had really felt about so many unspoken slights.

I wished I had shown him more love and attention, as Stella had. I loved my Uncle Rodrigo. What I loved best about him was the way he protected me. He cared about me, and he showed it whenever the legalistic trials took place at church meetings before Sunday communion.

Stella was not a member of the church, so she never had to face the communion meeting. But during her year with us, our cavorting drew plenty of criticism from members. Try as I might not to be seen, it was useless. Florianópolis was just too small a city for anonymity, and invariably I was spotted. Then at the next communion trial, someone would recommend my expulsion from the church.

"I saw her in a restaurant with sinner boys!" came the accusation. Or, "She was walking in town with unbelievers!" Or, "My wife saw the girl with her hair down in Florianópolis!"

And that's when dear Uncle Rodrigo stood up, slowly walked to the front of the congregation, and with all of the drama he could muster, said, "My dear brothers and sisters in the Lord, I come here as a servant of the Lord, and ready to defend another of God's handmaidens, our dear sister, Graça. I have always been proud of my niece and her many talents, which she uses for the glory of God: Her Hawaiian guitar playing, the accordion playing and most of all her angelic singing." He continued, "How can we judge our sister in the Lord? If there is one person here without sin, let him throw the first stone. Let him condemn our faithful servant of the Lord, our sister, Graça."

Uncle Rodrigo talked on and on about my unending virtues, until eventually, time would just run out. With no time to vote, the membership was forced to table the discussion until the next meeting, and I was allowed to go on with communion because the evening service was about to begin. I know Uncle Rodrigo did this on purpose, to spare me from castigation. But what I could never understand was why my father, when he was present for these meetings, averted his eyes when there were accusations against me. His eyes remained averted while Uncle Rodrigo extolled my virtues. Uncle Rodrigo was on my side, but where was my father?

I knew Dad didn't buy into all the accusations, or the rules themselves. From the beginning, rules handed down from Swedish missionaries to the Brazilian congregations were stricter and more prohibitive than in the United States. The whole thing about keeping the women's hair uncut, the constant tight braids, the segregation of the sexes, with men on one side of the church and women on the other, the admonition against short sleeves . . . it was foolish at a certain point. I knew he didn't think it made me a sinner every time I talked to a nonmember or let out my braids. I could see it in the way he cast his eyes down in the trials, and in the way he averted my questions later. But it was his church, his beloved and almighty church, and finally I understood the enormity of his loyalty to all that the church represented, whether it included or excluded me. It made him so much smaller and more fallibly human than I could ever before have believed he could be. All my life I had believed my father was just one little sliver beneath God on the totem pole of power and light, just one notch away from divine hero. And to a little girl, one notch is nothing. But now, with his bent head and avoidant eyes, my father was just a man, a man who could not, or would not, stand up for my goodness in his own church. It may not have been fair of me to be so devastated, so let down, by my father's mortality, but fairness does not govern the heart. I was crushed.

I was also in a quandary. If something didn't change, I would find myself thrown out of the church before long. Even dear Uncle Rodrigo couldn't stall the congregation forever. They wanted me out, and it was only a matter of time until they got what they wanted. To see me expelled would be an unthinkable humiliation for my parents. It would be ruinous for us all.

What could I do? I couldn't imagine cutting myself off from the friends I loved. Nor could I imagine being cut out of the church my father loved. And so I did the only thing I could think of, which was to avoid communion trials. I found any excuse I could to be absent from church for those services—too much studying, or a last minute trip to Urubici, or feigned illness. I drummed up anything to avoid the congregation's angry accusations. Dad said little about my absence from communion, and Mother clucked her tongue and complained, but half-heartedly. Ultimately we all recognized that the best solution was to avoid bringing the situation to a head with the congregation, who were biding their time to bring me to justice.

This marked the end of my blind trust and faith in my parents' beliefs and in their church. This was a new beginning for me in my search for a benevolent God, a loving God, a forgiving God, a just God. I sought evidence and comfort in the Bible, and returned again and again to a particular verse, Ephesians 2:8: "For it is by grace you have been saved through faith. And this is not from yourselves, it is the gift of God. Not by works so no one can boast."

Chapter Twenty-Eight

Horizons

I TURNED SEVENTEEN in 1951, the summer before we returned to America for good. Everyone's emotions were running high that summer, even Mother's. But the afternoon I found her sobbing in the kitchen was different. Her eyes were swollen and dark with a sadness I didn't recognize. She'd been praying on and off since early that morning, and her tears flowed at every little thing even more than usual. Finally, I asked her what was wrong.

"It's Sister Teresa," Mother said through tears.

Sister Teresa was a neighbor from over the hill, and Mother had talked to her that afternoon.

"Something very disturbing is happening," Mother sobbed. "Only the Lord can help them now."

Finally, Mother got the whole story out, of how Sister Teresa's husband was sexually molesting their two small daughters, only eight and nine years old. "She's desperate, Gracie!" Mother confided. "She doesn't know what to do." The pie crust she was rolling out tore apart under the force of her rolling pin. She balled up the dough violently and started again.

"Mother, what did you tell her?" I asked.

"I told her this was her cross to bear. I told her that there was nothing to do but pray that her husband would find the Lord."

"But, Mother!" I argued. "What about the two little girls?" I was horrified at her acceptance of their fate, of relying on God alone to intervene.

"He is their father, Grace," she said, rolling pin flying. "There is nothing that can protect them from him, only God."

I was angry and sad and yet I felt the truth of what Mother said. I watched her as she fit the crust into the pie tin, the lines of her face furrowed in concentration, her hands working in the skillful confidence accrued over a lifetime of practice. She was right, she was tragically right. No law enforcement would come to the rescue of these little girls, and there was absolutely nothing that their mother, Sister Teresa, could do. I had heard enough stories like this one before, but never involving people I knew so well.

Sister Teresa had no way out. She had four young children, two girls and two boys, and they were dirt poor. If she fled her abusive husband, she would have no way to support her family, except maybe prostitution. Her children would literally starve. Divorce was not legal in Brazil; therefore, remarriage was doubly out of the question. Sister Teresa and her children were trapped in a special kind of hell from which no one could save them; even a man as powerful as my father could not help.

IN JANUARY, Dad announced that the inauguration of the new Florianópolis church—the one he'd been raising money for and constructing since our arrival back in Brazil—would take place on the twentieth of April. This might have been a premature announcement, as the church was far from done. None of the walls were even up. And besides, Aunt Elizabeth was due to arrive in Brazil the first week of February, and Dad would be extra busy showing her around various places in Brazil. He was working day and night.

But this was especially a nice time for me, since his work on the church construction—doing the work and supervising the workers—kept him from much travel. Still, almost grown up as I was, I preferred my father to be home.

Stella and I were frantically preparing for final exams. We left Coqueiros and went to Urubici for almost three weeks in January to study, and of course, to sin, in my mother's eyes. But Urubici was a lot quieter than Coqueiros, especially in the summer. We returned to Coqueiros the last week in January, and both of us were ready. We had studied as much as we could. Dad was exhausted, still working day and night on the Florianópolis church.

"Why is Dad in such a hurry to finish the church?" I asked Mom.

"Ask your dad himself when he comes home," she said flatly.

Dad came home for dinner late that night—it was after nine o'clock. I waited for him to finish eating and then, finally, I worked up my courage to ask the question. This took some courage, as I was afraid of what the answer might be. "Why are you in such a hurry to get the church done, Dad? Aunt Elizabeth will be here and you know we have to show her Brazil, especially Urubici."

Dad took a deep breath, which he usually did when he had something important to say. "Gracie, we are going back to America as soon as the church is completed. I just purchased a ticket for us on Braniff airlines. We leave on May 5 from Rio de Janeiro."

I couldn't believe what I was hearing. "But why? We have only been here for three years. Aren't furloughs for missionaries supposed to be every six years?"

"Yes, but the Lord has laid it on my heart to move to Germany, and I must leave Brazil and work on finding new financial support before your mother and I can make the move abroad. It should take us about one year in the United States."

"What about me?" I asked, tears welling up in my eyes.

"Gracie, by then you will be nineteen years old. No doubt you'll be going to a Bible school and maybe even getting married. You won't want to come with us, most likely. We shall see."

There would be nothing to see. I did not want to move to Germany with them, I was sure of that. I was crying because I did not want to leave Brazil. I rushed to my room and told Stella, "Stellóca, I don't want to go, I want to stay here."

But we both knew that was impossible. And it was so unfair! I loved Brazil. I didn't want to leave my friends again, especially Stella. I was ready for college, I felt at home in Brazil, and I had a future in Brazil. Back in the United States I'd be an outsider all over again.

Aunt Elizabeth arrived the first week of February. Mother and Dad took her to Rio Grande do Sul. The church was coming along well. The roof was even on. Stella and I were busy with our exams—more than a week's worth of full-time test taking, oral and written. But unlike for the practice exams we took six months before, this time we were well prepared. We both passed easily, and as soon as we got the good news, Stella left for home in Urubici. I was heartbroken to see her go.

As soon as Mother and Dad returned from their trip with Aunt Elizabeth, I strongly suggested that Aunt Elizabeth must see Urubici. Mother and Dad agreed and in March we left for a one-week week trip. At least now I could have a proper goodbye with Stella.

"Stellóca," I begged, "promise me you will come to America as soon as you finish your studies."

Stella answered, "You can be sure of that. My dream is to come to America some day, and especially to be with you. But Graçóca, I'm afraid that when you get to America you will forget all about us."

"Stellóca, I promise that I will return to Brazil as soon as I can," I said. "You know that I feel more like a Brazilian than an American, and I can't imagine being so far away from you, dearest friend."

We both cried, and I felt my heart was bruising.

The inauguration of the Florianópolis church lasted three days with visitors in attendance from all over the state and the country. Dad was so very proud. But I couldn't shake away my sadness enough to celebrate.

On the morning of May 5, Mother and Dad and I said goodbye to Uncle Rodrigo and Aunt Martha, to Rudolfo and Edison. I walked out to the back of the house and ran down the rocks to our beach a final time, cupped my hands into the clear water and splashed it on my face.

"Come quickly, Grace! We must go!" My father's voice was still staccato, still powerful.

I looked out to the horizon, veiled in predawn haze, and could barely distinguish the line between sea and sky.

"Grace, we'll miss the plane!" It was Mother now, shrill and angry.

I imagined myself on that day eight years before, in a small white boat under a cloudless sky, skipping Sunday school, singing with my little friend, rowing toward a deep blue sea as my parents called from shore.

"Grace!" My father's voice was panicked now. Maybe he worried I was hurt, had fallen into the sea and gotten pulled out by a riptide, away, away, away. I could hear footsteps and scattering stones on the rocks above me, and I wanted to shout something out—that I was alive, that I was coming. But nothing could escape the swollen, constricted space of my throat.

I thought of Luiz, and how he had never come with the band and serenaded me outside our front door. He had kept his promise, and now I regretted it. What would it have mattered? It would only have brought one more accusation at one more communion trial. I would miss him so terribly, wild Luiz, with his skinny arms and legs and his fast ways, his cigarettes and his love of music and life, and his big heart. He would never love me any more than his adopted American sister, but that was enough, just to be in his orbit.

I thought of Stella, her sinful curls and her stubborn freckles, and I pictured her wide smile and the way she loved me, just loved me. A wave of *saudades* crashed over me and a sob shook my body so forcefully that I dropped to my knees.

My father's footsteps approached. "Grace," he said. His voice trembled a little. "Please."

His hand on my back was warm and familiar—an order I understood. I would have to stand up and climb that rocky cliff. I would have to get on that plane. I would have to start all over again. And this time, I would have to carry the burden of more questions than answers. I thought of Stella's smile again, and the way she lavished it on me, on Uncle Rodrigo, on Maria the prostitute, and I felt so grateful for the questions she created, just by being who she was.

"I'm ready, Dad," I said.

I stood up and looked out at the water. It was fully light now, and the haze was lifting. Already there was a bit of the morning sun's heat in the breeze. Together, Dad and I climbed the rocks up to our house one last time as the sea lapped steadily back and forth below us, and the sky stretched out above our heads, an endless open blue.

Epilogue I

A S SOON AS DAD'S FUNERAL SERVICE WAS OVER, a procession of cars went to Turlock, where the burial took place at the Turlock Memorial Park Cemetery. Pastor Joe Wright, one of Dad's Modesto pastors, conducted a short memorial at the grave sight.

Then we got in the cars to drive to a luncheon given by the ladies of the church. I sat in the limousine with my husband Bill, our daughters Angela, Beth and Martha, my sister Dorothy, and Mother. As we left the cemetery I had another surprise.

Mother took a deep breath, and sighed, saying loudly, slowly, and emphatically, "I will never have to bake another pie."

Dorothy and I looked at each other in shock. What did she mean by this? After thinking about it for a few minutes, the only way to interpret what she said was that her job as Mrs. John Peter Kolenda was over. She had done a perfect job. According to everyone she scored very high marks. Dad adored her, and was always very proud of his Marguerite. In their last years together, they had grown even closer. It was not unusual to see Mother on Dad's lap, talking to him and kissing him. They sang together, read the Bible together, laughed together, and prayed together. But Dad was gone and now she could be Marguerite, not Mrs. J.P. Kolenda. And she never baked another pie, cookies, or anything else for that matter.

Mother came to Minneapolis to be near me, and lived in a Christian retirement home. She let me cut her hair, wore a permanent wave, and loved to wear the colorful fancy dresses I bought her. I saw my mother as an entirely different person. She laughed, she seemed more relaxed, and to me it was like experiencing a very different person from the mother I knew in Brazil. She missed Dad intensely, and at times she was almost angry with God for letting her live so long without her John. Then her prayers were answered on July 22, 1988. Just four years after Dad passed away, Mother went to be with her Lord, and with her beloved husband John Peter Kolenda.

Epilogue II

WHEN MY firstborn daughter, Angela, started growing older, I found myself calling her "Dorothy" by mistake. At the same time, I found that when I talked to my sister, I absent-mindedly referred to her as "Angie." As my own little girls grew up and I found myself immersed in the emotional intensities of motherhood, my mind and heart raced with questions about my sister all over again, questions I thought I had left behind. Questions I wished would go away. Questions like, why did Dad show such love and affection for Dorothy, while Mother scorned her so? Why?

And then there was that accusation Mother cast at Dorothy: "You're just like your father," an insult that on its surface made no sense. I must have heard Mother shout this insult at Dorothy a million times. While I certainly got used to it, it remained confusing no matter how many times I heard it. After all, being like our father should have been a good thing. And learning of Dorothy's adoption, and that my father wasn't her father, didn't make it any clearer. Somehow, Mother spoke as if she knew Dorothy's father, and disdained him. So, who was Dorothy's father? Would Mother have spat that particular accusation at Dorothy over and over again all through the years if she didn't know who Dorothy's father was?

Over the years, as Bill and I raised our daughters, the question of Dorothy returned to me again and again. I couldn't shake the thought that somewhere, somehow, there was a secret that meant something, that could explain something vital and profound.

By the summer of 2000, both Mother and Dad had been gone many years, and still my questions burned. Bill and I were driving that summer by Dorothy's house in Martinez, near San Francisco, on the way to our home in Nevada. As the gold and brown hues of the western landscape rolled past the car window, I wondered out loud again about whether, maybe, Dorothy and I were related.

"I can't shake the need to know, Bill," I said, turning to watch his profile as he drove. "I really need to solve this."

My husband urged me to do whatever I needed to do to find out Dorothy's paternity. So the next day, I called my sister. "Dorothy," I said, "do you ever wonder whether we're related—by blood, I mean?"

"Ha," Dorothy laughed. "I'd bet my last dollar—and I haven't got that many—that there's some secret lurking somewhere. What it is, I couldn't tell you, but I wouldn't be the least bit surprised if it turned out we're half-sisters, God forbid."

The force of what Dorothy suggested took a moment to sink in, but as it did, I realized that it wasn't the first time I'd considered the horrible possibility that Dad had fathered a child out of wedlock, during his marriage to Mother. It was unthinkable. "Dorothy, don't even say that," I breathed into the phone.

"Saying it doesn't make it more or less true," Dorothy said plainly. "It either is or it isn't. I hope to God it isn't, but we'll never know for sure, now will we?"

"I can't even imagine how to deal with that if it is true," I said. "But maybe we could find out. Maybe we should find out." My voice was shaking.

"Spit it out," Dorothy said. "Say what you mean."

I took a breath and held it in for a moment. Then I plunged. "What I'm saying is that I think we can find out, and I think we have to find out. But the only way is to have a DNA test done. Will you do it?"

"Ha, why wouldn't I?" Dorothy said. "Like I already said, knowing the terrible truth or not knowing it doesn't make it one bit more or less terrible."

My doctor found a lab in Los Angeles with a specialty in this type of testing. In just a few days, they'd sent us all the equipment and instructions to get the test rolling. We had our blood drawn at a local lab and sent in samples. It would take two weeks to get the results back. Those were two of the longest weeks of my life. Both Dorothy and I, and even Bill, were on pins and needles. At the end of the two weeks, there was no word from the lab. We waited nervously, and we waited some more. Four weeks later, we'd still heard nothing. I contacted the lab. The manager said that they'd repeated the tests several times, and wanted to do it again to be absolutely sure of the results. Our minds were literally swimming with possibilities by now. Was it Dad? Could it be true? Or maybe one of his brothers? We'd lived almost seventy years without knowing any of this, and now every minute felt like a century.

Dorothy and I prayed hard that it wouldn't be Dad. We both admired and loved him too much to begin to think about dealing with the implications of this terrible possibility. Sometimes, during the weeks of waiting, I cried myself to sleep, torn by the thought that everything I believed about my father for my whole life might be about to come crashing down.

Finally, after six excruciating weeks, we got the results. There was a zero percent chance that Dorothy and I were sisters. Tears poured down my cheeks at the news. I felt like I could breathe again for the first time in weeks, or maybe longer. After all, this question had been germinating for more years than I had been able to admit. I thanked God out loud when I read those words, "zero percent." But there was more to the picture than that. As it turned out, there was an eighty-five percent chance that Dorothy and I were cousins. Cousins!

So, Dad wasn't Dorothy's father, but we were related somehow. What a relief on both counts. First, our father hadn't deceived our mother and us for our whole lives. How could we not be relieved to know that? Dad had made his mistakes, yes, but to find out about a lifetime of deception and sheer hypocrisy would have been a very heavy burden indeed. His

sincerity and the purity of belief in his ideals is what made it easy to forgive him for the damage those same ideals caused. To find out the ideals
themselves were false would be more heartbreak than I could imagine.
But still, there was a secret. There was a deception. Dorothy and I were
related all along, just as we suspected. This explained so much. But who
was Dorothy's father?

"Most likely it was Ernie," Dorothy announced after a moment's
thought. It was as if somehow she'd already known this without having
thought about it consciously. And it did make some sense. After all,
Dorothy's birth mother was a member of Dad's church in Flint, and
during those years, just after Uncle Ernie's divorce, he'd lived with Mother
and Dad for a while. And he did have a widespread reputation as a "lady's
man." Even as a child, I'd understood that much.

And then there was Mother's deep disdain and dislike for Ernie. She
made this very obvious. Whenever Dad wanted to visit Ernie, Mother
protested vehemently. And, of course, there was her perennial and previ-
ously inexplicable insult to Dorothy: "You're just like your dad." If Ernie
was Dorothy's dad, this insult made perfect sense coming from Mom, who
never could stand Ernie.

The more Dorothy and I thought about it and talked it over, the more
convinced we became that this was in fact the solution to a lifelong mystery.
We knew that Mother had been given no choice in the adoption—it had
been Dad's idea and Mother was forced to go along with it. And since
Dorothy was not only born out of wedlock but also the result of a family
shame, Mother, in her black-and-white judgment, could only deem her
a bad seed, start to finish. That left Dad with the job of trying to make
up for Mother's bitterness and nastiness toward Dorothy. After all, Dad
was family oriented, he was a Kolenda, and he was loyal. He couldn't let
outsiders raise his own brother's daughter. He, as a good married man,
and a preacher besides, had to do the right thing.

Dorothy and I cried and laughed together on the phone almost every
day during the weeks after getting those lab results. It seemed there was
no end to the "evidence" for Ernie being Dorothy's father. The more we
thought and talked about it, the more memories surfaced and added to the

equation. I even recalled something odd about when we had first returned to the United States in 1946 and stayed with Ernie and Goldie. I hadn't understood at the time why my aunt and uncle were so nervous about my spending time alone with Ernie's daughter, Faith. I loved Faith, after all, and wanted to be with her as much as possible. Now I can understand Aunt Goldie's great concern as she pleaded with me not to say anything to Faith about Dorothy. With the understanding that Ernie was actually Dorothy's father, Aunt Goldie's strange request that day made perfect sense. She must have assumed that I not only knew that Dorothy was adopted, but also that Ernie was her natural father. She assumed I knew! But Faith didn't, and Goldie didn't want the shameful secret shared.

With this new knowledge, the rainy afternoon in Modesto at my father's funeral took on a whole new light. What was at the time a confusing spectacle was now clear to me for what it was: An expression of unspoken gratitude and remorse, love and pain, pent up over a lifetime. The scene was as vivid to me now as it was all those years ago. I could still see Ernie just as he was that afternoon, wild with emotion. How must it have felt for him, after years of strained relations with his brother, to simply lose all control in his grief? Why, he'd practically lifted Dad right out of his casket. Why?

I finally felt I knew what Ernie was thinking in that moment, and how much reason he truly had for loving his brother John.

I also must say that we will never be absolutely certain that Uncle Ernie was Dorothy's father. Dorothy could have been fathered by other Kolenda or even Dad's cousin, Kelterborn. But I have no doubt that Mom, Dad, Uncle Ernie and Aunt Goldie believed that Dorothy was indeed Ernie's child. Even so, Dorothy's mother may have lied in order to get her child adopted by my parents. I have also learned that testing for a father, without his actual DNA renders the results inconclusive. It is interesting that when testing for the mother, without her specific DNA, the results are more conclusive. For both Dorothy and me there remain some questions, but there is great comfort in knowing we are genetically related.

I didn't have any more reason to love Dorothy—that much was already in place, and always had been. But I had reason to be grateful for a deeper and more complete understanding of so much of what was painful in our growing up years. This secret, the way it had festered in the currents beneath the surface of our childhood, now explained everything about the way Dorothy was treated, and the way she had to have felt about me. Knowing doesn't make it better, exactly, at least, not in the sense of healing all the scars. It's profoundly sad that in those days, particularly within the extremes of religion, these things were looked on as so shameful. I understand, at least on some level, why my parents felt so compelled to keep their secret.

Today, at seventy-five years old, I see my youth from a compassionate distance. But the lifeblood of those years in the subtropics, spent in the shadow of my father's great love for me and also his unquestionable beliefs, still pumps through my veins. Everything about that time remains vibrant: The smell of the sea, the deep undulations of my father's voice from the pulpit—his constant preaching of the "end of times"—and the cadence and rolling beauty of the Portuguese language as he spoke it.

I married Bill Deters who was not Assemblies of God; he was raised a Christian Scientist. My horrified parents, on a mission in Germany at the time, flew back to save my soul. When I refused salvation, carrying on with the wedding over my parents' protests, my break from their church became permanent in my eyes and in theirs.

Like so many others raised in religious extremism, I spent my first fifteen years fearing God, and the next fifty-eight trying to balance rebellion and faith. Early in our marriage, Bill and I explored religions—Catholic, Mormon, Judaism, Unitarian, and various Protestant sects. We fit in best with mainstream Protestantism, but I could make do with any church, as long as it wasn't dogmatic or fanatical in any way. Today we are at home at St. Patrick's Episcopal Church in Incline Village, Nevada. Meanwhile, the rest of my extended family is nearly all Assemblies of God. In keeping with my life's thesis of incongruities, I love them deeply. I have no desire to change them. I also do not have a need to have them understand and accept why I left a system that condemned me.

As I drive the winding roads of Incline Village in the new millennium, on my way for an afternoon of volunteer work at the church thrift shop, I find myself ticking off my list of things to do on a busy day. I wonder about my children and my grandchildren and how they are finding their own way in this crazy, complicated world. And I find myself so grateful for Bill, for our three daughters, for our home above Lake Tahoe. But I also find myself yearning for Brazil, wishing to return again, as we do every five years or so. A rush of love for my childhood family, for all of them, including my parents, Dorothy, and even my Uncle Ernie, fills me. And I feel an ache of hope and prayer—and, from someplace deep within, a steadfast belief—that God is infinitely loving and forgiving.

In Memoriam

Divine Betrayal is dedicated to the memory of David Brendah, my cousin and son of David and Ann Brenda.

David and I corresponded regularly via e-mail. David was the only relative, aside from my children, who showed excitement and support for my memoir. David discovered that the Kolenda family was descended from German Jews, and David was in the process of doing extensive historical research on the Jewish branch of our family, another carefully concealed family secret. David also discovered that several Kolendas were killed in Nazi Concentration camps, during WWII.

The Author

G RACEANN KOLENDA DETERS was born in Michigan in 1934 and lived in Brazil as a missionary kid from 1939 to 1952. Grace graduated from Cox College of Nursing and Health Services in Springfield, MO, received a bachelor's degree in Nursing Education from the University of Minnesota and a master's degree in Human Development from St. Mary's University of Minnesota. Grace has taught nursing, counseled inmates in a men's prison, run businesses with her husband, traded securities and raised three lovely daughters. She lives with her husband in Incline Village, Nevada, where recently they celebrated their 50th wedding anniversary.

She can be reached at graceann@divinebetrayal.com

The Writer

Jeannine Ouellette is an award-winning writer and editor. She has published several books, including *A Day Without Immigrants* (Compass Point Books, 2007); *Hurricane Katrina* (Abdo and Daughters, 2007); and *Mama Moon* (Orchard Books, 1995). Her work has also appeared in dozens of magazines including *Ladies' Home Journal, Utne Reader, Rake Magazine, On the Issues,* and a wide variety of regional parenting magazines, as well as many web sites, including Discovery Channel's Planet Green. Jeannine's niche is family life and motherhood, and one of her essays on this topic is included in *Women's Lives: Multicultural Perspectives* (McGraw Hill, 2003). She has greatly enjoyed serving as a collaborating writer and editor with many authors.